Juli —
    Here is whe[r]
Hope this book will help you to
continue your education.

— Frank

May 1990

READING ROUSSEAU IN THE NUCLEAR AGE

TEMPLE
UNIVERSITY
PRESS
Philadelphia

Grace G. Roosevelt

READING ROUSSEAU IN THE NUCLEAR AGE

With full translations of
Jean-Jacques Rousseau's "État de guerre"
and of his "Extrait" and "Jugement"
of the Abbé de Saint-Pierre's
Projet de paix perpétuelle

Temple University Press, Philadelphia 19122
Copyright © 1990 by Temple University. All rights reserved
Published 1990
Printed in the United States of America

The paper used in this publication meets the minimum
requirements of American National Standard for Information
Sciences—Permanence of Paper for Printed Library Materials,
ANSI Z39.48-1984

Library of Congress Cataloging in Publication Data

Roosevelt, Grace G., 1941–
Reading Rousseau in the nuclear age / Grace G. Roosevelt.
p. cm.
"With full translations by the author of Rousseau's "The State of War" and his
"Summary" and "Critique" of Abbé Saint-Pierre's Project for perpetual peace."
Includes bibliographical references.
ISBN 0-87722-679-2(alk. paper)
1. Peace.   2. War.   3. Rousseau, Jean-Jacques, 1712–1778—Contributions in
international relations.   4. Rousseau, Jean-Jacques, 1712–1778—Contributions in
education.   I. Rousseau, Jean-Jacques, 1712–1778. État de guerre. English. 1990.
II. Rousseau, Jean-Jacques, 1712–1778. Extrait et jugement du projet de paix
perpétuelle de M. l'Abbé de Saint-Pierre. English. 1990.   III. Title.
JX1946.R58   1990
327.1'72—dc20   89-36960
                                                                         CIP

For Frank

Contents

vii

Preface

The purpose of this book is to expand the contemporary relevance of Jean-Jacques Rousseau's political and educational thought through a comprehensive study of his writings on war and peace. In pursuing this purpose, my intentions are to make Rousseau's understanding of international relations accessible not only to Rousseau scholars and to specialists in international relations theory but also to undergraduate students of political philosophy and to educators interested in new perspectives on the quest for peace. Thus in what follows I have tried to summarize and explain Rousseau's ideas as clearly as possible and have included in each chapter some reference to the personal and intellectual context within which those ideas took shape. For similar reasons, I have also translated all the titles and citations of Rousseau's work into English and have included, in the Appendices, full translations of Rousseau's unpublished manuscript on "The State of War" and of his forty-page "Summary" and "Critique" of the Abbé de Saint-Pierre's *Project for Perpetual Peace*. This is the only place where complete translations of these writings appear together in a single volume.

I would like to thank the many teachers, librarians, colleagues, friends, and family members who, while they cannot be held responsible for the contents of this book, played a crucial role in its formation. For sparking an initial interest in Rousseau, I am deeply grateful to Robert McClintock, and for developing a positive framework within which to study questions pertaining to war and peace, I am indebted to Dietrich Fischer. Mme. Marys Schmidt-Surdez and M. Daniel Ryser provided gracious and much-needed assistance in the Rousseau archives of Neuchâtel and Geneva, and the staffs of the New York Public Library, the New York University libraries, and the Columbia

University libraries have always been helpful and accommodating. I also wish to thank the members of the North American Association for the Study of Jean-Jacques Rousseau for giving me the opportunity to present the results of my research at their biannual colloquium in 1987, and the editors of *History of Political Thought* for giving me permission to reprint here parts of my article "A Reconstruction of Rousseau's Fragments on the State of War." John Broughton, Julian Franklin, Robert McClintock, Maxine McClintock, Douglas Sloan, and Jonas Soltis contributed useful feedback on earlier versions of the manuscript, as did Robin Bromley, Marc Crawford, Frances Foster, Louisa Goodyear, Luther and Carol Gulick, James T. Johnson, Barbara Milton, Etta Mooser, Richard Pollak, Betty Reardon, Tom Roderick, Janet Skupien, and Barbara Walton. For more recent critical readings of the manuscript in its entirety I am indebted to Howard Cell, Nicole Fermon, Henry Jackson, Friedrich Kratochwil, and Bill Paringer, and for her careful review of the translations I am grateful to Mary McAlpin. Jane Cullen and Mary Capouya, my editors at Temple University Press, have been a pleasure to work with and have guided the manuscript through its final stages with intelligence, skill, and kindness. Special thanks go to my friend Diane Wolkstein who, over the years, has always helped those around her to see what is important and what is not, and who has contributed invaluable insight and advice to the shaping of this book. My sister Cullen Reynolds and my three children, Phoebe, Nick, and Amie Roosevelt, have been generous with their concern for the progress of the manuscript and with their moral support, as have my students and colleagues in the General Studies Program at New York University, particularly James Colaiaco.

The most important source of encouragement has been my husband Frank, who has played as important a role as Rousseau in my political education. In this project he has provided attentive editing, sound technical advice, patient listening, probing questions, fruitful bibliographical references, warm loyalty, and, best of all, his strong affection. His steadfastness and generosity have made my work possible, and it is to him that this book is dedicated.

INTRODUCTION

SETTING OUT

The political writings of Jean-Jacques Rousseau have provided the vocabularies for many different responses to historical experience. During the French Revolution, *sans culottes* and aristocrats alike used Rousseau's writings to confirm their perceptions of the upheavals that surrounded them; in the nineteenth century, radicals and romantics looked to Rousseau for an affirmation of their age's yearnings for freedom and self-expression; and in the first half of the twentieth century, political observers of various persuasions used Rousseau's writings to support an ideological debate about the origins of totalitarianism and nationalism.[1]

The history of the past twenty-five years has brought a comprehensiveness and seriousness to Rousseau studies rarely seen earlier, a sign perhaps of recent deep-seated concerns about the effects of material progress on politics and morality. As the editor of a 1978 issue of *Daedalus* titled "Rousseau for Our Time" has pointed out, "his writings cannot be avoided by those who care to reflect on the moral and political unease of our day."[2] Among these more recent examinations of Rousseau's political writings, Roger Masters, Allan Bloom, and others have stressed the relationships between Rousseau's writings and classical political theory and have pointed to the close connections in Rousseau's work between politics and education;[3] Maurice Cranston and Robert Derathé have related Rousseau's thinking to other seventeenth- and eighteenth-century political theorists;[4] and Stephen Ellenburg, Michel Launay, and James Miller have reiterated Rousseau's faith in participatory politics and democratic freedoms.[5] Although a number of these

3

scholars have provided crucial insights into the contemporary relevance
of Rousseau's political thought, however, few of them have taken more
than a passing glance at his writings on war and peace.

But today the complex realities of international life call for a new
examination of Jean-Jacques Rousseau as a political educator. In an
age when biological life can be extinguished in an instant by weapons
whose explosive power rivals the energy of the sun, when the internal
politics of the smaller nation-states are at the mercy of competitive
"superpowers," and when the language of politics has everywhere become corrupted by the language of the marketplace, any suggestion
that the prophetic philosopher who gave the world the revolutionary
ideals of "natural man," "sovereignty of the people," and "the general
will" might also have left ideals that could inspire new ways of thinking
about international relations surely merits close attention.

Reading Rousseau in the Nuclear Age is based on the recognition that
although the principles of political justice set forth in Rousseau's *Social
Contract* have been carefully studied for over two hundred years, little
attention has been given to the principles of justice among states that
he set forth in his less extensive but equally insightful writings on
"The State of War" and on the Abbé de Saint-Pierre's *Project for Perpetual Peace*. In addition, while many scholars have pointed to the close
links between Rousseau's political writings and his educational writings, none has shown the extent to which his educational insights reflect
a lifelong concern to limit war and promote peace.

It is significant to the purposes of this book that Rousseau's own
most comprehensive reference to his writings on war and peace can
be found in the final pages of his great treatise on education, *Emile*.
Toward the end of Book V the tutor proposes to his twenty-year-old
pupil that the two of them set out on a trip through Europe to look for
a peaceful and well-governed community where Emile and his beloved
Sophie might settle to raise a family. In the paragraphs that follow
Rousseau provides the reader with a list of the questions that the tutor
and his young companion will use to guide their judgments of the political institutions that they observe along the way. Most of the questions
on this list, as Rousseau himself indicates in a footnote, constitute a
summary of the contents of the *Social Contract*—a strategy that reveals
the close connection Rousseau saw between the "principles of political right" of the *Social Contract* and the educational principles of *Emile*.
The last few questions on the list, however, go well beyond the *Social
Contract*'s focus on justice within the state and review the important
issues concerning relations among states that Rousseau had raised in
his lesser-known writings on "The State of War" and on the Abbé de
Saint-Pierre's *Project for Perpetual Peace*.

"Once we have thus considered each species of civil society in itself we shall compare them in order to observe their diverse relations," Rousseau proposes, after his summary of the ideal social contract. But what the study of relations among states will bring to the fore, he goes on to say, is the prevalence of war, with nations "attacking, resisting, and destroying one another" to such an extent that he and Emile will have to ask themselves whether civil society perhaps has not accomplished "either too much or too little" and whether it might not be better to have "no civil society in the world than to have many."[6]

In this passage Rousseau is pointing to the paradox that while it is assumed that individuals submit themselves to the laws of civil government as a means of gaining security, the tendency of governments to be continually in conflict with one another means that in fact the lives of individuals are less secure than they might be without any government at all. Rousseau refers frequently to this paradox in his writings on war and peace, but here in *Emile* it leads him to ask whether this "mixed condition" of law within states and lawlessness between them is not the main cause of tyranny and war, and, he asks, "Are not tyranny and war the greatest plagues of humanity?"

The travellers' observations of the state of war that predominates in international relations lead directly to their examination of possible remedies for the "mixed condition" that might be found in peace leagues and confederations. At this point Rousseau mentions in particular the proposal for a European peace confederation made by the Abbé de Saint-Pierre and suggests that he and Emile consider "what can make it durable and how far the right of confederation can be extended without jeopardizing that of sovereignty." "Finally," Rousseau says at the end of the passage, "we shall lay down the true principles of the right[s] of war, and we shall examine why Grotius and others presented only false ones."[7]

The questions pertaining to international relations that Rousseau lists in the final pages of *Emile* provide both a summary of his writings on war and peace and a synopsis of the subject matter of this study. Changing Rousseau's order of presentation somewhat, I begin in Part I with a close look at "the state of war" that Rousseau saw prevailing among civil societies and then look closely at his unpublished attempt to find the "true principles of the rights of war" and "why Grotius and the others presented only false ones." In Part II of the discussion I turn from Rousseau's writings on war to his writings on peace and explore in depth first his writings on the general will and then the "Summary" and "Critique" that Rousseau wrote in 1758 of the Abbé de Saint-Pierre's *Project for Perpetual Peace*. Finally in Part III I suggest how Rousseau's writings on war and peace inform his educational philosophy. Here I show that both in his *Considerations on the Government of Poland* and in *Emile*, one of Rousseau's primary concerns is to nurture nonthreatening forms of personal security that can serve to promote international security.

When they are looked at in the context of his mature political and educational principles, what Rousseau's writings on war and peace bring to the fore is an understanding of the relationships between human nature, the state, and the war system that is as relevant to present concerns as it was to Rousseau's own time. War is not natural to human beings, Rousseau argues in his writings on "The State of War," but it is natural to states, especially to states caught up in the interdependencies and rivalries engendered by military alliances and international trade. How, then, are we to get beyond the miserable paradox of relative peace within states and the continual threat of war between them?

Because he sees war as endemic to the system of interdependent states, Rousseau offers little hope that limitations on war will evolve either out of the universal acceptance of natural law or out of the customary laws that exist among states or even out of the extension of international trade. Instead, he maintains that since war is a political institution, the achievement of peace requires deliberate political will, and in his political writings he suggests two possible paths that, depending on the context, citizens might choose to get beyond the war system. First, in his discussion of the ideal social contract, Rousseau stresses that while there is no "general will of the human race" that can be relied on to bring about peace, the experience of responsible civic life within a small and unified republic can nurture habits of willing generally that might eventually be applied to those who live beyond one's national borders. In his responses to the Abbé de Saint-Pierre's *Project for Perpetual Peace* Rousseau offers a second and very different way to get beyond the war system. Assuming a context dominated not by small self-sufficient republics but by large commercial empires, Rousseau argues that a permanent peace could be achieved if states were willing to establish a system of collective security that would effectively enforce international law. Although it is clear in his "Critique" of the plan that Rousseau had few illusions about the willingness of the European "princes" of his own day to agree to the Abbé's *Project*, it is also clear from Rousseau's eloquent portrayal of the advantages to be gained from it that he was not without hope that the political forces of the future might someday make the Abbé's vision of perpetual peace a reality.

Thus Rousseau's political writings do not point to a solution, but they do point to a choice. In order to get beyond "The State of War" and to gain a more effective system of individual security, sovereign peoples have the choice either to limit themselves to relatively autonomous forms of political association or to develop larger organizations for peace that can institute new means of preventing international war. And, as Rousseau indicates in his educational writings, the necessary political choice between self-sufficiency and interdependence also involves a pedagogical choice, for to form human beings whose primary concern is to preserve the integrity of their own state calls for educational methods that stress patriotism, whereas to form human beings whose primary concern is to preserve international peace requires educational methods that stress humanitarianism. In *Considerations on the Government of Poland* and in *Emile* Rousseau insisted that such contrasting aims cannot be pursued at the same time; however, given his portrayal of the evolutionary nature of the general will, such aims may not be mutually exclusive in the long run. Looked at closely, Rousseau's writings on the general will suggest that given enough time and political awareness, nations that were once jealously patriotic can develop into polities whose main concerns are peace and security for other nations as well as for themselves.

PERSPECTIVES

Although Rousseau's writings on war and peace have not received the public attention they deserve, they have by no means been neglected completely. In the early years of the twentieth century, when the expectations of a permanent peace were high, a number of scholars optimistically looked to Rousseau's writings for signs that a world without war was at hand. Among the most notable attempts to explore his writings from this standpoint were Georges Lassudrie-Duchène's *Jean-Jacques Rousseau et le droit des gens* and J. L. Windenberger's *Essai sur le système de politique étrangère de J.-J. Rousseau: La République Confédérative des petits États*—the former stressing Rousseau's contributions to international law and the latter speculating about Rousseau's conception of a "confederative republic" among small states that could encourage peace among large ones.[8] During approximately the same period as Lassudrie-Duchène's and Windenberger's work, C. E. Vaughan was in the process of putting together his still widely used collection, *The Political Writings of Jean-Jacques Rousseau*, and although Rousseau's more extensive political writings filled up most of the space in his two-volume work, Vaughan took the implications of Rousseau's shorter writings on war and peace very seriously. He not only gave close attention to these writings in his "Introductions" but also published, in 1917, his own translations of some excerpts from "The State of War" and *A Project for Perpetual Peace* in which he made allusions to the relevance of Rousseau's writings for the effort to establish a permanent peace once World War I was brought to an end.[9] In a similar vein, an edition of Rousseau's *L'État de guerre and Projet de paix perpétuelle* published in 1920 by Putnam included a preface stressing how Rousseau's work fits into the larger history of the quest for peace.[10]

In the second half of the twentieth century the scholarly perspective on Rousseau's understanding of relations among states has been very different from what it was before the realities of two world wars, an ineffectual United Nations, and the frightening excesses of the nuclear arms race. In general, the recent interest in Rousseau's views has come from the field of international relations theory rather than from the field of Rousseau studies, and it has stressed Rousseau's understanding of the war system rather than his vision of peace. The seminal work from this standpoint is Kenneth Waltz's *Man, the State, and War* in which Rousseau appears as the main spokesman for what Waltz calls the "third image" explanation of the origin of war, one that puts responsibility for international conflict not on human nature or on states themselves but on the "system" of interdependent states.[11]

Waltz's stress on Rousseau's structuralist understanding of the war system was followed by a chapter on Rousseau in F. H. Hinsley's *Power and the Pursuit of Peace* where Hinsley argues that because of a "confusion" evident in all of Rousseau's mature political writing between his moral views and his deep sense of history, his essays on war and peace are fraught with an "inconclusiveness" and "defeatism" that "closed Rousseau's eyes to all ideas of progress." Hinsley concludes that, like the fundamental principles of the *Social Contract*, any principles that might be drawn from *A Project for Perpetual Peace* in particular constitute nothing more than "an ideal laid up in heaven" that fails to be of any relevance today.[12]

In a similarly pessimistic but more deeply probing analysis titled "Rousseau on War and Peace," Stanley Hoffmann takes issue with the categories constructed by Waltz and argues that Waltz's use of Rousseau to represent the third image of international relations is somewhat misleading, since Rousseau also saw the cause of war to lie in the way actual states are constituted. Like Hinsley, however, Hoffmann concludes that Rousseau's implied solutions to "The State of War" that prevails in the relationships between states offer little hope for an end to the international anarchy that has persisted from the eighteenth century to the present. Within the context of an insightful and thought-provoking comparison of Rousseau's basic differences with Hobbes and Kant, Hoffmann dismisses the *Project for Perpetual Peace* as "utopian" and argues that because the modern world has repudiated Rousseau's ideals of the frugal, autonomous community, his work is "hardly relevant to the world in which we live."[13]

The present study is based on the belief that the earlier "pacifist" and the more recent "realist" uses of Rousseau have failed to do justice to the full richness of his thought and that a more comprehensive examination of Rousseau's writings on war and peace is now in order. In what follows I attempt to show that Rousseau is neither a pessimist nor a utopian but a political educator who provides his readers both with an analysis of the structural persistence of war and with a vision of the political possibilities for peace. Crucial to this synthesis are Rousseau's writings on education. Although education is seldom discussed by international relations theorists, in Rousseau's work education provides a necessary dimension of the relationship between what is and what ought to be and can lead us to understand that for Rousseau questions about war and peace pertain not only to the system of interdependent states and to the particular constitution of states but also to the way human beings are educated and socialized. In Waltz's terms, Rousseau's writings on education help us to see that Rousseau's political thought combines first, second, and third images of international relations.

The juxtaposition of Rousseau's writings on war and peace with his writings on education can also add a dimension to our understanding of the essential unity of Rousseau's *oeuvre*. Rousseau scholars have long been perplexed by the challenge of reconciling the qualities of humanitarianism and moral autonomy that are so clearly the aim of Emile's education with the demands for strict civil obedience and collective loyalty that would be required of a political community modeled on the principles of the *Social Contract*.[14] Once Rousseau's "Summary" and "Critique" of the Abbé de Saint-Pierre's *Project for Perpetual Peace* are given the attention they deserve, however, a means of resolving this apparent contradiction in Rousseau's work comes into view. As becomes evident in Part III, Rousseau's *Considerations on the Government of Poland* presents us with an educational program that seems appropriate for the closely knit polity of the *Social Contract*, whereas the pedagogy of *Emile* provides an apt preparation for the interdependent world of the *Project for Perpetual Peace*. Rousseau's writings on war and peace thus help us appreciate the extent to which his pedagogical ideals are based on the moral needs of specific political contexts.

TEXTUAL FOUNDATIONS

In addition to limitations in their approach and scope, previous examinations of Rousseau's international relations theory have been limited by uncertainties concerning the actual archival record of Rousseau's writings on war and peace. For example, much of the earlier work accepted as true a rumor about a lost sequel to the *Social Contract* that purportedly contained an elaboration of Rousseau's views on confederations. But this rumor, it has now been discovered, is almost certainly false. In addition, both the earlier and the more recent studies of Rousseau's theory of war have used as their textual source Rousseau's "fragments" on "The State of War." Yet these fragments, I have recently found, actually constitute a coherent though unfinished manuscript that Rousseau would probably have titled "Principles of the Rights of War" but whose pages have for nearly a century remained out of order. Although detailed accounts of these recent findings appear elsewhere,[15] a brief summary of them here can serve both as part of the justification for a new and more comprehensive study of Rousseau's writings on war and peace and as an introduction to those writings themselves.

The rumor that Rousseau had once drafted a sequel to the *Social Contract* arose during the French Revolution when an eccentric and disillusioned aristocrat claimed that he had been given a copy of the work by Rousseau himself. In a political pamphlet published in 1790 in Lausanne, Switzerland, Louis-Emmanuel Henri Alexandre Launay, Count d'Antraigues, stated that Rousseau had given him a 32-page draft of a sequel to the *Social Contract* that discussed "the means by which small states could co-exist with great powers by forming confederations" and that d'Antraigues had been authorized by Rousseau to use in whatever way d'Antraigues thought "might be useful."

D'Antraigues's account goes on to say that in July of 1789 (which would have been during the turbulent weeks either before or after the storming of the Bastille), "re-reading this piece of writing and struck by the sublime ideas of the genius who had composed them," he determined to have the work published. Before doing so, however, he consulted with a friend who warned him about "what deadly use might be made of the writings of the great man whose new ideas I was about to publish."

> My friend predicted that the sound ideas which this great man offered would be misunderstood, that whatever this new piece of writing might contain that was impractical and dangerous for the monarchy would be precisely that which people would want to bring into realization, and that harmful ambitions would find support in this great author in ways that could weaken, and perhaps destroy, the authority of the King.

Like other discontented aristocrats at the time, d'Antraigues had evidently found republican ideals easy to admire when such ideals could be used by the aristocracy to bolster its position against the King. But as soon as the liberating rhetoric of the *Social Contract* moved out of the Paris salons into the Paris streets and the "sovereignty of the people" became the rallying cry not of the *philosophes* but of the *petite bourgeoisie*, the Count d'Antraigues's own class loyalties came to the fore. At that point he could feel only scorn for those who might take Rousseau's writings literally.

> How they would have sullied it—those who, disdaining to study the writings of this great man, have denatured and debased his principles; those who have not seen that the *Social Contract*, an isolated and abstract work, is not applicable to any actual people in the universe. What part would such bad disciples of such a great man have taken from this work —that his friendship conferred on me, in the case that it "might be useful"!

In his passionate concern to avoid any move that might provide Rousseau's "bad disciples"—that is, the revolutionaries of 1789—with any more writings that might be used to "weaken, or perhaps destroy, the authority of the King," d'Antraigues says that his sense of duty compelled him to have the manuscript destroyed.

> This work, which the wisdom of others preserved me from publishing, will never be; I have seen too well, and from too close a vantage point, the danger that would result for my country. After having communicated it to one of Rousseau's true friends, who lives near the place where I am now, it will no longer exist, except in our memories.[16]

What is one to make of this account? Since d'Antraigues's name is never mentioned by Rousseau either in his published work or in his correspondence, the story of d'Antraigues having been given a sequel to the *Social Contract* might not have been taken seriously if Rousseau himself had not hinted in a number of his published writings that he had once intended to write such a work. As he tells us in the *Confessions* and elsewhere, the *Social Contract* was originally only a part of a larger work that Rousseau had titled "Political Institutions" and that he had begun to work on as early as 1743–1744 when he was a secretary to the French ambassador to Venice. Combining his firsthand observations of the political decadence in Venice during the War of the Austrian Succession with a close study of "the history of morals," he had come to see that "everything pertained radically to politics" and that "no people would ever be anything except what their government made them to be." This insight, he says, then led him to questions about "the best possible government," and from there to the question "What is law?" and to "a whole chain of questions on this order of importance. I saw that all of this was leading me to large truths, useful to the well-being of the human race, but above all to the people of my homeland."[17] A hint of the scope of his ambitions at this time can be found in the section on "Political Institutions" in Book V of *Emile* where Rousseau states that the investigations of the feasibility of the Abbé de Saint-Pierre's *Project for Perpetual Peace* "lead us directly to the questions of public

right which can complete the clarification . . . of political right." [18]
Since the subtitle of the *Social Contract* is "Principles of Political Right,"
and since "public right" is how eighteenth-century theorists generally
referred to legitimacy in relations among states (or what is now referred
to as international law), the statement suggests that Rousseau intended
to write a sequel to the *Social Contract* that would focus on those questions concerning international relations that he was raising in the final
paragraphs of *Emile*.

When the *Social Contract* finally appeared in 1762, Rousseau again
reiterated that it was originally part of a larger and more comprehensive
project. "This short treatise" he says in his foreword, "is taken from a
more extensive work, which I undertook in the past without considering my strength, and [which I] have long since abandoned." In Chapter
xvi of Book III Rousseau again mentions his intended sequel: In reference to the danger of small states being subjugated by large ones,
he says in a note that he had intended to deal with this matter "in the
sequel to this work when in dealing with foreign relations I would have
discussed confederations." In the *Social Contract*'s conclusion Rousseau
makes the same point again: "What remains to be done is to buttress the
State by its foreign relations, which would include international law,
commerce, the right of war and conquest, public law, alliances, negotiations, treaties, etc. But all that," he concludes ruefully, "constitutes
a new object, too vast for my limited purview." [19]

Given Rousseau's numerous suggestions that the *Social Contract* was
once part of a larger project that would have included the study of foreign relations, many students of Rousseau's writings on war and peace
have accepted d'Antraigues's account of having been given a draft of
the work by Rousseau. Basing their views on the work of d'Antraigues's
biographer and on the discovery of other objects that d'Antraigues
claimed to have received as gifts from Rousseau, both J. L. Windenberger and C. E. Vaughan, for example, concluded that there is "no
good reason for doubting" d'Antraigues's story, [20] and Windenberger in
particular structured his whole analysis of Rousseau's foreign policy
on speculations about what Rousseau's lost manuscript might have included. Later research done by Alfred Cobban and R. S. Elmes on the
Count d'Antraigues's correspondence pointed to a similar conclusion:
Although they admit that independent confirmation of any friendship
between d'Antraigues and Rousseau is "entirely lacking," they go on
to say that "one can hardly imagine d'Antraigues sowing his private
papers as well as his published works with references to Rousseau for
the purpose of deceiving posterity." [21]

With the most recent edition of the *Correspondance complète de J.-J.
Rousseau*, however, the Count d'Antraigues's claims are for now, at least,

laid to rest. In a section of the Appendices titled "Les Fabrications du comte d'Antraigues," R. A. Leigh emphatically states that despite appearances to the contrary, "there is not one word of truth" in the Count d'Antraigues's claim to have corresponded with Rousseau. Leigh supports this conclusion by pointing out that passages from d'Antraigues's private papers that Cobban and Elmes had conjectured might be based on authentic letters from Rousseau are actually based on correspondence that by 1790 was already *well known*. The editor ends this entry with a final stab at d'Antraigues: "But Rousseau wasn't mentioned for nothing. . . . It is well known that in 1789 and even before, it was a badge of civic virtue, or of respectability to have enjoyed the friendship of Jean-Jacques. The Count d'Antraigues must have greatly needed it."[22]

Where does such a scathing evaluation of the Count d'Antraigues's story leave one? Although it is clear from many of Rousseau's published writings that he did originally intend to write a sequel to the *Social Contract*, it is also very clear from the body of evidence currently available that Rousseau never actually completed such a work and that the Count d'Antraigues's reference to it was either simply one of many deceitful lies or—as is perhaps more likely considering the consistency with which he actually did go about "sowing his private papers as well as his published works with references to Rousseau with the purpose of deceiving posterity"—the symptom of some deep psychological delusions.

Recent research thus indicates that a manuscript pertaining to international relations that was once thought to exist probably never did exist. Other recent findings, however, show that what was once considered Rousseau's unpublished "fragments" on "The State of War" in fact represent a carefully composed, though unfinished, introduction to a work that would probably have been titled "Principles of the Rights of War." This actual manuscript may be able to demonstrate better than the one imagined by the Count d'Antraigues what Rousseau would have wished his work on "Political Institutions" to include.

Originally part of a large collection of notebooks and preliminary drafts of his writings that Rousseau gave to his friend Pierre-Alexandre Du Peyrou for safekeeping during the years when he was fleeing from the consequences of the publication of *Emile*, the fragment known as "The State of War" consists of three sheets of paper, each approximately ten and one-half by seven and one-half inches, that have been folded in half and written on on both sides, thus making twelve medium-size pages of very compressed and heavily reworked text. Because of the uncertainty about the correct order in which the three folded sheets are meant to be read, however, the manuscript has re-

mained something of an enigma ever since it was first published by
Édouard Dreyfus-Brisac as an appendix to his annotated edition of *Du
Contrat Social* in 1896. Despite repeated reshuffling by J. L. Winder-
berger and C. E. Vaughan (in 1906 and 1914, respectively), the version
that appears in the 1964 Pléiade edition of Rousseau's *Oeuvres complètes*
is noticeably lacking in logical coherence. The most glaring incon-
sistency is that the manuscript begins with the word "But"—a clear
indication that the first page of the manuscript is not its original beginning. There are other problems as well. The argument shifts back and
forth between an explicit attack on the political philosopher Thomas
Hobbes and an implicit attack on the international jurist Hugo Grotius;
a paragraph that begins "These examples" follows a paragraph containing principles, not examples; and finally and most important, a passage
that rings with the eloquence and power of a Rousseauean beginning
is buried in the middle of the text, after specific details about the definition of war. "I open my books about rights and morals," Rousseau
suddenly booms out, "and inspired by their suggestive discourses, I
deplore the miseries of nature, admire the peace and justice established
by the civil order, bless the wisdom of public institutions, and find
consolation for being man by seeing myself as a citizen."

As he continues, the reader begins to hear a note of irony in his tone:

> Well instructed as to my duties and happiness, I close the books, leave
> the lecture-room, and look around me. There I see unfortunate peoples
> groaning under an iron yoke, the whole human race crushed by a hand-
> ful of oppressors, and an enraged mob overwhelmed by pain and hunger
> whose blood and tears the rich drink in peace. And everywhere the
> strong are armed against the weak with the formidable power of the law.

The passage goes on to describe, with bitter irony, the contradiction
between the civil order that is extolled in the books of scholars and
jurists and the violence that is all too prevalent in the actual world,
especially on the fields of war. This leads Rousseau into a frontal attack
on the assumption that war is "natural" to mankind and thence to the
argument, familiar to readers of the *Discourse on the Origin of Inequality*,
that "the error of Hobbes and the *philosophes* is to confuse natural man
with the man that they have before their eyes, and to transport into
one system a being which could only exist in another."[23] As one comes
to the end of the fragment, the question arises, wouldn't this whole
section of the text, beginning with "I open my books about rights and
morals," more appropriately be placed at the *beginning* of the fragment,
before the page that starts with "But"?

Finally, to complicate matters even more, there is an additional fragment included in the appendix of the Pléiade edition, which has been

given the title "War and the State of War." This fragment was discovered by Bernard Gagnebin as recently as 1965, at which time it was acquired by the Rousseau archives in Geneva.[24] Gagnebin provocatively mentions that this fragment probably "relates to" the larger fragment on "The State of War" at Neuchâtel, but until 1985 apparently no one had tried to find out exactly how the two fragments might relate to each other.

Puzzled by these inconsistencies while I was translating "The State of War" in preparation for this book, I became interested in visiting the Rousseau archives in Neuchâtel to examine the manuscript myself. When I was finally able to do so, I found that by simply refolding two of the three pages of the manuscript in the opposite direction from the way they had been folded before, the logic of Rousseau's argument falls into place and the whole sequence of his ideas becomes more clear. When this is done the eloquent passage beginning "I open my books about rights and morals" appears at the beginning of the text, the polemic against Hobbes becomes a coherent unit, and the page beginning with "But" takes its place as the centerfold of the document. Moreover, once the larger Neuchâtel fragment on "The State of War" is put into its proper order, the smaller Geneva fragment that was discovered in 1965 fits right into the manuscript before the page beginning "These examples."

With the Neuchâtel manuscript on "The State of War" in a more logical order and the Geneva fragment in its proper location, what has long been regarded as two separate fragments becomes a single, well-developed exposition consisting of four integral parts. First there is the grand "overture" in which Rousseau eloquently alerts his readers to the horrors of war and to the "manifest contradiction" in the way civil life is organized. Next comes a substantial central section (titled "Concerning Civil Society") in which Rousseau proceeds from a critique of the concept of "natural" war (explicitly directed against Hobbes) to an analysis of war between states (implicitly directed against Grotius), and in which Rousseau rigorously attributes the origin of war to the nature of the state itself. This is followed by a somewhat parenthetical section (titled "The General Idea of War between State and State") in which Rousseau describes the specific methods that states use to harm one another. Finally there is a fourth section (titled "Fundamental Distinctions") in which he turns his attention from questions of actual war to questions of legitimate war. ("Up until now I have been speaking of the natural state, . . . now I am speaking of the legitimate state.") This final section is obviously incomplete, since it only touches upon the huge subject of "the rights of war," and it leads one to surmise that the exposition here is the one Rousseau was referring to in his 9 March

1758 letter to M.-M. Rey in which he stated that "my Principles of the Rights of War are not at all ready."[25] At the same time, however, it is interesting to note that Rousseau ends the manuscript with a discussion of the relationship between slavery and the rights of war, for that is precisely the relationship he analyzes at greater length in Chapter iv of Book I of the *Social Contract*.

In between the last two sections of the reconstructed manuscript is a page of the Geneva fragment that has been crossed out by Rousseau and that includes a fairly long digression on the distinction between "war" and "the state of war." This lengthy digression does interrupt the flow of Rousseau's argument, which is probably why he crossed it out. Nevertheless, since the definition of "the state of war" that Rousseau gives us here so presciently describes the "cold war" that has characterized the relationship between the United States and the Soviet Union for the past thirty years, one is tempted to disregard Rousseau's editing and keep the digression in the text.

While the restoration of the manuscript's original page sequence does not change the textual basis of Rousseau's theory of war in any substantive way, the new arrangement of "The State of War" does allow for some shift in emphasis and perspective. First of all, with the section titled "Fundamental Distinctions" coming at the end of the manuscript rather than in its middle, one can see Rousseau making a clear progression from "natural war" to "legitimate war"—that is, from unlimited war to war that is limited in its scope and purpose. As I argue in Chapters 1 and 2, this subtle shift indicates that Rousseau's writings on war, which were drafted in the mid-1750s, provided the context for the larger development of his political thought that is evident in the difference between the second *Discourse*, which was published in 1755, and the *Social Contract*, which was published in 1762. Looked at in this way the reconstructed text gives strong support to the view that Rousseau's reflections on relations among states helped to stimulate his reflections on relations within states.[26]

Even more important, perhaps, the newly discovered logic and coherence of Rousseau's manuscript on "The State of War" provide clear evidence of the profound seriousness with which Rousseau approached the whole question of relations among states. This seriousness is especially evident in the paragraphs that now appear at the beginning of the manuscript. Following the symphonic opening referred to above, in which Rousseau contrasts the complacent "books on rights and morals" with the oppression, pain, and hunger that he observes in the *de facto* realities of civil life, Rousseau turns his attention to the realm of international relations where the situation is even worse:

I lift my eyes and look into the distance. There I see fires and flames, deserted countrysides, pillaged villages . . . I draw near. Before me is a panorama of murder—ten thousand slaughtered men, the dead piled up in heaps, the dying trampled by horses—and everywhere the sight of death and agony.

"And all of this," Rousseau remarks sarcastically, "is the fruit of peaceful institutions. . . . Barbarous philosopher," he cries out, probably addressing Hobbes, "come read us your book on a battlefield!"

When he begins to discuss how he himself can best respond to such horrifying ironies, Rousseau again sets his own views in opposition to "the books about rights and morals" of previous political philosophers:

I will limit myself, as I always have done, to examining human institutions by means of their principles; to correcting, if it is possible, the false ideas given about them by self-interested authors; and, at the very least, to insuring that injustice and violence do not shamelessly take on the names of right and equity.

In the remaining pages of his unfinished manuscript on "The State of War," Rousseau examines the human institution of war by means of its principles, corrects the false ideas given about war by "self-interested" authors like Thomas Hobbes and Hugo Grotius, and tries to prevent the realities of injustice and violence from being deliberately obscured by the rhetoric of right and equity. It is this effort that is the focus of the next two chapters.

PART I

THE STATE
OF WAR

1

WAR AND HUMAN NATURE

A RESPONSE TO HOBBES

"Who can imagine without shuddering the insane system of a natural war of every man against every man?" asks Rousseau vehemently in "The State of War."

> What a strange animal this man must be who believes that his own well-being depends upon the destruction of his species! . . . But it is to extremes such as these that the desire, or rather the fury, to establish despotism and passive obedience has led one of the greatest geniuses that ever lived.[1]

As the context of this passage makes clear, and as readers familiar with political thought can guess, Rousseau's angry outburst here in "The State of War" is directed against the seventeenth-century political philosopher Thomas Hobbes, who in *De Cive* and *Leviathan* had posited a natural war "of every man against every man" as the theoretical origin of civil society. Although Rousseau learned much from Hobbes's bold and cogent writings, he was never able to accept the assumptions about human nature that underlie Hobbes's analysis of political sovereignty. In the tension between Rousseau's deep respect for Hobbes's "genius" and his equally deep aversion to the notion that human beings are "naturally" aggressive and warlike, one can perhaps find an appropriate starting point not only for Rousseau's writings on war and peace but for his other political writings as well.[2]

Unlike most of the other authors who provided the stimulus for Rousseau's political thinking, Hobbes is never mentioned in the *Con-*

fessions, and thus there are no clues about exactly when it was that Rousseau first encountered Hobbes's philosophy. Maurice Cranston's biography of Rousseau, for example, mentions only that works by Hobbes were probably available to Rousseau both while he was still living in Chambéry with Mme. de Warens and later when he had settled in Paris and was working as a secretary for Mme. Dupin.[3] Nor do scholars know exactly which editions of Hobbes's political writings Rousseau was most familiar with. He might have read only the earlier work titled *De Cive*; Robert Derathé, however, argues that references by other political thinkers had probably whetted Rousseau's appetite for the later and more complete work, *Leviathan*.[4]

But whatever the source, Rousseau's knowledge of the main arguments of Hobbes's political philosophy was firmly based, and a brief review of those arguments can help set the stage for an examination of the critique of Hobbes that Rousseau began in the *Discourse on the Origin of Inequality*, developed in "The State of War," and fully formulated in the *Social Contract*.

IN HIS introduction to the 1651 edition of *Leviathan*, Hobbes reminds his readers of the old saying "read thyself." Since man's passions show a remarkable "similitude," he says, whoever honestly looks into himself and reflects on his own process of thinking, hoping, and fearing shall thereby "read and know what are the thoughts and passions of all other men upon the like occasions."[5] Against this assertion Rousseau will later maintain that Hobbes's attempt to describe the passions of all men was extremely limited. "I have said before and can not repeat too often," he argues in his unfinished manuscript on "The State of War," "that the error of Hobbes and the *philosophes* is to confuse natural man with the man that they have before their eyes."

Fundamental to Hobbes's view of human nature is a definition of happiness that is perhaps as familiar to our own world as it was to Hobbes's world. The felicity of this life, he says in Part I of *Leviathan* (which is titled "Of Man"), does not consist in some "final end" or "greatest good" as was claimed by the moral philosophers of ancient times; happiness is not something static. Instead, he says, it is "a continual progress of the desire from one object to another, the attaining of the former being still but the way of life to the latter." Happiness is thus a drive, not a state of being; and the emphasis is on motion, not on attainment. It is interesting to see in this definition also a hint of the importance that we today give to what is called "life style." Objects, or things, Hobbes recognizes, can be sought after as a means to other objects or things.[6]

The assumption that happiness is an inherently insatiable drive leads

Hobbes to see human life in its original natural state as dominated by an ever-compelling need to conquer and consume. "In the first place," he says, "I put for a general inclination of all mankind a perpetual and restless desire of power after power that ceases only in death." Given the need to assure the gratification not only of present but also of future desires, human beings cannot assure the power and means to live well that they have at present without the acquisition of more power. And because the only way one person can attain his desire is to "kill, subdue, supplant, or repel" another, such competition finally leads to "contention, enmity, and war."[7]

The emphasis in these pages of the *Leviathan* is on the necessary connection between survival and aggression. In the Hobbesian state of nature there is no way to resist the whirlwind of ever-growing violence; one must kill or be killed. Human life in its original ungoverned condition is thus inevitably a life of constant violence and competition: "During the time men live without a common power to keep them all in awe, they are in that condition which is called war, and such a war as is of every man against every man." In such a condition, Hobbes goes on to say,

> there is no place for industry . . . no culture of the earth; no navigation, . . . no commodious building, . . . no knowledge of the face of the earth, no account of time; no arts; no letters; no society; and, which is worst of all, continual fear and danger of violent death; and the life of man solitary, poor, nasty, brutish, and short.[8]

In such a situation of anarchy one cannot even speak in terms of "right" and "wrong"; for, Hobbes asserts, "where there is no common power, there is no law; where no law, no injustice. Force and fraud are in war the two cardinal virtues."[9]

The stark, brutal clarity of Hobbes's description hits hard. Like Rousseau more than two centuries ago, we cannot read such words "without shuddering." And yet Hobbes insists that such a picture is not an exaggeration. To convince his readers of the veracity of his account of the "war of every man against every man" that would characterize a society that lacked a "common power," Hobbes points out that a parallel condition exists in the international realm where there is a similar lack of legal constraint. Even when they are not actually fighting one another, Hobbes says, "Kings and persons of sovereign authority, because of their independency, are in the state and posture of gladiators, having their weapons pointing and their eyes fixed on one another." But having made the analogy between ungoverned individuals and warring states, Hobbes insists that civil anarchy is a much more fearful danger even than international anarchy, for international war at least preserves the "industry" of the sovereign's subjects, whereas internal war destroys society completely.[10]

Hobbes's purpose, however, is not to describe the horrors of modern war but to construct a hypothetical rationale for an absolute sovereign who might bring about peace. After describing the state of nature Hobbes points to what he saw as the only means of getting out of the miserable condition of war by presenting the concepts of natural right, natural law, contract, and covenant. Their fear of violent death and of each other must persuade men to enter into a covenant by which they "lay down" or alienate their instinctual natural *rights* of self preservation in the name of the rational natural *laws* of treating others as one would wish to be treated oneself.[11] In other words, men need to agree together to trade freedom for peace, or else face death.

But what is to hold men to the performance of their covenants? Once again "the passion to be reckoned upon is fear"—in particular the fear of some power that "can keep them all in awe." What is needed, according to Hobbes, is for men to "confer all their power and strength upon one man, or upon one assembly of men . . . and therein to submit their wills every one to his will, and their judgments to his judgment" so that the covenants of peace will be maintained.[12] Only fear can motivate men to so submit themselves. For Hobbes, the only thing we have to hope for is fear itself.

The sovereign power that Hobbes hopes fear can give rise to may be brought about either by institution or by force, he argues in the part of *Leviathan* titled "On Commonwealth." His clear enunciation of sovereignty by institution, whereby a people choose to submit to a sovereign for the sake of mutual protection, has rightly made Hobbes one of the originators of the "social contract" tradition in political theory. On the other hand, to Rousseau's consternation one hundred years later, Hobbes also accepts conquest as a legitimate means of generating sovereignty. "The vanquished, to avoid the present stroke of death," he says in the chapter entitled "Of Dominion Paternal and Despotical," "covenants either in express words or by other sufficient signs of the will that, so long as the life and liberty of his body is allowed him, the victor shall have the use thereof at his pleasure."[13]

Whether instituted by will or by force, the resulting sovereignty is absolute. Hobbes insists that subjects have no authority to change the form of government, or accuse the sovereign of injustice, or have any jurisdiction over the means of peace and defense or over what doctrines are fit to be taught to the people, nor can they legislate any of the rules concerning property rights. While he seems to recognize that his argument for an absolute ruler will meet with disapproval, Hobbes is adamant that repression is the only alternative to war. "Though of so unlimited a power men may fancy many evil consequences, yet the consequences of the want of it, which is perpetual war of every man against his neighbor, are much worse." [14]

As Robert Derathé points out in his excellent study *Jean-Jacques Rousseau et la science politique de son temps*, Hobbes's dark doctrines had few admirers in the years leading up to and including the eighteenth-century Enlightenment: Leibnitz, Bayle, and Barbeyrac, Derathé observes, had all written critically of the English philosopher's "false principles." [15] And yet it was Rousseau who was known as his age's most vigorous critic of Hobbes. In the entry titled "Hobbisme" written by Diderot for the *Encyclopédie* it was Rousseau who was singled out as representing most clearly an anti-Hobbesian view. "The philosophy of M. Rousseau, of Geneva," the article reads, "is almost the inverse of that of Hobbes," and after summarizing their opposing philosophies Diderot goes on to imply that the differences between Hobbes and Rousseau can be explained by the different historical contexts of their lives: "One of them was born in the midst of disorder and factionalism; the other lived in society and amongst intellectuals. Different times, different circumstances, different philosophers." [16]

Diderot's speculations about the origin of Hobbes's doctrines may be plausible. Hobbes himself, who was born in 1588 during the general apprehension in England over the approaching Spanish Armada, once wrote that he and fear were "twins." [17] But Diderot's hint that Rousseau's more benign view of human nature was somehow rooted in his life as an intellectual is less convincing. In the first place, Rousseau spent most of his formative years in small towns in the Swiss and French Alps, far from the sophisticated intellectual society of the Enlightenment. In the second place, according to his *Confessions*, Rousseau's initiation into the Parisian salon society of the *philosophes* was what marked the beginning of his "miseries." Hence, although Rousseau's acquaintance with society may explain his view of society as corrupting, it cannot explain Rousseau's passionate affirmation, throughout his writings, that man is naturally *good*. For that aspect of his argument with Hobbes we need to search farther back into Rousseau's earlier life, before he became an accepted, though reluctant, member of "society."

The most significant fact about Rousseau's early life is his mother's death, which occurred only ten days after he was born. As Rousseau was later to say, his birth "cost my mother her life." [18] His mother's untimely death obviously had repercussions on many of the external circumstances of Rousseau's life, and it can be seen as the initial cause of the sequence of events that began with his father's leaving home when Jean-Jacques was ten years old, the young boy's later need to be apprenticed to the "oafish and violent" M. Ducommun, his subsequent truancy and departure from Geneva, his conversion to Catholicism, his various menial jobs for rich families in Turin, and finally his ten-year sojourn with the lovable but irresponsible Mme. de Warens, whom he always would call "Maman."

But his mother's death undoubtedly had equally powerful repercussions on Rousseau's emotional experience. For one need not be thoroughly versed in psychoanalytic theory to see that the knowledge of having been the cause of a parent's death is perhaps the heaviest burden a child can bear. In the account of his life that Rousseau so openly presents to us in his *Confessions* it is thus not surprising to find (indeed it would be surprising not to find) that questions about guilt and innocence assume an unusual importance for him.

While the *Confessions* is, as the title implies, Rousseau's honest avowal of all his "sins," the work is also, perhaps even more, a poignant attempt to demonstrate his innocence, particularly the innocence that is asserted in the face of unjust accusations—both real and imagined. The compelling need to hold on to his own sense of innocence can be seen again and again in Rousseau's story—from his descriptions of himself as a bashful blunderer in the salons of Paris and his account of the events leading up to his disastrous break with the French Ambassador to Venice, to his lengthy justification of his decision to abandon his children to a foundling home and his compulsively documented fears of disloyalty on the part of his friends.

But perhaps the most significant episode in the *Confessions* illustrating the theme of innocence is the famous incident involving Mlle. Lambercier's broken comb. Mlle. Lambercier was the sister of the pastor living on the outskirts of Geneva to whom Jean-Jacques and his cousin were sent for their first formal education when they were about ten years old. Her comb had been laid to dry on a stove near the room where Rousseau was studying; when Mlle. Lambercier returned to use it, the comb was found broken, and Jean-Jacques was accused. He denied having touched the comb, but "appearances were too strong for me, and all my protests were overruled." The result was repeated beatings, which still failed to bring forth a confession. Finally, Rousseau says, he "emerged from that cruel ordeal shattered but triumphant." To meet with injustice in such an irrational form had indeed "shattered" Rousseau's illusions about life: "Even today," he wrote forty years after the event, "I am conscious that memory of childhood's delights stops short at that point." But Rousseau also saw the experience as some form of "triumph." Being innocent of breaking the comb was symbolic of a larger innocence, and he would henceforth side with all those who were innocent but falsely accused. "The feeling was only a personal one in its origins," he reflects, "but it has since assumed such a con-

sistency and has become so divorced from personal interests that my
blood boils at the sight or the tale of any injustice, whoever may be the
sufferer and whatever may have taken place, in just the same way as if
I were myself its victim."[19]

In the need to make innocence "triumphant" we may have a clue
about the source of Rousseau's objection to Thomas Hobbes's portrayal of an aggressive and warlike natural man. Although Rousseau
agreed with many of Hobbes's observations about relations among
states, Rousseau could not tolerate Hobbes's underlying assumption
that human survival originally required human aggression. Instead,
Rousseau needed to believe that mankind, himself included, was in-
nately innocent (that is, innocent "at birth") and that the survival of
one human being does not necessarily entail the killing of another.
Throughout his life Rousseau's writings show that while he respected
Hobbes's genius, he could not "read himself" into Hobbes's account of
natural man.[20]

NATURAL MAN

Rousseau's first reference to Hobbes is in the *Discourse on the Sciences and
Arts* where, in his sweeping critique of the luxuries and technologies
that have corrupted human morality, Rousseau mentions that "thanks
to typography and the use we make of it, the dangerous dreams of
Hobbes and Spinoza will remain forever."[21] But it is only in his second
discourse, *On the Origin of Inequality*, that Rousseau confronts Hobbes's
view of human nature head-on, and, I might add, it is there that one
first sees him using "typography" to construct a different "dream."

"The philosophers who have examined the foundations of society
have all felt the necessity of going back to the state of nature, but none
of them has reached it," Rousseau says in his Preface to the *Discourse on
the Origin of Inequality*. "All of them . . . speaking continually of need,
avarice, oppression, desires, and pride, have carried over to the state
of nature ideas they had acquired in society: they spoke about savage
man and they described civil man." In the preface Rousseau prepares
his readers for a new vision of human nature by showing where previous versions have been wrong. Although Hobbes is not here mentioned
by name (he is, however, singled out frequently in the *Discourse* itself),
Rousseau begins with a statement that right away seems to be taking
issue with the first book of *Leviathan*. "The most useful and least advanced of all human knowledge seems to me to be that of man," Rousseau asserts in his opening sentence, and then continues, "and I dare say
that the inscription of the temple of Delphi alone contained a precept
more important and more difficult than all the thick volumes of the

moralists."[22] By referring to the Delphic oracle's inscription, which he
assumes his readers remember is to "know thyself," Rousseau immediately evokes Hobbes's advice, in his introduction to *Leviathan*, to "read
thyself." At the same time, however, Rousseau's assertion that the science of man is the one that is the "least advanced" implies that Hobbes
treatise "On Man" did not succeed in advancing our true knowledge
of ourselves in any positive way. A third hint of Hobbes's background
presence in the preface comes in the next few sentences where, in
speaking of the difficulty of separating out "man as nature formed him"
from "what circumstances and his progress have added to or changed"
in him, Rousseau makes an analogy between the human soul that has
already been corrupted by social progress and a statue of the sea god
Glaucus that time and erosion had so disfigured that it looked less like
a god than a "ferocious beast"—an image undoubtedly aimed at the
"beastly" qualities that Hobbes posited as natural in human beings.[23]

Perhaps with Hobbes's division between "On Man" and "On Commonwealth" in mind, Rousseau divides his *Discourse on the Origin of
Inequality* into two parts. The first part describes in full man in his
natural state—his capacities and his needs, his instincts and behaviors.
The second part then sets forth a hypothetical account of the stages of
development that divide "natural" man from "civil" man. The text as a
whole is to be read neither as anthropology nor as history; instead, in
the same spirit as *Emile*, which appeared eight years later, the book aims
to provide standards with which to evaluate political life. As Rousseau
explicitly asserts, the effort "to separate out what is original from what
is artificial in the present nature of man" is a necessary aspect of the
effort "to judge our present state correctly."[24]

The solitary natural man that Rousseau describes in the *Discourse
on the Origin of Inequality* is very different from the one portrayed in
Hobbes's *Leviathan*. Once he has "stripped" the human being of all
the artificial faculties he could have acquired only after many stages
of political and intellectual development, Rousseau says, and once he
has carefully considered him "as he must have come from the hands of
nature," he sees

> an animal less strong than some, less agile than others, but all things
> considered, the most advantageously organized of all. I see him satis-
> fying his hunger under an oak, quenching his thirst at the first stream,
> finding his bed at the foot of the same tree that furnished his meal; and
> therewith his needs are satisfied.[25]

With the phrase "and therewith his needs are satisfied," one immediately senses that Rousseau is far from the Hobbesian world of the
"restless desire of power after power"; likewise he is far from a world

in which happiness itself is defined as the "progress of the desire from one object to another." Instead, the disproportion between desires and the means of satisfying them is precisely how Rousseau, later in *Emile*, will define *unhappiness*. "Our unhappiness consists," he explains, "in the disproportion between our desires and our faculties," a disproportion caused by the artificial stimulations of social life. True happiness, in contrast, results when our desires and our powers are in equilibrium, when our needs are so limited that we can easily satisfy them ourselves. "A being endowed with senses whose faculties equaled his desires," he argues, "would be an absolutely happy being."[26]

In contrast to the spiraling competitiveness that constitutes the central drama of the early chapters of Hobbes's *Leviathan*, the balance between man's desires and his ability to satisfy them best exemplifies Rousseau's account of original life in the state of nature. Without artificial objects or social comparisons to arouse his imagination, without competition or jealousy, primitive man has few ideas, few needs, few fears. Deprived of "enlightenment," "his desires do not exceed his physical needs, the only goods he knows in the universe are nourishment, a female, and repose; the only evils he fears are pain and hunger," and, Rousseau adds, again putting his vision in opposition to that of Hobbes, "not death, because an animal will never know what it is to die."[27]

Because his needs are limited to the ability to satisfy them, natural man is not only happy but strong. Contrary to the common assumption that strength is revealed by aggressiveness, Rousseau maintains throughout his writings that strength is based on self-reliance. Dependency, in contrast, engenders weakness. Taking issue with a notion that Hobbes had put forth in *De Cive* comparing man to a "robust child," Rousseau says that one needs to ask whether Hobbes's robust child is dependent or free, for "to be robust and to be dependent are two contradictory suppositions in the state of nature. Man is weak when he is dependent and he is emancipated before he is robust."[28] To be strong, in other words, human beings need to be free. Later, in his *Considerations on the Government of Poland*, Rousseau will apply the same standards to nation-states that he applies to natural man: to be "robust" in one's foreign policy is above all to be free of dependencies of any kind—a conception that might be relevant to the defense postures of certain nation-states today.

At this point it is important to understand that underlying the differences between Hobbes's and Rousseau's assumptions about happiness and strength are different interpretations of self-preservation or "self-love." Unlike Hobbes, who had represented human history as the expression of a single biological drive for self-preservation, Rousseau

distinguished between two very different self-preserving instincts—
one that he called *amour de soi*, and the other that he called *amour propre*.
As he defines them in a note to the first part of the second *Discourse*,
"[*amour de soi*] is a natural instinct which inclines every animal to watch
over its own preservation," while "[*amour propre*] is only a relative sentiment, artificial and born in society, which inclines each individual to
have a greater esteem for himself than for anyone else." Thus *amour de
soi* compels us to satisfy those essential biological needs that we share
with animals—nourishment, rest, procreation; while *amour propre* compels us to compare ourselves with other men, to want to see ourselves
as superior to them, and to desire more than we need. Our natural
amour de soi is always good, but our socially stimulated *amour propre*
makes us "competitors, rivals, or . . . enemies."[29] As I indicate in the
chapters that follow, this important distinction lies at the foundation of
much of Rousseau's political and educational thought and provides the
crucial link between his writings on war and peace and his writings on
education.

According to Rousseau's distinction between *amour de soi* and *amour
propre*, then, the competitiveness that Hobbes describes in such familiar
terms—the ceaseless striving for power after power—is not generated
by the self-preserving instincts that the human being has naturally;
instead, the Hobbesian world of competition is generated by the self-
preserving instincts that develop only after people have come together
to form societies. In other words, it is not natural man but social man
who poses the problem, according to Rousseau, and in the second
part of the *Discourse* he shows how far apart, both conceptually and
historically, he believed the two to be.

Rousseau further differentiates his view of self-preservation from
that of Hobbes by adding a "softening" element to *amour de soi:*

> There is, besides, another principle which Hobbes did not notice, and
> which—having been given to man in order to soften under certain cir-
> cumstances, the ferocity of his [*amour propre*] or the desire for self-
> preservation before the birth of [*amour propre*]—tempers the ardor he has
> for his own well being by an innate repugnance to see his fellow-man
> suffer.

"I speak of pity," Rousseau explains, an instinctive feeling of commis-
eration for one's fellow beings that can sometimes be observed even in
animals, and he gives the examples of the hesitancy of horses to trample
a living being underfoot or the mournful lowing of cattle when they
see their fellow creatures being slaughtered.[30]

In "The State of War" Rousseau carries this aspect of his argument
with Hobbes further by pointing out that if human beings were naturally as destructive and aggressive toward one another as Hobbes as-

serts, such hostility would come to dominate every human relationship: "The fierce hatred of humanity would eat away at the heart of man. He would mourn at the birth of his children, rejoice at the death of his brothers, and kill every sleeping man he happened to come across." Benevolence and compassion would be seen as contrary to nature. Instead, "in spite of our prejudices and in spite of ourselves," our more benevolent feelings not infrequently come to the fore and "speak to us from the depths of our hearts and often lead us back to the truth we have abandoned as fantasy." In the second *Discourse* this argument is anticipated by Rousseau's sober assertion that without such natural feelings of compassion the human species would have perished long ago.[31] Social man's major challenge, Rousseau makes clear in his later writings, is thus to create political and educational institutions that effectively sublimate the more destructive aspects of *amour propre* and build upon the self-preserving aspects of compassion and *amour de soi*.

His happiness assured by his independent satisfaction of limited needs, his instincts of self-preservation mitigated by pity, Rousseau's man in the state of nature is thus a creature who is essentially at peace. Since human beings in their natural state had no "commerce" among themselves and thus had no occasion to develop *amour propre* or any of the attitudes that are fed by *amour propre* (admiration, jealousy, contempt); since they had no notion of "thine and mine" or any idea of justice, "their disputes would rarely have bloody consequences," and certainly could never lead to anything resembling a war. In "The State of War" Rousseau asserts even more emphatically that "it is not in natural man that one finds the great propensities for war." War, he points out, is a long-lasting condition requiring constant relationships among men. In the state of nature, in contrast,

> Everything among individuals is in a continual flux which incessantly alters one's interests and ties. The subject of a dispute thus appears and disappears in almost an instant, a quarrel begins and ends in a day, and while there may be conflicts and killings there is never, or at least very rarely, long-standing enmity or general war.

"In the state of nature there is thus no general war of every man against every man," concludes Rousseau, and, in a phrase that resounds with significance for our present age, he adds "the human race was not created simply in order to destroy itself."

THE ORIGIN OF WAR

If it is not in natural man that one finds "the great propensities for war," how, then, does war arise? In the second part of the *Discourse on the Origin of Inequality* Rousseau prepares the ground for his later argu-

ment that war originates not in human nature but in states by setting
forth a genealogy of moral and political life that shows how the state
of nature was gradually transformed into a "state of war" and how the
peaceful and timid creature that nature first created becomes the competitive, insecure aggressor that Hobbes's *Leviathan* describes. Like a
series of carefully joined dioramas in a museum of natural man's history, the central sections of the *Discourse* lead from one scene of man's
development to the next, until the furtive, animal-like creature whom
we originally encounter in the state of nature has finally become the
competitive Hobbesian man in whom we recognize ourselves.

Rousseau begins in the shadows of prehistory, with the natural man
at his most primitive, and here one meets again the shy, indolent being
whom Rousseau first introduced in the first part of the *Discourse*. As the
human race multiplies and spreads, primitive man becomes aware of
other beings similar to himself and might find occasions to compete or
cooperate with them. But at this stage such chance encounters are spo-
radic and unreliable, and short-term self-interest always predominates
over long-term collective interest.[32]

Gradually, however, Rousseau shows this primitive man procuring
the means of his survival in ever-more-inventive ways; gradually,
knowledge and inventiveness stimulate each other until people finally
learn to build crude huts and shelters. With this change comes the first
"great revolution" in human life—the establishment and differentiation
of families. Family life gives rise to "the sweetest sentiments known to
man: conjugal love and paternal love," but the resulting possibilities for
cooperation and leisure also make possible the fabrication of commodities that human beings had never felt in need of before. The desire
for new products, Rousseau observes at this point, "was the first yoke
they imposed upon themselves without thinking about it, and the first
source of evils they prepared for their descendants."[33]

What explains the gradual aggregations of families into larger units?
When did different languages evolve? At this stage Rousseau describes
floods and earthquakes breaking up the continents, forcing groups of
families to flee to higher ground, and gradually islands of more settled
life begin to appear. With their own languages and loyalties but as yet
little concept of private property or formal law, this stage of tribal
groupings, which Rousseau describes as "a golden mean between the
indolence of the primitive state and the petulent activity of our *amour
propre*," is probably the happiest and most durable epoch.[34] But now
the introduction of private property, brought about by the coordination of developments in agriculture and metallurgy, marks a "second
revolution" that soon causes the colorful scenes of tribal life to recede
into memory. Once again it is man's imaginative response to a natural

phenomenon that initiates the change: From the chance observation of an erupting volcano comes the discovery of how to make iron, and from the resulting division of labor between mining and farming arise all the classic categories of political economy. Labor now needs control and coordination, and as Rousseau describes the resulting economic transformations, "vast forests were changed into smiling fields which had to be watered with the sweat of men and in which slavery and misery were soon seen to germinate and grow with the crops." [35]

From here on, the scenes depicting natural man's history are painted in more lurid hues. Contrived inequalities gradually replace natural differences between men; "to be" and "to seem" become two altogether different things; and, subjected continually to new needs, man becomes ever more subjected to his fellows. With vivid imagery the reader is shown how both rich and poor begin to make "of their force or their needs a sort of right to the goods of others, equivalent according to them to the right of property." Inequality leads to violence and disorder, and soon "nascent society gave way to the most horrible state of war." [36]

With this tableau of the human race at "the brink of its ruin," one has finally arrived at a scene that very closely resembles Hobbes's war of every man against every man. At the same time, however, it is clear that the human being presented here is many stages removed from the state of nature where his story first began. And, as in Hobbes's version of human life, the warring individuals in Rousseau's account will also, at this point, be forced to make a pact for law and order. But unlike the peacekeeping covenant that Hobbes described, the civil order instituted in the *Discourse on the Origin of Inequality* is only a clever deal made among the rich to formalize their oppression of the poor. For Rousseau maintains, in opposition to Hobbes, that agreements constituted out of fear and inequality are nothing but forms of usurpation, and that laws so derived can only have the effect of giving new "fetters to the weak and new forces to the rich." [37]

Most important, Rousseau's account of the origin of inequality stresses that the apparent peace gained by the institution of *de facto* civil society only brings on a new, more violent, and more destructive "state of war." For no sooner are the antagonisms between rich and poor successfully suppressed by the constraints of civil society than war between those societies breaks out in ever-more-virulent forms. The bodies politic, now living in a kind of Hobbesian "state of nature" in relation to one another, "soon experienced the inconveniences that had forced individuals to leave it; and among these bodies that state became even more fatal than it had been among the individuals of whom they were composed."

Hence arose the national wars, battles, murders, and reprisals which make nature tremble and shock reason, and all those horrible prejudices which rank the honor of shedding blood among the virtues. The most decent men learned to consider it one of their duties to murder their fellow-men; at length men were seen to massacre each other by the thousands without knowing why; more murders were committed on a single day of fighting and more horrors in the capture of a single city than were committed in the state of nature during whole centuries over the entire face of the earth.

"Such are," Rousseau concludes, "the first effects one glimpses of the division of the human race into different societies."[38]

By arguing that conflicts between states are "more fatal" than conflicts between individuals in the state of nature, Rousseau sets himself apart both from Hobbes and from those contemporary theorists who argue that since states provide individuals with at least a minimum of law and order (and, as Hobbes pointed out, since wars can actually help support the "industry" of the sovereign's subjects), international war is less destructive than the anarchy that would exist among individuals in a society without states. It is obvious from the above passage that Rousseau sharply disagrees with this view. Instead of accepting international war as an unfortunate but necessary price to pay for the state system, Rousseau will ask, both in *Emile* and in his "Summary" of the *Project for Perpetual Peace*, whether it might not be better to have "no civil society in the world than to have many." His willingness to demand whether the destructiveness of war does not call into question the whole system of sovereign states indicates convincingly that Rousseau was not the unequivocal "nationalist" that he is often made out to be.[39] Unlike Hobbes, who was haunted by the specter of civil war, Rousseau perceives that the enforced suppression of civil conflict brings on the more widespread effects of international war.

It is important to note also that, unlike Hobbes's absolutist alternative between anarchy and despotism, Rousseau's genealogy of social life allows for political consciousness to develop in slow and complex ways. Rousseau's stress on the evolutionary aspect of political consciousness will appear both in his writings on the general will and in his writings on education; here, however, what is significant is that in the final scenes of the *Discourse on the Origin of Inequality* the human scale that is depicted is very different from the one with which Rousseau began. From natural man as a self-sufficient individual, to the family as a unit, to tribes, to class groupings, and on to the consolidation of nation-states, the reader is now finally looking at human life on a supranational scale. It is a modern world view, and Rousseau's underlying point, that the modern state system itself—a plurality of disorganized political bodies continually in conflict with one another—is the source of war, provokes one to want to know more about his prophetic understanding of the origin of war on the level of global political relations. But here the exposition ends. Rousseau's purpose in the *Discourse on the Origin of Inequality* was to show that human nature is not warlike, and he has made his point. Instead of elaborating on "the state of war" among civil societies, Rousseau returns in the closing pages of the *Discourse* to a wide-ranging discussion of the "institution" of civil societies and the reasons why *de facto* governments founded on inequality inevitably degenerate into despotism. It is only in his manuscript on "The State of War," which he wrote shortly afterward, that Rousseau again takes up the questions about global politics touched upon in the second *Discourse* and begins to explore in greater depth the relationship between civil society and international war.

Again stressing the negative consequences of the state system, Rousseau observes near the beginning of "The State of War":

> When I reflect upon the condition of the human race, the first thing I notice is a manifest contradiction in its constitution. As individuals we live in a civil state and are subject to laws; but as nations each enjoys the liberty of nature. The resulting continual vacillation makes our situation worse than if these distinctions were unknown. For living simultaneously in the social order and in the state of nature we are subjected to the evils of both without gaining the security of either.

This "double condition" that we find ourselves in, Rousseau goes on to say, "is the true origin of public calamities."

Rousseau will mention the contradiction in the human condition again in his "Summary" of the Abbé de Saint-Pierre's *Project for Perpetual Peace* and finally once again in Book V of *Emile*. In "The State of War," however, Rousseau restates his differences with Hobbes concerning the origin of war. His first point is a reiteration of the argument that was developed in the second *Discourse* about natural happiness being limited to physical necessity and about it being only in society that men develop greed and passions and the propensity for war.

> Man is naturally peaceful and shy; at the slightest danger his first movement is to flee; he only becomes emboldened by force of habit and experience. Honor, self-interest, prejudice, vengeance—all the passions that can make him brave the perils of death—are far from him in the state of nature. It is only after having associated with one man that he determines to kill another. He only becomes soldier after having been made citizen. It is not in natural man that we find the great propensities for war. But I need not dwell on a system that is as revolting as it is absurd, and that has been refuted a thousand times.

War thus does not take place between individuals in the state of nature; nor, Rousseau goes on to say, does war take place between individuals in a civil state, since their relationships are governed by laws; nor does it even take place between kings as individuals. Real war, as distinct from quarrels or brigandage or even armed skirmishes, is a long-term condition that occurs only between states themselves. This provocative concept is examined more closely later in connection with Rousseau's response to the work of Hugo Grotius, the great theorist of the rights of war; at this point, however, it is necessary only to point out that the idea was restated even more radically in the *Social Contract*: "It is the relationship between things," Rousseau says there, "not between men that constitutes war. . . . The state of war cannot arise from simple, personal relations, but only from proprietary relations."[40]

Also reiterated in "The State of War" are the final scenes of *de facto* political development that Rousseau had described in the second *Discourse*. "From the first formed society the formation of all the others necessarily follows," and thus "the whole face of the earth is changed: everywhere nature has disappeared and human art has taken its place; independence and natural liberty have given way to laws and slavery." In a pointed reference to what he feels to be Hobbes's failure to describe man's basic nature, Rousseau adds, "the philosopher searches for man and does not find him."

In "The State of War" Rousseau also, once again, lays bare the dynamics of civil repression. The natural freedom and independence that are inhibited by the institution of civil laws have "broken loose" and are now to be found in the relationships among states, and "these great bodies, left completely to their own impulses, produce shocks whose terror is proportional to their mass." At this point in the manuscript Rousseau gives voice to questions about the origin of war that will lead him into the most significant part of his discussion. "But, one may ask, if each of these political bodies has a stable base, why must they come into conflict? Should their own constitutions not keep them in peace? . . . Can political bodies not be self-sufficient?" Why, in other words, do states naturally find themselves in conflict with other states? Since, according to Rousseau, man alone in the state of nature can live and let live, why cannot states do the same?

Rousseau's answer to these questions constitutes a unique and compelling theory about the inherent instability of the modern state system —a theory that Stanley Hoffmann and F. H. Hinsley find pessimistic, but that both advise their colleagues in the field of international relations to take notice of.[41] In introducing his theory, Rousseau reminds his reader that he is "reasoning about the nature of things and not about events that could have a thousand particular causes that have nothing to do with basic principles." He also asserts that in order to answer the question why political bodies cannot coexist peacefully the way natural man does, one must look closely at the way political bodies are constituted. "For although it may be true that theoretically each one could be self-sufficient, we will find that in fact their relations with each other cannot help but be more intimate than the relations among individuals are."

Rousseau proceeds to explain the surprising notion that states are necessarily more "intimate" than individuals in terms that recall the distinction between *amour de soi* and *amour propre*. "Natural man," he says, "after all, has no necessary ties to his fellow men; he can survive in good health without their assistance," and, given the abundance of the earth's natural fruits, can subsist quite well on his own. In addition, the human organism has built-in limits that keep a human being's *amour propre* within certain bounds: "His life is short, his years are numbered; fortune cannot stretch his stomach; his passions multiply in vain. . . . His ideas may convince him of his grandeur, but in his life he is always small." Constitutionally capable of being autonomous, natural man is therefore also capable of living at peace.

In contrast to the self-sufficient and naturally limited natural man, the state is an artificial being with no fixed or necessary limits to its size. Since a state's boundaries are potentially limitless and yet also necessarily contiguous with the boundaries of other states (except in the case of a state that happens to be an island), it cannot help but compare itself with its neighbors. Consequently, its capacities for aggressive expansionism are boundless:

> The state . . . can always expand, and yet it always feels weak as long as there are other states that are stronger than itself. Its security, its defense, demand that it try to appear more powerful than its neighbors; and it can only grow, feed itself, and test its strength at their expense.

"The inequality of men has limits that are put in place by the hands of nature, but the inequalities of states can grow incessantly, until one alone absorbs all the others."

The power of a state, unlike that of an individual, is thus necessarily relative: It is forced to "compare itself in order to know itself." Using the terms Rousseau applies to the motivational drives of individuals, one can say that a state's *amour de soi*, or instincts of self-preservation, inevitably degenerate into *amour propre*, or competitive greed. Like the Hobbesian natural man, Rousseau's *de facto* state is a being that needs to be aggressive simply to survive.

And, as in the Hobbesian account of the state of nature, the activity of unrestrained passions constitutes aggression's driving force.

But in Rousseau's analysis, there is a difference, for he regards the activity of the passions not as a fixed "given" of human biology but as a relative energy that increases only as other forms of strength decline. Again Rousseau's touchstone for strength is self-sufficiency, and again his diagnosis of the causes of international conflict is acutely relevant to today's world.

Rousseau's understanding of the political weaknesses that generate aggression begins with the notion that relative to the individuals composing it, the *de facto* state lacks any permanent bond of unity or integrity. Unlike the human body's muscles or nerves, which are an integral part of the human organism, the "members" of a state are potentially self-sufficient individuals who have their own separate existence outside the existence of the state. Hence, "when one considers how inferior the public force in the body politic is to the sum of private forces, how much there is, so to speak, of friction in the play of the whole machine, one will find that, all due allowance being made, the frailest man has more strength for his own preservation than the most robust state."

To compensate for its relative weakness, the state must assume a high level of action for itself; passions must supplement actions, and "its will must become animated to the extent that its strength becomes slack." Like a married couple whose frenzied habits of work and conspicuous consumption serve to conceal the internal tensions in their relationship, the aggressiveness of nation-states serves to keep the social fabric from falling apart. "War is the health of the State!" was the angry cry of a disillusioned American progressive and social critic named Randolph Bourne when he heard of his country's entry into World War I.[42] But the words might just as appropriately be used to summarize the antiwar writings a century and a half earlier of Jean-Jacques Rousseau. Because he so clearly sees the intimate relationship between internal tension and external aggression, Rousseau attempts both here in "The State of War" and in the *Social Contract* to demystify war and reveal it as a purely political convention.

"It seems that we have made it our task to reverse all the true ideas about things," Rousseau says in summing up his differences with Hobbes about the origin of war.

> Natural man is above all inclined to rest; to eat and to sleep are the only needs he knows, and hunger alone pulls him from his idleness. And yet we have turned him into a furious being who is always ready to torment his fellows because of passions that he knows nothing of. Conversely, we consider the passions that are aroused by all the stimulations of society not to exist. A thousand writers have dared to say that the State is without passion and that there is no "raison d'état" other than reason itself. And yet anyone can see that the essence of society consists in the activity of its members and that a State without motion would be dead.

Hobbes had said that human life itself is "but motion," and from that presumed need for forward motion he derived his vision of the war of every man against every man.[43] Rousseau sees it differently: Natural man on his own merely seeks sustenance and repose; it is the state that is motivated by the frenzied need to conquer and consume.

Rousseau's ironic judgment on the origin of war—that "all the horrors of war arise from the efforts that were taken to prevent it"—can leave one with a deep pessimism about global politics; alternatively, his understanding of the origin of war can lead one to ask, as it later leads him to ask in his writings on the Abbé de Saint-Pierre's *Project for Perpetual Peace*, whether in our political evolution we have not accomplished "either too much or too little." I explore Rousseau's responses to this question more fully in Chapter 4, but at this point it is necessary to complete the examination of Rousseau's critique of Hobbes by looking at Rousseau's understanding of the relationship between force and law.

THE RELATIONSHIP BETWEEN FORCE AND LAW

One of the more intriguing passages in "The State of War" comes right after Rousseau's observations about the contradiction between civil life and international life. "The perfection of the social order consists, it is true, in the conjunction of force and law. But for this it is necessary that law direct force," he says. Rousseau then goes on to deplore the fact that according to the assumption that "princes must be absolutely independent," it is force that usually predominates in international relations, and so, in the end, "the vain name of justice serves only to safeguard violence."

The hint in the above passage that Rousseau is calling into question the whole concept of state sovereignty is dealt with in Chapter 4. More important at this point is to look at Rousseau's assertion that the perfection of civil order requires that law direct force, for this is a theme that Rousseau takes up once again at the beginning of the *Social Contract*. Although the discussion of the relationship between force and law in the *Social Contract* leads us somewhat beyond the question of whether or not war is rooted in human nature, it is nevertheless an important topic to include within the context of Rousseau's critique of Thomas Hobbes.

Hobbes's main contribution to modern political theory is his argument that political life is based on deliberately enacted covenants, undertaken by individuals, for the sake of self-preservation. This emphasis on secular choice, on politics as an "artificial" creation of the human will, places Hobbes theoretically in the classical liberal tradition of those who believe that the state originates not in "nature" but in covenants or "conventions."[44] Indeed, the compelling portrayal that Hobbes gives of a political community arising out of conscious choice and his insistence on moral norms deriving from a secular sovereignty are undoubtedly the reason for Rousseau's paradoxical reference, in "The State of War," to Hobbes as "one of the greatest geniuses that ever lived."

Yet, as we have seen in the summary of Hobbes above, Hobbes seriously compromises his allegiance to the liberal tradition by leaving open the possibility that political authority can be established by "acquisition" as well as by "institution." By arguing that sovereignty can arise out of conquest as well as by free choice, Hobbes in effect lets nature and the use of force into his theory by the back door. This very unliberal side of Hobbes is expressed even more blatantly in *De Cive* than it is in the chapter from *Leviathan* cited on page 24 above. In *De Cive*, Hobbes states:

> In the . . . foregoing . . . we have treated of an institutive or framed government, as being that which receives its original from the consent of many, who by contract and faith mutually given have obliged each other. Now follows what may be said concerning a natural government: which may also be called acquired, because it is that which is gotten by power and natural force.[45]

Although Hobbes in *Leviathan* tries to qualify his statements about the use of force by saying that "it is not . . . the victory that gives the right of dominion over the vanquished but his own covenant," nevertheless, since the "covenant" in such a situation is extracted by the threat of death, the effect is the same, and the use of force thus becomes a justifiable basis for asserting political sovereignty.

In contradistinction to Hobbes, Rousseau in the *Social Contract* denies that political rule can rightfully be founded on the use of force. The word "rightfully" is crucial here, for while Rousseau recognizes that states have been founded by conquest, his purpose in the *Social Contract* is explicitly to elucidate not what *is*, but what *ought to be*. Unlike the second *Discourse*, which aimed to explain the "Origin of Inequality among Men," the *Social Contract* aims to put forth the "Principles of Political Right." The intention to focus not on "fact" but on "right" can be seen in the very first chapter of the *Social Contract* where after the famous opening words, "Man is born free, and everywhere he is in chains," Rousseau goes on to ask, "What can make [this change] legitimate?" What, in other words, can "make right" mankind's transition from the condition of natural freedom to the condition of civil obedience?[46]

Rousseau proceeds to answer his own question by asserting what a legitimate political order cannot be based on, and in disposing of the unacceptable alternatives he first confronts the assumption that legitimate political authority can be established by force or conquest. He begins by arguing that if one accepts the notion that the use of force is a legitimate means of getting a people to obey, then one must also accept the legitimacy of those same people using force to overthrow their oppressors. "For in recovering its freedom by means of the same right used to steal it, either the people is justified in taking it back, or those who took it away were not justified in doing so." But the principle that serves as the basis for a legitimate civil order must be a pure and absolute right, Rousseau argues, not one that is fraught with contradiction and arbitrary applications. Therefore, it is not in the use of force that one can find the fundamental principles of political legitimation.[47]

In contrast to Hobbes, whose allowance for the use of force to establish despotic rule leaves room for natural inequalities rather than deliberate choice to be the basis of sovereignty, Rousseau insists that political life cannot be based on nature in this way, but must instead be based on pure conventions, or agreements. Natural differences such as those between fathers and children, masters and slaves, gods and men, or the strong and the weak cannot logically provide the basis for legitimate political authority, Rousseau argues in Book I of the *Social Contract*, and in the course of his argument he reiterates his conviction that "might" cannot make "right." "Force is a physical power," Rousseau asserts. "I do not see what morality can result from its effects. Yielding to force is an act of necessity, not of will."[48]

Having shown that political authority is not something that is "natural," Rousseau then considers whether political authority could be based on the "convention" of voluntary slavery. I look at this question more closely in connection with Rousseau's responses to Grotius in the next chapter; for now, suffice it to say that Rousseau also eliminates slavery as a legitimate basis for political order. He sums up the arguments he has made thus far by observing that,

> even if I were to grant everything I have thus far refuted, the proponents of despotism would be no better off. There will always be a great difference between subjugating a multitude and governing a society. If scattered men, however many there may be, are successively enslaved by one individual, I see only a master and slaves; I do not see a people and its leader. It is an aggregation, if you wish, but not an association. It has neither public good nor body politic.[49]

In searching for a form of convention or covenant that can provide the basis for legitimate political rule, the problem then becomes, as Rousseau sees it, to "find a form of association that defends and protects the person and goods of each associate with all the common force, and by means of which each one, uniting with all, nevertheless obeys only himself and remains as free as before." This, he goes on to explain, is the fundamental problem that can be solved only by the social contract.

Although Rousseau agrees with Hobbes that sovereignty, once established, is the sole source of law, the social contract that Rousseau proposes is very different from that of Hobbes; it is also very different from the brutal manipulation of those without property by those with property that Rousseau had described in his *Discourse on the Origin of Inequality*. Instead of alienating their sovereignty to a despot for the sake of their mutual survival, Rousseau insists that in all forms of government sovereignty must remain with the people; and instead of being motivated by fear, the common interest must be motivated by a sense of the general will.

I explore Rousseau's conception of a social contract based on the general will further in Chapter 3; here it is necessary only to stress the importance of Rousseau's new conception of the relationship between force and law. By insisting that law and "right" must be based not on force but only on agreement, Rousseau in effect purifies the classical concepts of both nature and convention. For deprived of warring instincts, human nature can be assumed to be originally good; at the same time, deprived of any organic "natural" basis for authority, the state can be seen as being only as effective as it is deliberately made to be by the people's concerted will.

UNTIL NOW, the focus has been on Rousseau's understanding of war and human nature as that understanding developed in reaction to the political philosophy of Thomas Hobbes. By examining Rousseau's criticism of Hobbes's views about natural man, the origin of war, and the relationship between force and law, we have seen that Rousseau's writings on war helped him to construct an alternative to Hobbesian political theory founded on the convictions that man is naturally peaceful, that war is thus not a product of nature but of *de facto* political life, and that the rightful basis for political order is not conquest by a despot to keep men all in awe but the deliberate association of free individuals.

But by directing one's attention to the Hobbesian critique in "The State of War," one gains only a partial appreciation of Rousseau's important assertion that war is a relation not of men but of states. For in the latter half of Rousseau's unfinished manuscript the argument against Hobbes merges into an argument against Grotius, and Rousseau turns away from speculations about war and human nature and moves toward his definition of war as a purely political relationship. To continue the exploration of Rousseau's understanding of the relations among states, it is now necessary to examine closely his response to the *Rights of War and Peace* of Hugo Grotius.

2

WAR AND THE STATE

A RESPONSE TO GROTIUS

In the opening paragraph of the "Prolegomena" to his *Rights of War and Peace*, Hugo Grotius points out that while many people have undertaken to explain or summarize the internal civil law of various states,

> few have dealt with that law which exists *between* several peoples or rulers of peoples, whether it be that derived from nature herself or instituted by Divine decrees or created by custom and tacit agreement; and no one at all has so far discussed it generally and in systematic fashion, although it is of importance to mankind that this should be done.
>
> Rightly indeed has Cicero called this a pre-eminent science, including as it does . . . the whole law of war and peace.[1]

Written in 1625, Grotius's long and complex attempt to analyze "that law which exists between peoples or rulers of peoples" is rarely read today, although it is considered by students of legal history and of what is known as just-war doctrine to be one of the seminal works in the history of international law. In the eighteenth century, however, Grotius's *Rights of War and Peace* was widely read, and as Robert Derathé has observed, was a crucial stimulus to the political writings of Jean-Jacques Rousseau.[2]

As the "Prolegomena" indicates, one of the central themes of Grotius's work and of the just-war tradition in general (as that tradition developed from Christian just-war doctrine during the Middle Ages and up through Grotius's time to modern theories about international law) is the question whether the laws governing the relations among states are to be found in "nature herself or instituted by Divine decrees

43

or created by custom and tacit agreement"—that is, whether international law can be derived from natural law or from religion or from the "customary" laws between nations. As is evident in the discussion of Rousseau's critique of Hobbes in the last chapter, and as one learns from Rousseau's testimony in the *Confessions*, questions about the source of law were central to all of Rousseau's political writing. It has also been pointed out that among the topics he intended to treat in his "Political Institutions" were "the true principles of the rights of war" and "why Grotius and others presented only false ones."[3] Since these questions about the source of law and the rights of war form the background for Rousseau's "The State of War," it is necessary to become acquainted with his response to Grotius and to the other theorists of the just-war tradition of which Grotius's work was such an important part.

UNLIKE his consistently critical response to Hobbes, Rousseau's early references to Grotius show that Rousseau initially shared his contemporaries' general admiration for Grotius and for the "natural law" school of jurisprudence of which Grotius was then considered to be a leading light. As early as 1740, in his "Project for the Education of M. de Sainte-Marie," which he wrote when he was a tutor to the young sons of M. de Mably, Rousseau, repeating the conventional pedagogical wisdom of the day, proposes the reading of Hugo Grotius as the important last step of the curriculum. "Finally," he says,

> if it happens that my pupil remains long enough in my hands, I shall venture to give him some acquaintance with moral and natural law through the reading of Puffendorf [sic] and Grotius, because it is becoming in a good man and a man of intelligence to know the principles of good and evil, and the foundations on which the society of which he forms a part is established.[4]

In his "Dedication to the Citizens of Geneva," which Rousseau placed at the beginning of his *Discourse on the Origin of Inequality* fourteen years later, Rousseau makes an even more respectful reference to Grotius. Reminiscing about the community of artisans and activists of which he and his father—in Rousseau's recollection at least—were proud and well-informed partisans, he says of his father, "I see him still, living from the work of his hands, and nourishing his soul on the most sublime truths. I see Tacitus, Plutarch and Grotius mingled with the instruments of his trade before him."[5] As anyone familiar with Rousseau's admiration for Plutarch and Tacitus will know, to be situated beside those great names is indeed a mark of honor. Plutarch's *Lives* were Rousseau's favorite reading as a child, and it was Plutarch whom Rousseau later credited with having created in him "that proud and intractable spirit, that impatience with the yoke of servitude" that he experienced throughout his life. Tacitus's *Histories* of Rome were equally significant for Rousseau's intellectual development; he undertook a translation of Tacitus during his visit to Geneva shortly after he completed the second *Discourse*, and Tacitus's account of Rome's early independence and frugal virtues underlies much of the spirit of Book IV of the *Social Contract*. Here in his dedication to the second *Discourse*, then, Grotius is found in very good company. One might even surmise that by mentioning the names of Plutarch, Tacitus, and Grotius, Rousseau was deliberately trying to raise the Genevans' consciousness of themselves as individuals, as citizens of the state, and as citizens of the world.

By the time Rousseau published the final chapters of *Emile* and the opening chapters of the *Social Contract* eight years later, however, his references to Grotius had changed completely. Instead of being associated with his heroes Plutarch and Tacitus, Grotius is now identified with Rousseau's archenemy, Hobbes; and instead of providing a lesson in morals, Grotius is presented as an example of "bad faith." "The science of political right is yet to be born," Rousseau asserts boldly in the closing pages of *Emile*,

> and it is to be presumed that it never will be born. Grotius, the master of all our learned men in this matter, is only a child, and what is worse, a child of bad faith. When I hear Grotius praised to the skies and Hobbes covered with execration, I see how few sensible men read or understand these two authors. The truth is that their principles are exactly alike.[6]

In the *Social Contract*, which appeared in the same year as *Emile*, one reads an equally sharp condemnation of Grotius: "His most persistent mode of reasoning is always to establish right by fact," Rousseau asserts; and, in terms that implicitly put Grotius in the same category as Hobbes, he continues, "one could use a more rational method, but not one more favorable to tyrants."[7] How can this apparent turnabout in Rousseau's assessment of the work of Hugo Grotius be explained?

As I plan to show, part of the reason for Rousseau's changing assessment of Grotius can be found in the ambiguities inherent in Grotius's work, and part can be found in the rather slow development of Rousseau's own convictions about what constitutes "legitimate" behavior in international relations. In order to elucidate the complex dynamics of Rousseau's response to Grotius, I focus on the three themes of natural law, the rights of war, and the relationship between slavery and right, and I again move from the second *Discourse* through "The State of War" to the *Social Contract*. The parallels between the treatment of Grotius here and the treatment of Hobbes in the last chapter are not accidental;

although Rousseau began the second *Discourse* with an assessment of Grotius that was very different from that of Hobbes, as his own political thought developed, gradually his responses to Grotius and Hobbes began to converge.

Grotius tells the reader of his "Prolegomena" that he undertook his study of *The Rights of War and Peace* because

> being fully convinced . . . that there is some law common to all nations which applies both to the initiation of war and to the manner in which war should be carried on, there were many and weighty considerations impelling me to write a treatise on the subject of that law. I observed everywhere in Christendom a lawlessness in warfare of which even barbarous nations would be ashamed. Nations would rush to arms on the slightest pretext or even without cause at all. And arms once taken up, there would be an end to all respect for law, whether human or divine, as though a fury had been let loose with general licence for all manner of crime.[8]

Grotius makes it clear in what follows that his concern about the "licence" of war does not lead him to believe that "all arms should be forbidden"; pacifists, like his fellow Dutchman, Erasmus, he says, seem to be acting on the principle that "to straighten a bent stick one must bend it strongly the other way. But this attempt to force too much to an opposite extreme often does more harm than good." Instead, what Grotius wants to find, he says, is "a remedy . . . for both schools of extremists—for those that believe that in war nothing is lawful and for those for whom all things are lawful in war."[9]

With this as his goal, Grotius divides *The Rights of War and Peace* into three parts. Book I lays the groundwork for his presentation by defining "What War Is, and What Right Is," and by discussing possible answers to the question "Whether War Can Ever Be Just." In Book II Grotius focuses on the causes of war, in particular on what constitutes a just or legitimate cause of war (i.e., the *jus ad bellum* of just-war doctrine), and in Book III he addresses the issue of what constitutes just behavior in war—the acceptable way to conduct war (i.e., *jus in bello*). Throughout his lengthy treatise, Grotius's method is to assert a specific principle and then to support it with a weighty accumulation of testimony from classical and Christian literature—a method that prompted Rousseau to comment that the only difference between Hobbes and Grotius was that the former supported his arguments with sophisms and the latter with "poets."[10] Yet it is this emphasis on precedent rather than principle that has made modern legal historians see Grotius's work as an important benchmark in the history of international law.

In Book I, which he devotes mostly to a definition of terms, Grotius distinguishes between "private war" (war waged by individuals), "public war" (war waged by those who have legitimate authority to wage war), and "mixed war" (war waged by individuals on one side and authorities on another, for example, revolutionary war), but in subsequent passages these distinctions sometimes get blurred, and civil law is frequently used as an analogy or even a precedent for international law.

In the first book Grotius also defines sovereignty and provides arguments and testimony to refute the opinion of those "who hold that everywhere and without exception sovereignty resides in the people." To refute this notion, Grotius uses examples from both Jewish and Roman law to show that historically anyone has the right to engage himself in private servitude, and if an individual may do so, argues Grotius, "Why, then, would it not be permitted to a people . . . to submit itself to one person, or to several persons, in such a way as plainly to transfer to him the legal right to govern, retaining no vestige of that right for itself?"—a line of reasoning similar to the one later used by Hobbes to justify despotic government. Grotius also defends the rights of absolute monarchy with the argument that "sacred and secular history alike bear witness" to the "fact" that "there have been kings who did not derive their power, even in a general way, from the will of the people."[11] As can be guessed, these arguments later provoked an outcry from Rousseau and led him to criticize Grotius for always tending to "establish right by fact," a method that could not be more "favorable to tyrants."

In Book II, however, a number of precepts serve to remind Grotius's readers of the exemplary norms that should govern relations among states, particularly those that call themselves "Christian." In his discussion of legitimate causes for going to war, Grotius, like other theorists of the just-war tradition, distinguishes three valid reasons for going to war: self-defense, recovery of property, and punishment for crimes. He emphasizes, however, that the most valid justification for war is self-defense and that, for example, "wars cannot justly be waged against those who are unwilling to accept the Christian religion."[12]

Book III of *The Rights of War and Peace* is more problematical than Book II. Here, in his discussion of *jus in bello*, or what constitutes legitimate conduct in war, one may find the source for Rousseau's jab at Grotius in a footnote in Book I of the *Social Contract*. Quoting the Marquis d'Argenson's observation that "learned research on public right is often merely the history of ancient abuses and people have gone to a lot of trouble for nothing when they have bothered to study it too much," Rousseau comments wryly that "this is exactly what Grotius has done."[13] For in the lengthy discussions that Grotius devotes to topics such as the rules governing the declaration of war, or who is to be considered an enemy, or the treatment of prisoners, one cannot help feeling that his principles are embedded in such a labyrinthine tangle of qualifications and counterexamples that it is hard to know exactly what Grotius believes the rights or laws of war to be.

In his discussion of the declaration of war, for example, Grotius says that the law of nature, which is primarily self-preservation, does *not* require that a declaration of war be made, but by the law of nations "it is honorable and praiseworthy to make it."[14] He gives us a similar but perhaps even less excusable equivocation regarding the question of who is to be considered the enemy. In Chapter iv of Book III one may be shocked to read that all the people residing in the enemy territory are to be considered a part of the war, and thus that "the slaughter even of infants and of women is made with impunity, and that this is included in the law of war." Moreover, "this also extends to captives and even to those who wish to surrender."[15] Grotius admits, however, that what is permissible in killing enemies may not be without "moral wrong," and in a later chapter he argues that though such behavior is "permitted," men who consider themselves rational and Christian should consider "moderation" in their treatment of noncombatants.

In Grotius's discussion of prisoners, one finds precepts that sound even more problematical. Basing his argument on the premise that conquest gives the right to rule over conquered people and become their master, Grotius states that "according to the law of nations all persons captured in a war that is public become slaves" and that "there is no suffering which may not be inflicted with impunity upon such slaves." Grotius's reasoning here is somewhat questionable: Since the victors actually have the right to kill their captives, he argues, the decision to spare their lives and make them slaves can thus be considered a kind of "self-restraint" on the part of the conquerors.[16] Although he typically modifies this principle in later chapters that counsel "moderation," Grotius's apparent justification of any and all forms of torture of prisoners goes quite far beyond the norms formulated by other theorists in the just-war tradition, both before and after Grotius.

But it is possible to read Grotius's work in different ways. What has made *The Rights of War and Peace* susceptible to varying interpretations is the extent to which he applies different sets of religious, moral, and legal standards to each of the phenomena for which he is attempting to provide guidelines. As is evident in the quotation from the "Prolegomena" that opened this chapter, one of Grotius's intentions in *The Rights of War and Peace* was to analyze whether the laws that govern relations among states are "derived from Nature herself or instituted by Divine decrees or created by custom and tacit agreement." Grotius's answer, at times to the dismay of anyone who tries to read through *The Rights of War and Peace* today, appears to contain elements of all three approaches. To pursue this question further, it is necessary to take a brief look at Rousseau's response to Grotius's notion of the law derived from nature herself—that is, natural law.

NATURAL LAW

From Saint Augustine's writings about what constitutes just or legitimate war, on up through the Middle Ages, just-war doctrine generally (though not exclusively) was based on biblical texts and on what the Christian schoolmen interpreted as divine law.[17] By the sixteenth and seventeenth centuries, however, when expanding Christian nations found themselves at war with non-Christian peoples and when the Protestant Reformation had split European Christendom into two hostile camps, those searching for criteria with which to restrain war and keep it within more reasonable bounds began to look beyond religious doctrine for more universal guidelines that would include Christians and non-Christians alike. It was then that one saw the emergence, in just-war theory, of the concept of natural law, a concept that had been rediscovered in the writings of Aristotle, Cicero, and the Stoics, and that was first used simply to reinforce but later to include both divine law and customary law. From the Catholic theologians of just-war theory such as Suarez and Victoria in the sixteenth century, up through Grotius in the seventeenth and Pufendorf and Vattel in the eighteenth century, and finally to Paul Ramsey in our own time, natural law concepts and terminology "weave in and out of just war tradition much as a thread of a particular color might be subtly woven in and out of a length of tweed fabric," as James T. Johnson explains in *Just War Tradition and the Restraint of War*.[18]

But in contrast to his predecessor, Francisco Victoria, and his follower, Samuel Pufendorf, both of whom argued clearly for the primacy of natural law as a guideline to waging war justly, Grotius, as we saw in the preceding section, seems at times noncommittal about which order of criteria—natural, conventional, or divine—should take precedence over the others. In general Grotius seems to move from what is "permissible" in war by the law of nature, which allows a wide range of actions, to what is "permitted" by the law of nations or *ius gentium* (the customary and tacit norms observed by different peoples), which imposes tighter limits, to what is recommended as charitable conduct for a Christian, the law that Grotius sometimes calls the "law of love," which is even more restrictive. Thus while "natural law," according to Grotius, might appear to allow almost any acts of belligerency that would serve the purposes of self-defense, the customary laws of nations and the "moderation" of rational (Christian) men prescribe more restrictive norms. Although the double and sometimes triple standards for what constitutes a legitimate cause for war or legitimate conduct during war makes reading Grotius somewhat taxing, the emphasis he gives to the customary "law of nations" gives him an important role in the development of international law. For contemporary international law theory has generally rejected the notion that there is any universalistic or absolutist "natural law" governing the relations among states; instead, the emphasis is on precedent and on positive law.

In the eighteenth century, however (and this is a point that makes Rousseau's initial response to Grotius somewhat difficult for twentieth-century students to understand), Grotius's readers did not see this novel emphasis in *The Rights of War and Peace* as clearly as we do today. For his Enlightenment readers, Grotius was thought to be a key founder of the "natural law" school of jurisprudence, and was considered to be a part of the same tradition of thought as Pufendorf (and other followers, such as Burlamaqui and Barbeyrac), who clearly made natural law the prior standard of morality. In other words, while we today stress the degree to which Grotius veered from the natural law tradition of jurisprudence and emphasized precedent and utility in international relations, eighteenth-century readers stressed the degree to which Grotius broadened the concept of natural law and included in that law both relations among states and relations among individuals. Like other Enlightenment readers, Rousseau at first viewed Grotius as one of the fathers of the natural law school of jurisprudence; only gradually did Rousseau depart from his own contemporaries' assessment and begin to see Grotius more as a theorist of the rights of war than as a theorist of natural law.

WHILE the main thrust of Rousseau's *Discourse on the Origin of Inequality* may have been to put forth an alternative to Hobbes's natural man, it is very clear from Rousseau's preface that an equally important intention of the *Discourse* was to criticize certain assumptions on the part of Grotius, Pufendorf, and others (whom Rousseau refers to as the "modern jurists") about natural law. Like other theorists in the natural law tradition (but unlike Hobbes), Grotius had defined natural law as a "dictate of right reason" that leads individuals to form social groupings: "The very nature of man, which even if we had no lack of anything would lead us into mutual relations of society, is the mother of the law of nature," he asserts in the "Prolegomena" to *The Rights of War and Peace*.[19] What Rousseau objects to in this definition of natural law is the tendency to posit as "natural" the human characteristics of reason and sociability that he believes can have evolved only after several stages of human development.

Rousseau's conviction that reason is not necessarily "original" or "natural" in man is explored to its fullest extent in *Emile*, but the spring-board for that mature analysis can be seen in the preface to the *Discourse on the Origin of Inequality*, where Rousseau begins to question the assumption that natural law is known through reason.

> All the definitions of these wise men, otherwise in perpetual contradic-
> tion to one another, agree only in this, that it is impossible to understand
> the law of nature and consequently to obey it without being a great
> reasoner and profound metaphysician: which means precisely that men
> must have used, for the establishment of society, enlightenment which
> only develops with great difficulty and in very few people in the midst
> of society itself.[20]

It is not reason that gives rise to political life, Rousseau is hinting here; instead, it is political life that nurtures reason.

Another characteristic that Rousseau finds arbitrarily arrived at by the theorists of natural law is the human attribute of sociability. Although he develops his critique of this assumption more fully in the *Discourse* itself and later in his early draft of the *Social Contract*, in the preface the device of positing innate "sociability" as the foundation of natural law comes under subtle but pointed attack:

> Writers begin by seeking the rules on which, for the common utility, it
> would be appropriate that men agree among themselves; and then they
> give the name "natural law" to the collection of these rules, without other
> proof than the good which they judge would result from their universal
> application. This is surely a very facile way to compose definitions and
> to explain the nature of things by almost arbitrary conveniences.[21]

Although Rousseau does not yet name Grotius in any of these attacks on the "modern jurists" of the natural law tradition, as one of the presumed fathers of that tradition, Grotius's presence would have been very much felt by his eighteenth-century readers.

In the first part of the second *Discourse* Rousseau unveils a picture of a natural man that implicitly challenges the assumptions of Grotius and his followers about the characteristics of natural law. As we saw in the last chapter, the primitive human being abiding by the law of nature whose portrait Rousseau so vividly painted is a creature not of sociability but of solitude; and what motivates his behavior is not reason but instinct—particularly the instinct of *amour de soi*, or self-preservation mitigated by pity. "It is in this natural sentiment [of *amour de soi*], rather than in subtle arguments," Rousseau insists, "that we must seek the cause of the repugnance any man would feel in doing evil, even independently of the maxims of education. Although it may behoove Socrates and minds of his stamp to acquire virtue through reason, the human race would have perished long ago if its preservation had depended only on the reasonings of its members."[22] And later, in "The State of War," Rousseau expresses this idea in even more explicit terms: "If natural law were inscribed only on human reason," he says, in a section where he is implicitly directing his arguments against Grotius,

> it would hardly be capable of directing most of our actions; but [natural law] is also indelibly engraved in the human heart. It is from the heart that natural law speaks to man more powerfully than all the precepts of philosophers. It is from there that it cries out to him that he may not sacrifice the life of his fellow man except to save his own, and that even when he sees himself obliged to do so, he cannot but feel a sense of horror at the idea of killing in cold blood.

From this passage in "The State of War" one might believe that Rousseau intended to develop a new concept of natural law that would make its touchstone not human reason but human sentiment, and from which could be derived a standard on which to base the restraint of war that would be more definitive and humane than the one set forth by Grotius. In fact, however, Rousseau never developed a concept of natural law for the conduct of international relations; nor did he accept as a useful standard for judging the legitimacy of war the concept of a "law of nations" or *jus gentium*, which Grotius had made so central to his own theories of war and peace.[23] In "The State of War" Rousseau states clearly that there is a fundamental weakness in such a concept:

> As for that which is commonly called the law of nations, it is clear that without any real sanction, these laws are only illusions that are more tenuous even than the notion of natural law. The latter at least addresses itself to the heart of individuals, whereas decisions based on the law of nations, having no other guarantee than the utility of the one who submits to them, are respected only as long as those decisions confirm one's own self-interest.

In a context devoid of any legitimate power to enforce such laws, Rousseau is suggesting, *ius gentium* or the customary laws of nations become simply excuses for the perpetuation of violence.

In his later discussion of the rights of war, Rousseau provides an alternative to the whole just-war tradition by seeking to establish the limits of war not on the concepts of natural law or even the law of nations, but by means of the definition of war itself. This discussion constitutes one of Rousseau's most significant contributions to the history of international law.

THE RIGHTS OF WAR

With his assault on the "modern jurists" of the natural law tradition in the second *Discourse*, Rousseau was obviously beginning to look at Grotius's writings more critically than he had done fourteen years earlier when he was a tutor for the sons of M. de Mably. But still Rousseau had not addressed Grotius's doctrine on the *Rights of War and Peace* in any fundamental way. Part of the reason for this delay may be the fact that Rousseau himself was, early in his life, occasionally quite quick to "justify" war. In 1740 when he was in Lyon, for example, he wrote a poetic drama called "The Discovery of the New World," in which he described, in terms that verge on a kind of cultural imperialism, France's ability to "conquer" the Americas by her "sweet" and "tender" culture. (Also addressing Europe, "Destiny" says, "If there remain in your climes any barbarian peoples/[France] will tame them, and by her uncommon concern/Will bring sweet manners to their inhuman hearts.")[24] And later, in his *Discourse on the Sciences and Arts*, when he is deploring the weaknesses of "all these modern warriors who are so scientifically disciplined" and the "enervation" of military valor by modern luxury and learning, he occasionally seems to confuse "virtue" with "conquest," especially when he is referring to Rome. ("The only talent worthy of Rome is that of conquering the world and making virtue reign in it," he has Fabricius say, in a strident tone.)[25]

Rousseau's nostalgia in the first *Discourse* and elsewhere for the tradition of "armed civic virtue" in ancient Sparta and republican Rome has caused a number of critics to see Rousseau as an apologist for more modern forms of nationalism and militarism.[26] In the correspondence that Rousseau had with his readers after the publication of the first *Discourse*, however, one finds Rousseau's later views about the rights of war beginning to emerge. In a letter in which he is responding to King Stanislas of Poland's argument that progress in the sciences and arts had led to wars being both less frequent and more just, Rousseau responds tartly, "Whatever period you are talking about, how can war be more just for one side without being more unjust for the other?" and in his "Final Response," addressed to M. Bordes, Rousseau develops a distinction, which had been absent from the first *Discourse* itself, between aggressive and defensive wars, and sharply criticizes France's colonial incursions in terms that are very different from the chauvinistic attitude he had expressed ten years earlier in "The Discovery of the New World." If the barbarians were unjust, he says, "What were we, then, I ask you, when we made that conquest of the Americas which is so highly praised? What was that but the means by which men who have cannons, charts, and compasses can also commit injustices?"[27] Here it becomes clear that although Rousseau may have admired the citizen militias of ancient times, he was unequivocally opposed to standing armies and the rationalized techniques of modern war.

But while the correspondence he engaged in after the publication of the first *Discourse* undoubtedly helped Rousseau sharpen his critique of modern war, even by the time he wrote the second *Discourse* in 1754, his assessment of Grotius still had not developed in any consistent way. On the one hand, he had implicated Grotius in his assault on the assumptions of the "modern jurists" about natural law in the preface to the *Discourse*; on the other, he had put Grotius alongside Tacitus and Plutarch in his dedication.

A year or two later, however, by the time he began drafting "The State of War" and other fragments, Rousseau was already clear about his desire to find alternative principles for the rights of war. This change may have come from a closer reading of Grotius than Rousseau had done before, or it may be that by the mid-1750s a more critical attitude toward the natural law jurists was simply "in the air." There is evidence of this attitude in the disparaging comments by the Marquis d'Argenson about the just-war theorists that Rousseau quoted in the *Social Contract*, and in a letter to a friend in 1758 Voltaire mentions that despite the law of nations of Grotius and Pufendorf his own niece had been insulted and dragged in the mud at Frankfurt.[28] But whatever the prompting, in "The State of War" and a number of other unpublished fragments, Rousseau embarked on an implicit critique of Grotius that became, in the *Social Contract*, a full-scale, explicit attack, not only on Grotius but on the underlying assumptions of all just-war theory that attempts to ground the rights of war in any form of transcendent law.

THE OPENING wedge for Rousseau's critique of Grotius in "The State of War" can be found in Rousseau's argument that war does not exist between individuals, a theme that had been implicitly present in the *Discourse on the Origin of Inequality* but that, as was pointed out in the last chapter, is developed in full in "The State of War." Whether one is referring to individuals in the state of nature or to individuals in the civil state or even to individuals who happen to be kings, Rousseau argues, the conflicts between them cannot be called actual wars because such conflicts lack the permanency that war presupposes. This idea, which he had first formulated in reaction to Hobbes's notion of a natural war of "every man against every man," becomes the starting point for Rousseau's critique of Grotius. For if there is no such thing as a war between individuals, then by definition there is no such thing as the distinction between "public" war and "private" war that Grotius had described in Book I of *The Rights of War and Peace* and that he had used as a precedent for much of his further discussion of war. Since war originates not in human nature but in the "system" of international relations, Rousseau will finally conclude, war can by definition only be "public" and must be treated as a political "convention" or institution.

Rousseau leads his reader to an understanding of the concept of war as a political institution by means of a fairly long digression that proceeds first through the manuscript's section titled "The General Idea of War between State and State" and then through a description of "What the State of War Is." (The first section, he admits, is an "immense detail" that is not really "within my subject matter," and the second section is crossed out in the original.)[29] He begins this somewhat circuitous but illuminating discussion with a comment about the close links between the internal constitution of states and their international relations. Having discovered among political bodies "a general relationship which tends towards their mutual destruction," Rousseau says (reminding the reader of the preceding section of the manuscript, which had focused on the origins of war), "it remains for us to see what exactly it is that constitutes their existence, their well-being, and their life, so that we may then be able to identify the kinds of hostilities by which they are able to attack each other and harm each other." This brings him to an observation about the constitution of the state that comes very close to the ideas expressed in his article on "Political Economy" and in his *Social Contract*:

> It is from the social pact that the body politic receives its unity and its *moi commun*. The government and the laws determine the robustness of its constitution, the hearts of the citizens give it its life, their courage and customs determine its durability, and the only actions which it undertakes freely and which it can be accountable for are those dictated by the general will.

In Rousseau's later writings these ideas are developed further: Here in "The State of War" he states only briefly that it is by the actions dictated by the general will that "we can judge whether the being which produced them is well or poorly constituted." The way a state conducts itself in the world, Rousseau is implying, indicates something about the basic political structure of the state.

Rousseau proceeds to argue that so long as there is the required political commitment, the social pact will continue to survive. And because the social pact is not "a charter made out of parchment" but a conviction that is "written into the general will," the social pact is not at all easy to destroy. Nevertheless, there are innumerable ways that the social pact can be torn apart: "If the body is invulnerable, its separate members can be struck at one by one; . . . if the source of its life cannot be reached, that which maintains it—the government, laws, customs, holdings . . . can still be destroyed. When everything that preserves it is annihilated, the state will finally die."

Contained in the meaning of the word *war*, then, are not just overt acts of violence but also espionage, economic exploitation, and cultural subversion—that is, any deliberate attempts to "weaken" the enemy state. As Bernard Gagnebin has pointed out, "On this point, as on so many others, Rousseau distinguished himself from the writers of his time," most of whom (such as Grotius and Vattel) had argued that war consists in the use of force. Rousseau, however, extends the notion of war to include all forms of willful political destruction.[30]

Rousseau supports his view of the political nature of war by giving examples of the Greek republics that attacked one another "less in order to take away each other's liberty than to change the form of their governments" and examples of Roman leaders who understood that a useful tactic for conquest was simply to allow an enemy state to perish from the "effeminate and sedentary arts" that could destroy it from within. But for twentieth-century readers modern history provides even more examples to fit Rousseau's definition of war as an attempt to destroy the "social pact" of another state: The conflict between the United States and the Soviet Union has been characterized more by a rivalry between opposing political and economic ideologies than by the overt use of force and violence.

Indeed, Rousseau was one of the first to make a distinction between war itself and the state of war, a condition that we today would call a "cold war." War itself, he explains, is "the effect of a mutual, constant and manifest intention to destroy the enemy state" that takes the form of actual acts of war. If, however, the intention does not actually manifest itself as acts of war, there is said to be a "state of war." In a section of the Geneva fragment that is crossed out in the original, Rousseau describes this state of war more fully. When two self-declared enemies remain stationary and on guard but take no offensive actions against each other, Rousseau points out, the relationship has not changed as far as their intentions are concerned. Thus they are in a "state of war." "Long wars that people get tired of but that they cannot end ordinarily produce this state," Rousseau explains. He concludes this definition with a warning: "Sometimes, far from being lulled into inaction, the animosity needs only to wait for a favorable moment to surprise the enemy, and then often the state of war that produces this release is more dangerous than would be war itself."

Rousseau defines the situation that results from an imposed peace treaty or truce also as simply a continuation of the state of war. It is clear from his previous definitions, he says, that a truce, a cease-fire or a "Peace of God" all constitute a "modified" state of war in which the two enemies "tie their own hands" without losing or disguising the will to harm each other. "They make preparations, pile up weapons and materials for a siege, and all the non-specified military operations continue apace. This is enough to show that the intentions have not changed." Further on Rousseau asks rhetorically, "What are such forms of peace in the end but a continual war that is all the more cruel because the enemy can no longer defend itself."

Throughout this section Rousseau's tone is somewhat puzzling. The objectivity with which he lists the various ways that political bodies are able to "attack each other and harm each other" makes this part of the text at moments sound like a "how-to" manual for war. But unlike the natural law theorists who claimed that nature itself is the source of moral norms, Rousseau, like Hobbes, firmly believed (and this point becomes clearer in Chapter 3) that morality develops only with the establishment of political societies. In "The State of War" what is being described is the behavior of political bodies that in effect are in a state of nature in their relations with one another. In such a context, they are thus outside any framework in which it would be appropriate to judge that behavior as right or wrong.

Instead of trying to discuss "The General Idea of War between State and State" in moral terms, therefore, Rousseau limits himself to examining the institution of war by means of its "principles." He emphasizes the essentially political nature of war—that war is a conflict between political entities rather than a conflict between human beings. "For the objective of all the harm inflicted on one's enemy at war is to force him to accept those things which he will have to suffer even more from when at peace," says Rousseau in words that anticipate Clausewitz's dictum, over a half-century later, that war is the pursuit of politics "by other means."[31] There is a difference, however, because for Clausewitz the purpose of war was the destruction of the enemy, not specifically the destruction of the enemy state—a distinction that has significant implications for the concept of war itself.

Rousseau's stress on the political nature of war provides the starting point for a number of unambiguous and logically consistent limitations on the rights of war that eventually appear in Book I of the *Social Contract*. It must also be acknowledged, however, that by defining war as a relationship between states rather than a relation between human beings, Rousseau's definition excludes wars that are the result of religious fanaticism or ethnic hostility, such as the twelfth-century Crusades or the twentieth-century campaigns against the Jews. Does such a limitation undermine the effectiveness of Rousseau's inquiry?

Here it is important to keep in mind the underlying purpose of Rous-

seau's definition. By insisting that war be understood as a deliberate
political choice rather than as an inevitable tendency rooted in human
nature, Rousseau conveys the hope that a sovereign people will judge
the risks of war in terms of their long-term general will, or common
good. Only when citizens understand war as an artificial consequence
of conventional politics, and not as a natural consequence of innate aggressiveness, is there the possibility that the use of war will be opposed
or at least limited.[32] Although Rousseau himself, as Alfred Cobban has
pointed out, would probably be appalled at the extent and the ferocity
of the wars that, since the eighteenth century, have been perpetrated by
democratic governments in the name of the general will,[33] it is also true
that Rousseau's definition can serve to remind his readers of their own
responsibility for the foreign policy decisions of their governments and
their responsibility to resist war rather than promote it.

At the end of the section on "What the State of War Is," Rousseau
leads his readers into a crucial transition that occurs only a page before the manuscript breaks off. Anticipating the objection that if war
is so natural to states, then why should states be expected to observe
the formality of declaring war, Rousseau says, "Until now I have been
speaking of the natural state, [but] now I am speaking of the legitimate state." This important statement is followed by a new section of
the manuscript subtitled "Fundamental Distinctions" that begins with
the plea that his readers remember he is looking "not for that which
makes war advantageous to the one who wages it, but for that which
makes it legitimate." It is thus at this point that Rousseau finally introduces the specific precepts that derive from his "principles of the rights
of war." Moreover, it is here, perhaps for the first time in Rousseau's
political writing, that one sees him making an explicit transition from a
description of *de facto* political society to an analysis of legitimate political society, from what politics *is* to what politics *ought to be*. This shift
in the manuscript on "The State of War" can thus be seen to herald
the larger shift in Rousseau's thought represented by the difference between the descriptive emphasis of the *Discourse on the Origin of Inequality*
and the normative emphasis of the *Social Contract*. Finally, it is here
too that Rousseau probably came to realize that Grotius's method of
establishing "right by fact," that is, of basing moral guidelines for war
on the customary laws and actual practices of war in the past, was a
method favoring only "tyrants."

Rousseau embarks on his discussion of the actual rights or laws of
war by spelling out the full definition of war that he has been leading
up to thus far. Since war cannot take place between individuals, he
asks, "Whom therefore does it take place between? Who can really be

called enemies?" and his answer refers one back to the point made at the end of the last chapter about the necessarily artificial or "conventional" character of political bodies: "To [the above questions] I answer that war takes place between public persons. And what is a public person? To this I answer that it is an artificial being that one calls sovereign, which is brought into existence by the social pact, and whose collective will carries the name of law." The notion that wars are relationships between states and not between men and that legitimate war can thus be neither "private" nor "natural" but must by definition be "public" and "artificial" brings Rousseau to an apparently paradoxical conclusion: "If war only takes place between artificial beings, then there need be no enmity between men, and one might therefore wage war without taking a single person's life." Again, the acknowledgment of the possibility of ideological war is a logical conclusion of Rousseau's premises that states, rather than individuals, cause war and that states themselves are merely human constructs or "conventions." "As an artificial being," Rousseau reminds us, "the body politic is essentially only a creature of reason. Remove public convention, and at that instant the state is destroyed without the slightest alteration in all that comprises it."

Rousseau summarizes this argument as follows:

> What is it then to make war on a sovereign? It is to attack public convention and everything that results from it, for the essence of the state consists only in that. If the social pact could be broken apart in one blow, at that instant there would no longer be war; and by this blow the state would be killed without a single man having died.

According to Rousseau's understanding of war, then, there can be wars without battles or massacres if, solely because of the menace of enemy forces, the state dissolves and the social pact is broken.[34]

Having finally arrived at a definition of war as a political institution or "convention" between sovereign states, Rousseau is ready to deduce specific rights of war from his definition. But, unfortunately, just at this point, just as he is beginning to explore the particulars of just-war theory, his manuscript on "The State of War" breaks off. It is impossible to know exactly why Rousseau never completed the manuscript; in his letter to Rey in 1758 he simply states that his "Principles of the Rights of War are not at all complete." One can only speculate that Rousseau gradually came to see the futility of pursuing a discussion of the rights of war outside any context of political morality. In contrast to Grotius, who had believed that *The Rights of War and Peace* could become the basis for international law even without a supreme authority to enforce such law, but similar to Hobbes, who had argued that "where there is no common power there is no law," Rousseau seems to have concluded that with no overarching legal framework as its basis, the assessment of a political entity's "rights" becomes meaningless.

The above hypothesis would also explain both why Rousseau subsequently became interested in the Abbé de Saint-Pierre's project for a European confederation of states and why he decided finally to place the precepts resulting from his "Principles of the Rights of War" within the context of the *Social Contract*. While the rights of war may have little meaning outside any context of law, they do have meaning as the moral guidelines for the foreign policy of a legitimately constituted political community.

In the chapter titled "On Slavery" in Book II of the *Social Contract*, Rousseau repeats his definition of war as a relation not between men but between states and continues his response to Grotius about what constitutes the rights of war. By piecing together passages from the *Social Contract* with the final paragraphs of "The State of War" and with other fragments, one can compile a fairly complete picture of Rousseau's most fundamental precepts about the declaration of war, noncombatant immunity, and the treatment of prisoners—the traditional concerns of just-war theory and international law. What is original about Rousseau's formulations are not the precepts themselves, for those had evolved over several centuries of debate about the morality of war. Instead, what Rousseau offers is a fresh way of integrating the traditional concerns of just-war theory into a purely secular and political definition of war.[35]

For example, in contrast to Grotius's equivocation about whether war needs a formal declaration, Rousseau's views are uncompromising. In order to make war legitimate, he asserts at the end of "The State of War," war needs to be formally declared, and in the *Social Contract* he reemphasizes a point that had been mentioned by Grotius but not insisted on, namely, that declarations of war are not so much warnings to those in power as they are warnings to their subjects so that all mankind may be able to judge the war's legitimacy. "The foreigner—whether he be king, private individual, or people—who robs, kills or imprisons subjects without declaring war on the prince, is not an enemy, but a brigand," Rousseau insists.[36] In a related fragment he specifies further the formality that ought to accompany the beginning of hostilities between states: "If I wanted to deepen the notion of the state of war I would show easily that it can only result from the free consent of the belligerent parties; that if one party wants to attack and the other does not want to defend itself there is no state of war but only violence and aggression." Once more Rousseau is emphasizing that war is not "natural" but "conventional," that it is a decision to be undertaken only as an application of the law that reflects the general will, and only for the purpose of achieving political ends.[37]

In his discussion of noncombatant immunity, Rousseau again draws his principles from his definition of war as a politically, rather than naturally, motivated action. In contrast to Grotius's broad assumption that the enemy is anyone who happens to be in enemy territory at the time of war (an assumption that allows for the "justification" of killing women and children), Rousseau restricts the definition of enemy as much as possible and argues for the immunity of all those who are noncombatants. Since war is not a relation between man and man, but between state and state, Rousseau points out in the *Social Contract*, "private individuals are enemies only by accident, not as men, nor even as citizens, but as soldiers; not as members of the homeland but as its defenders. . . . Each State can have only other States, and not men, as enemies." Thus, "even in the midst of war, a just prince may well seize everything in an enemy country that belongs to the public, but he respects the person and goods of private individuals. He respects rights on which his own are based." According to Rousseau's principles, then, citizens who do not carry arms and are not defenders of the homeland should not be ranked among the enemies and should not be attacked during a war.[38]

In addition to providing a rationale for noncombatant immunity, Rousseau's understanding of the necessarily political character of war leads him to limit the rights a conqueror might have over those who have been defeated in war. Unlike Grotius, who had argued that the "natural law" of conquest brought with it the right to rule over conquered people and even, Grotius implies, to kill them, Rousseau states unreservedly in the *Social Contract* that since the purpose of war is the destruction of the enemy state and not the killing of people and since "war confers no right that is not necessary to its end," the conqueror has no right to kill the conquered or to make them his slaves.

> The end of war being the destruction of the enemy state, one has the right to kill its defenders as long as they are armed. But as soon as they lay down their arms and surrender, since they cease to be enemies or instruments of the enemy, they become simply men once again, and one no longer has a right to their lives.[39]

In a related fragment Rousseau formulates this same principle as follows: "People may kill in order to conquer, but there is no man so brutal that he would seek to conquer in order to kill."[40]

Rousseau's limitation of what constitutes legitimate treatment of a conquered people clearly has far-reaching implications. On one level, the limitation of the rights of conquest has the effect of pulling the rug

out from under Grotius's attempt to argue for the "right" of enslaving
a defeated people during war. Grotius had argued that the victor in a
war who enslaves the defeated in fact shows clemency, since he actually
has the right to do what is worse, which is to kill them. Rousseau explicitly rejects this argument: "If war does not give the victor the right
to massacre the vanquished peoples," he says, emphasizing once again
that the purpose of war is not to kill people but to defeat an enemy
state, "this right he does not have cannot establish the right to enslave
them."[41]

On another level, Rousseau's emphatic assertion that conquest extends no rights over those who are defeated has important implications
not just for the rights of war but for any political relationship. This
brings us to the point in our exploration of Rousseau's response to
Grotius where we are ready to examine Rousseau's critique of Grotius's assumptions about the relationship between slavery and right.
First, however, we should look back briefly over the terrain we have
just passed through. For by founding his rights of war not on the concepts of natural law or the customary laws of nations but instead on a
broad definition of war as intentional political harm, Rousseau radically
limits the rights of those who choose to participate in such intentions.
The limitation on the right to harm noncombatants that emanates directly from the definition of war as a relation not between individuals
but between states is a case in point; not only is such a concept extremely relevant to the present age of possible thermonuclear war but
it is also a concept that many argue has contributed significantly to the
formulation of international law. From the Brussels Conference in 1873
up through the Hague Conference in 1899 to more recent attempts
to devise universally acceptable guidelines pertaining to the waging
of war, the assumption that war is a relation not between individuals
but between states has provided the basis for many of the internation-
ally agreed upon standards for the declaration of war, the immunity of
noncombatants, and the treatment of prisoners.[42] Although Rousseau
himself seemed to have eventually decided that such precepts have little
meaning outside a political context, one can perhaps agree with his
own assessment that his principles "are not those of Grotius; they are
not based on the authority of poets, but are derived from the nature of
things, and are based on reason."[43]

THE CONTRADICTION BETWEEN
SLAVERY AND RIGHT

It is interesting to note that in his final draft of the *Social Contract* Rousseau's observations on the rights of war are placed in the chapter titled

"On Slavery." At first glance one might believe that this placement was a subtle suggestion on Rousseau's part that war is actually a kind of slavery. On closer study, however, one can see that the placement is an indication that Rousseau's analysis of the "principles of the rights of war" was intimately linked to his broader concern with "the principles of political right" and with his desire to refute Grotius's justification of slavery in *any* context. A hint of this confluence of public right and political right in Rousseau's mature thought can be found in a brief fragment that was probably drafted during the same period in which he was studying Grotius and drafting "The State of War." Shocked at Grotius's claim that the law of nations authorized the massacring of prisoners, Rousseau says (in a passage that provides a poignant reminder of the excesses of war in the twentieth century),

> Thank God we no longer see such things among Europeans. We'd be horrified by a prince who had his prisoners massacred. We become indignant even at those who treat them badly, and these abominable maxims which outrage reason and make humanity tremble are no longer familiar to anyone but the jurists who quietly make them the foundation of their political systems and who instead of showing us sovereign authority as the source of the happiness of man dare to show it as the torment of the defeated.[44]

In another related fragment Rousseau carries his critique of Grotius to the hilt:

> When a thousand ferocious peoples have massacred their prisoners, when a thousand learned scholars co-opted by tyranny have excused such crimes [a barbed reference to Grotius's allegiance to Louis XIII], is truth itself affected by such wrongs? Is justice affected by such cruelty? Let us not search for what has been done, but for what ought to be done, and let us reject these vile and mercenary authorities who want to make men into slaves, criminals, and malcontents.[45]

In the *Social Contract* Rousseau's "rejection" of Grotius and others who base sovereign rights on the "torment of the defeated" is developed in full. The argument follows from two different lines of thought that eventually converge at the end of the chapter "On Slavery." According to one line of reasoning, which is the one summarized earlier, Rousseau undermines the whole idea that conquest confers *any* rights over the defeated. War, being a purely political act, confers only the right to defeat the enemy state; the rights of individual people should therefore remain intact. Thus conquerors have no right either to kill the defeated or to make them their slaves.

Another line of reasoning reaches the same conclusion by another route, but it too has its source in Rousseau's reading of Grotius. Referring implicitly to Book I of *The Rights of War and Peace*, Rousseau directs his argument at Grotius's assertion that since a private individual can alienate his freedom and enslave himself to a master, a whole people can likewise alienate its freedom and subject itself to a king. Rousseau's response to Grotius on this point is crucial: An individual *cannot* alienate his freedom, Rousseau asserts, nor may a whole people do so. "To renounce one's freedom is to renounce one's status as a man," he affirms in words that have inspired human aspirations for freedom for over two hundred years. In Rousseau's view, man's freedom is his "everything" and "there is no possible compensation for anyone who renounces everything. Such a renunciation is incompatible with the nature of man."

While Grotius and others (including Pufendorf) had made an analogy between handing over one's property to a conqueror and handing over one's liberty to a sovereign, Rousseau was to argue all his life against this confusion between human liberty and private property.[46] Liberty cannot be exchanged or bought or sold; it is analogous not to property but to life itself, which no one has the right to "alienate."

> It is therefore an iniquitous exchange to make him buy his life, over which one has no right, at the cost of his freedom. . . . In taking the equivalent of his life, the victor has not spared it; rather than to kill him purposelessly, he has killed him usefully.[47]

By the end of his chapter "On Slavery" in the *Social Contract*, Rousseau's two-pronged argument with Grotius has thus demolished the "right" of slavery both from above and from below: Neither can a sovereign make slaves by conquest nor can a people become slaves by self-alienation. By attempting to argue for these so-called rights, Rousseau says, Grotius simply falls into redundancy: "By establishing the right of life and death on the right of slavery, and the right of slavery on life and death, isn't it clear that one falls into a vicious circle?"

In sum, slavery cannot be justified. "[F]rom every vantage point," Rousseau concludes, "the right of slavery is null, not merely because it is illegitimate, but because it is absurd and meaningless. These words *slavery* and *right* are contradictory; they are mutually exclusive."[48] Here it becomes clear why Rousseau's discussion of the rights of war appears in a chapter entitled "On Slavery." For by denying that human beings have any arbitrary rights over the freedom of others, Rousseau is undermining one of the justifications for offensive war. The logical extension of such an argument is that states that hold to the principles of freedom will be more likely to remain at peace. Indeed, this equation will appear years later, in his *Considerations on the Government of Poland*, where Rousseau argues that "anyone who wants to be free ought not to want to be a conqueror."[49]

WITH THE NOTION that slavery and right are mutually exclusive, Rousseau's response to Grotius merges with his response to Hobbes. In the preceding chapter, I showed how Rousseau's critique of Hobbes began in the second *Discourse*, was developed in "The State of War," and finally took the form of an alternative *Social Contract* in which sovereignty resides in the people themselves and in which force cannot be considered the basis for law. The present exploration of Rousseau's critique of Grotius, while it begins in the second *Discourse* with an assessment of Grotius that is very different from that of Hobbes, gradually evolves, again via "The State of War," into the *Social Contract*'s basic denunciation of any claim for slavery as the basis of political right. Rousseau's convergent criticisms of Hobbes's justification of despotism and Grotius's justification of slavery make it clear why Rousseau was moved to assert, in 1762, that Hobbes's and Grotius's principles "are exactly alike."

At this point, we can appreciate the extent to which Rousseau's unfinished manuscript on "The State of War" acts as a significant bridge between the *Discourse on the Origin of Inequality* and the *Social Contract*. Rousseau ended his *Discourse on the Origin of Inequality* in 1754 with a frightening scenario of civil repression and inequality within states and continual wars between them. Seven years later, he began the *Social Contract* with a vision of a legitimately constituted state in which conquest is not considered a right and where force cannot be the basis of law. In the interim between the two great works, in addition to publishing an article on "Political Economy," Rousseau drafted numerous notes and fragments pertaining to war and began working on the manuscript that we now know as "The State of War" but that was to be entitled "Principles of the Rights of War." Not only did this manuscript provide the context within which Rousseau was able to sharpen his assessment of Hobbes and Grotius, but, as I have tried to show in the past two chapters, the structure of the manuscript represents a spanning of the two famous works. The first two sections, where Rousseau points to the ironic contradictions between civil order and international anarchy and then argues against the idea of a "natural war of every man against every man," recall much of the underlying argument of the second *Discourse* (albeit in an abbreviated form and in a somewhat different sequence). The last three sections of the manuscript, where Rousseau analyzes what constitutes the "well-being" and "life" of a body politic and then goes on to hint at the criteria for "legitimate" war, anticipate Book I of the *Social Contract*—particularly Chapter iv where he explores in depth the definition of war as a political relation and deduces fundamental notions about the rights of war from that definition.

But more important even than representing a textual bridge between the second *Discourse* and the *Social Contract*, the manuscript on "The State of War" shows Rousseau making the crucial transition from questions of actual politics to questions of legitimate politics. This is perhaps the most important way that the writings on war contributed to the genesis of the *Social Contract*—and it is a development that could not be appreciated as long as the pages of the manuscript remained out of order. In Vaughan's edition of the text the statement "Up until now I have been speaking of the natural state . . . now I am speaking of the legitimate state" was buried in the middle of the argument, *before* the anguished descriptions of civil society as "miserable people groaning under an iron yoke" and of international relations as "a panorama of murder—ten thousand slaughtered men, the dead piled up in heaps." Given this sequence of ideas to go by, it is not surprising that many recent theorists have drawn cynical and pessimistic lessons from Rousseau's writings on war. But with the new arrangement, these parts of the exposition are reversed: Rousseau's initial focus is on *de facto* politics—the way things are organized—but toward the end he makes an explicit shift to legitimate politics—to the way things ought to be organized.

Seen in this light, the manuscript on "The State of War" takes its place alongside the article on "Political Economy" as an important indication of the development of Rousseau's political thought. At a time when questions about relations among states figure so largely in the discussions of relations within states, it is perhaps not inappropriate to stress that the vision of political right that Rousseau put forth in the *Social Contract* was in part rooted in his earlier attempts to limit and clarify the right of sovereign states to make war on one another.

Rousseau's clear assertion, at the beginning of the *Social Contract*, that slavery can no more be the basis for right than force can be a basis for law becomes the pushing-off point for his creation of a new form of political association that is based not on conquest or domination but on human freedom and collective will. The capacity for the political community described in the *Social Contract* to inspire political change within the nation-state has been carefully examined by a variety of recent writers,[50] but the possibility of applying Rousseauean political ideals to the context of relations among states has not yet been fully explored. A close look at Rousseau's writings on peace can provide the occasion for that discussion.

PART II

THE POLITICS OF PEACE

——— 3 ———

A GENERAL WILL OF THE
HUMAN RACE?

A RESPONSE TO DIDEROT

Chapters 1 and 2 have shown Rousseau "examining human institutions by means of their principles," "correcting . . . the false notions given about them by self-interested authors," and "insuring that injustice and violence don't shamelessly take on the names of right and equity." In reaction to Hobbes's picture of man as naturally warlike and in need of a fearful power to keep him "in awe," Rousseau constructed an alternative view of natural man as solitary and peaceful, and war as arising only with the institution of private property and the civil state. In reaction to Grotius's attempt to base the rights of war on natural law and a "law of nations," Rousseau put forth a definition of war as a purely political relationship and the rights of war as restraints on behavior that can be unequivocally deduced from the definition of war itself. In his critique of both authors, Rousseau's final concern was to counter their attempts to base law on force and "right" on slavery—examples of his desire to ensure that "injustice" does not shamelessly take on the name of "right" and that "violence" not be perpetrated in the name of "equity." Only when such concepts are demystified and examined critically in relation to their basic principles, Rousseau implies, can the ironic contradiction between the discourses of the moralists and the lived life of all of us be confronted and overcome.

In exploring Rousseau's effort to examine the true principles of right —both domestic political right and international public right—I have thus far been looking primarily at his attempt to limit the legitimation and scope of war. But, as is clear from the fragmentary nature of his writings on war, Rousseau eventually gave up on the effort to develop an extensive new set of "principles of the rights of war" as a solution to the contradiction between civil order and international anarchy. He never completed the manuscript that is now referred to as "The State of War," and he left only hints of what legitimate war might entail in his chapter "On Slavery" in the *Social Contract*.

Nevertheless, having abandoned just-war theory as the solution to the international dilemma that he had first described in the *Discourse on the Origin of Inequality*, Rousseau was not willing to give up on the problem altogether. In the period between 1755 and 1759, Rousseau's writings address not only the problem of war but also the hope for peace, and one can see him searching for a solution to the contradiction between civil life and international life both in his development of the concept of a general will and in his response to a plan for international security put forth by the Abbé de Saint-Pierre earlier in the eighteenth century. In this chapter, I focus on the concept of the general will, and in Chapter 4, I discuss Rousseau's responses to the Abbé de Saint-Pierre's *Project for Perpetual Peace*.

The concept of a general will may be a necessary part of any discussion pertaining to the possibilities of international peace. For without the conviction that common human aspirations can transcend particular national differences, the chances for peaceful coexistence of either individuals or nations seem slim. And yet in much of Rousseau's writing he appears to deny the possibility of the human race having any kind of "general will" for peace. In the second *Discourse* Rousseau argued persuasively *against* the assumption that man is naturally rational or sociable, and in "The State of War" he expressed the sobering notion that *de facto* civil societies have a built-in tendency to go to war. How, then, can one reconcile the obviously particularistic emphasis of Rousseau's political philosophy with the concept of a general will?

While today one associates the concept of the general will with Rousseau's *Social Contract*, the term was first used as a political concept not by Rousseau but by Denis Diderot in an article on "Natural Right" that he wrote in 1755 for Volume V of the *Encyclopédie*. Since Rousseau's concept of the general will as it appeared in the *Social Contract* seven years later can be seen as an important but subtle alternative to the concept of the general will presented by Diderot in his article on "Natural Right," it is appropriate at this point to look closely at Diderot's article and at the development of Rousseau's response to it.[1]

UNLIKE Rousseau's responses to Hobbes and Grotius, which were based solely on a reading of their texts (Hobbes and Grotius both having died several generations before Rousseau was born), Rousseau's response to

Diderot was based on a long personal friendship. Rousseau and Diderot met one another in 1741 when Rousseau first arrived in Paris trying
to promote his newly devised system of numerical music notation, and
the two resumed their acquaintance in the mid-1740s when Rousseau
returned to Paris after his stormy departure from the French Embassy
in Venice. Rousseau and Diderot were nearly the same age, they were
both sons of artisans (Rousseau's father had been a watchmaker, Diderot's father a cutler), and both had spent most of their postadolescent
years leading the kind of marginal and yet adventurous and experimen-
tal life that seems to be especially common among talented youth in
periods of intellectual ferment and social change.

More important, Diderot and Rousseau shared many interests. It
was probably their love of music that first drew them together—both
of them preferring the lighter, more melodic Italian music to formal
French compositions—but they also liked to play chess together and
shared an interest in classical literature, in the theater, and in science
and philosophy.[2] Rousseau says in his *Confessions* that he introduced
Diderot to the Abbé de Condillac, and that these three, later to be
joined by d'Alembert, met regularly together for dinner and conver-
sation at a small restaurant near Palais Royal called the Panier Fleuri.[3]
In retrospect, it is perhaps not an exaggeration to say that the French
Enlightenment owes much of its momentum to those conversations.

At one of their frequent meetings, Rousseau and Diderot had the
idea of starting a literary journal that would be called *Le Persifleur* ("The
Banterer"), but soon the project was pushed aside by the more serious
and demanding work of the *Encyclopédie*. The *Encyclopédie* had begun as
a fairly modest four-volume translation of the *Cyclopedia* that Ephraim
Chambers published in Scotland in 1728, but as soon as Diderot became the new venture's general editor, the project burgeoned into a
huge enterprise that would eventually fill seventeen volumes of print
and eleven volumes of engravings and would aim to collect and to
organize all of "modern" knowledge, especially the learning that had
proliferated in philosophy, technology, the arts, and sciences since the
beginning of the seventeenth century. A testament to the enormous
intellectual energy of the Enlightenment—its courageous criticisms of
orthodoxy, its curiosity about how the world works—the *Encyclopédie*
promised from the beginning to provoke as many questions as it would
provide answers. In this spirit of open dialogue Diderot wrote his
article on "Natural Right," and in this same spirit his closest friend,
Jean-Jacques Rousseau, later took up the line of reasoning about the
general will that Diderot put forth in that article and ultimately turned
Diderot's argument back upon itself.[4]

Diderot begins his article with the comment that although everyone thinks he knows what "right" is, the common man, when asked what it is, will silently refer to his own conscience, whereas the philosopher will get caught in a vicious circle of reasoning that will bring him right back where he started. For if the philosopher defines "right" as the foundation of justice, and justice as giving each person what is owed him, then when one asks the philosopher how such a concept of "owing" can arise in a state of nature where everything belongs to everyone, the philosopher will find himself in a quandary where he is reduced to admitting simply that "natural right" is certainly a difficult and complex concept. Given such confusions, says Diderot, we will have made a significant contribution to understanding if we can succeed in establishing principles that can help resolve the difficulties surrounding the definition of natural right.

At the center of Diderot's article is the question of where to look for standards of justice in a natural or "presocial" condition of human existence. Like other political philosophers before and since, what Diderot was wrestling with in his article on natural right was the attempt to find a grounding for moral norms that would overarch specific relativistic dogmas of religion or government. He broaches this question by describing the moral dilemma of a man in a Hobbesian state of nature who, while tormented by violent hostile passions, is also "rational" and recognizes that his own desire to harm others would require giving others the right to harm him. Diderot's description of this hypothetical "violent reasoner" typically takes the form of a dialogue inserted into the text. How could one respond, asks Diderot, if this violent reasoner said to us,

> I know that I bring terror and trouble to the human race; but it is necessary either that I am miserable or that I make others miserable; and no one is dearer to me than I am to myself. One can't reproach me for this abominable choice—I did not will it upon myself. It is the voice of nature which never expresses itself as loudly in me as when it speaks in my favor.[5]

But the violent reasoner will then have to admit, Diderot goes on to explain, that since he is "equitable and sincere,"

> if my happiness depends on my destroying the lives of those who hinder me, it is also necessary that any other individual can destroy my life if it hinders him. Reason requires this, and I will stand by it. I am not so unjust that I will expect a sacrifice of someone else which I am not ready to make myself.

The voice of the violent reasoner that Diderot creates here is very similar, both in tone and in underlying argument, to the natural man that Hobbes portrays in the first book of *Leviathan*. There, too, natural man was beset by passions of greed and competition that compelled him to seek power over others; there too, natural man's calculations of conflicting claims led him to understand the need to give up "natural rights" in favor of some superimposed rule of "natural law."[6]

But while accepting Hobbes's view of natural man, Diderot wants to avoid the Hobbesian conclusion that the violent reasoner must be *coerced* into civil society by the fear of an all-powerful despot. "How will we respond to the violent reasoner before stifling him?" Diderot asks. What Diderot is asking here is a fundamental question for ethical theory: On what basis can Enlightenment thought provide an alternative to Hobbesian reasoning before, or, better, without simply resorting to the use of force? What *is* the ultimate ground for morality in a presocial war of every man against every man?

To answer this question Diderot first explains why the individual himself is not a competent judge of his own claims in the state of nature. Even if he could make others accept his conditions, Diderot argues, the individual has no legitimate basis for knowing whether what is right for him is right for them.

But if the individual himself has no right to decide among conflicting natural claims, who does? To what "tribunal" can one bring the questions of natural justice? In the broadest terms, where do human standards of justice or "right" come from? At this point, Diderot introduces the concept of the general will—not just the general will of a particular society but the general will of the whole human race:

> It is to [the human race] alone that the right to decide belongs, because the good of all is the only passion it has. Individual wills are suspect; they can be good or evil. But the general will is always good. It is never wrong, it never will be wrong.

"It is the general will that the individual must consult to know his duties as man, citizen, subject, father, child, and when it is right for him to live or die," Diderot explains. And addressing his violent reasoner again, he says,

> Everything that you conceive of, everything that you meditate upon, will be good, grand, uplifted, sublime, if it is in the general and common interest. . . . Say often to yourself: "I am a man, and I do not have any other truly inalienable rights than those of humanity."[7]

Thus far, the general will sounds like a pure idea or ideal, but Diderot brings it down to the level of reality in response to the question of where the general will is "deposited." "In the principles of Right written by all civilized nations," he answers, somewhat as Grotius had done over a century earlier (but at this point the reader might begin to wonder if he or she has not somehow been trapped in the "philosopher's" vicious circle, since the article had begun with the intention to define *natural* or presocial right), "and in the social activities of savage and barbarian people"—even in certain behaviors of animals.

More significant for our present purposes than the occasional circularity in Diderot's argument are the qualities of the general will mentioned in the conclusion of his article. After reiterating the point that the general will is "a pure act of the understanding," that is, a concept grounded in reason, Diderot concludes,

> The consideration of the general will of the human race and of its common desire is the rule of conduct relating one individual to another within the same society, each individual to the society as a whole, and each society . . . to other societies.

The submission to the general will is thus the bond of all societies, even those formed by crime. Emphasizing a point that Rousseau will later question, Diderot goes on to argue that

> if one were to assume the notion of the species in a kind of perpetual flux, the nature of "natural rights" would not change, since it would be relative to the general will and to the common desire of the human race.[8]

The conclusion of Diderot's argument is that natural rights cannot be based on individual calculations of individual self-interest but must instead be based on a rational understanding of the general will of the human species as a whole. What Diderot calls the general will thus represents a desire that is common to the entire human race and that is always right—in both the moral and the legal sense of right.

Implicit in Diderot's portrayal of a general will of the human race is a tradition of thinking that reaches back to the Stoic notion of cosmopolitanism and to the concept of natural law that Victoria, Grotius, Pufendorf, and others looked to for a universal standard on which to base the restraint of war. The same tradition also reaches forward to the French Revolution's Declaration of the Rights of Man, Kant's vision of a "cosmopolitan" society, and the United Nations' Universal Declaration of Human Rights, which modern humanitarians have placed hopes on in their efforts to promote world peace. Central to that tradition is the conviction that we belong to the human race before we belong to our own society, that there are standards of morality that transcend ethnic, national, and religious differences, and that each person's identity as a human being should be put above his or her identity as a member of a particular group. Universal brotherhood, world citizenship, and goodwill toward all people are some of the ideals that have arisen out of this belief. How does the political philosophy of Jean-Jacques Rousseau relate to this tradition? Was Rousseau's concept of the general will similar to or different from Diderot's "general will of the human race"?

Rousseau gives his most direct response to this question, not in his article on "Political Economy" that appeared in the same volume of the *Encyclopédie* as Diderot's article on "Natural Right," but in an early version of the *Social Contract*—the "Geneva Manuscript"—that he probably drafted a few years later. In fact, in Book I of his draft, Rousseau devoted a whole chapter, "The General Society of the Human Race" —a chapter he chose not to include in the final version—to a critical discussion of Diderot's article. A close look at that chapter and at other passages in the "Geneva Manuscript" can help one more clearly understand Rousseau's provocative reformulation of Diderot's concept of the general will.

ON THE GENERAL SOCIETY OF THE HUMAN RACE

The first thing that a reader familiar with Rousseau's *Social Contract* may notice about the "Geneva Manuscript" is its subtitle. Instead of "Principles of Political Right," which is the subtitle of the final version, the draft version is subtitled "Essay about the Form of the Republic," a phrase that immediately brings to mind the *Republic* of Plato and signals to the reader that Rousseau is writing about political ideals rather than political realities.[9] This intention is reiterated in the brief opening chapter where Rousseau states explicitly that he will be focusing not on the maxims of government but on its nature. "It is therefore," he says, "not a question here of the administration of [the social body] but of its constitution."[10]

Having made clear that his focus will be on the constitution or nature of political societies, Rousseau moves immediately to the question at hand, which is whether the human species as a whole can provide the basis for the moral standards of political life—in other words, whether there is, as Diderot claimed, an inherent "general will of the human race" that rational beings can look to for the principles of social justice and political right. In order to remind his reader that the greedy, passionate man whom Hobbes had described is not natural man but man already several stages removed from the state of nature, Rousseau begins the chapter with a summary of one of the essential teachings of the *Discourse on the Origin of Inequality*. The needs of human beings in their natural state are so perfectly proportioned to their powers, Rousseau says, that each individual in a hypothetical natural state would do very well without the assistance of others and could thus lead an essentially autonomous existence. Once chance encounters or natural disasters cause people to come into contact with one another, however, the development of reason and imagination gives rise to new desires, and from then on the former delicate balance between needs and powers is drastically upset. With these developments, "the cooperation of the entire human race is barely enough" to satisfy man's desires, so extensive do they become. Reiterating a point that he makes both in the second *Discourse* and in *Emile*, Rousseau continues, "Thus the same causes that make us wicked also make us slaves. . . . The feeling of our weakness comes less from our nature than from our cupidity."[11] It is greed, in other words, that engenders dependence, "desires" that makes us "weak."

The dynamics of greed and dependence have important consequences for social life in the world as we know it. For at the same time as we are drawn toward others to gain their assistance in satisfying our needs, so our association with them breeds envy and competition; with dependency comes resentment. Here Rousseau is describing in general terms the same dynamic that he portrayed in detail in "The State of War."

> Our needs bring us together in proportion as our passions divide us, and the more we become enemies of our fellow men, the less we can do without them.

The terrible contradiction between need and envy makes any claims regarding the ability of universal humanity or "a general society of the human race" to provide infallible rules of justice a mere illusion, for, by definition, human bondage is a double bind:

> Such are the first bonds of general society; such are the foundations of that universal goodwill, which seems to be stifled as a feeling once recognized as a necessity, and from which everyone would like to benefit without being obliged to cultivate it.[12]

As for the notion that human beings all have a sense of a common species identity, Rousseau maintains that the concept of common identity "is as much a subject of quarrel as of union for men, and is as frequently a source of competition and jealousy as of mutual understanding and agreement."

Therefore, instead of providing an infallible guideline for "right," the society of the human race is in fact a "multitude of relationships lacking order, regulation and stability." Peace and happiness are only "momentary" for man, and nothing is permanent except "the misery that results from all these vicissitudes." "The kind of general society that mutual needs engender does not, therefore, offer any effective assistance to man once he has become miserable," Rousseau observes, referring to the time when humankind left its natural state. "We lost peace and innocence forever before we had appreciated their delights."[13]

THE GENERAL WILL AND NATURAL RIGHT

From general statements about human society's inherent lack of stability, Rousseau moves into a more specific critique of Diderot's argument for a "general will of the human race." But first, in a paragraph that he subsequently crossed out, Rousseau takes issue with the concept of natural law in a way that shows that he had many of the same objections to Diderot's claims about natural *right* as he had to Grotius's and Pufendorf's claims for natural *law*. (Indeed, in much of eighteenth-century writing, the terms natural right and natural law are used interchangeably.) The term human race, Rousseau points out, suggests only a collective idea that does not necessarily imply any real union among the individuals that constitute it. But even if, for the sake of argument, we attribute to the human race an innate feeling of common existence or unity—"a universal motivation which makes each part act for an end that is general and relative to the whole"—and even if we assume that there is a "natural law" that is at the basis of all human action, then "completely to the contrary to what we have supposed," Rousseau argues,

> we will find that the development of [*de facto*] society stifles humanity in men's hearts by awakening personal interest, and that concepts of the natural law, which should be called the law of reason, begin to develop only when the prior development of the passions renders all its precepts impotent.

"It is apparent from this," Rousseau asserts, "that the so-called social treaty dictated by nature is a true illusion." Besides, he continues, "if the general society did exist somewhere other than in the systems of philosophers," there would be a "universal language which nature would teach all men and which would be their first means of mutual communication."[14]

Although the above passage is crossed out in the manuscript, it indicates the direction of Rousseau's thinking in the next part of the chapter where he develops the same argument in a more direct response to Diderot. To make his position clear, Rousseau takes up the line of reasoning that Diderot had put in the mouth of the Hobbesian violent reasoner: Either I must be unhappy or I must cause others to be so, the reasoning goes, "and no one is dearer to me than myself." But having taken up the violent reasoner's words, Rousseau pushes his logic even further, and, in the process, takes Diderot's own line of reasoning to a conclusion that makes his "general will" solution to the violent reasoner's moral dilemma completely useless.

"I would try in vain," Rousseau says Diderot's violent reasoner would add,

> to reconcile my interest with that of another man. Everything you tell me about the advantages of the social law would be fine if while I were scrupulously observing it toward others, I were sure that all of them would observe it toward me.

"But," he says, and one hears the voice of today's political realists and the voice of all those who have ever been skeptical of the humanitarian desire to trust "the enemy" to abide by universal moral laws,

> what assurance of this can you give me, and could there be a worse situation for me than to be exposed to all the ills that stronger men would want to cause me without my daring to make up for it against the weak? Either give me guarantees against all unjust undertakings or do not expect me to refrain from them in turn.[15]

Here Rousseau brings his reader up against the same problem that Diderot's article on "Natural Right" had tried to solve, which is to find a basis for moral "right" that avoids the trap of resorting to the use of force. But, as Rousseau makes clear, the problem is that any appeal to a higher moral law will inevitably fail to satisfy the logic of a "violent reasoner." For the violent reasoner's intimation of his own passions leads him necessarily to distrust the passions of others, no matter how long a benevolent humanitarian might preach the virtues of a universal morality. Even if I agree to restrain my hostility toward others, the hostile person will say, what will restrain my enemies' hostility toward me? "What assurance can you give me" that they too are abiding by the moral law? "Give me guarantees!" has forever been the heartfelt cry of moral skeptics—from the early Greeks' skepticism of the Persians' ability to negotiate in good faith in the fifth century B.C.[16] to our own age's skepticism of the Soviet Union's commitment to arms control agreements. But such assurances and such guarantees require an internal trust—a trust both of ourselves and of others—that, as Rousseau has already poignantly pointed out in his exposition of the relationship between desires and weakness, is eroded by the very needs that made human beings socially dependent in the first place. As he had done in the second *Discourse* and in his manuscript on "The State of War," Rousseau is again insisting that prepolitical society is amoral and that there can be no reliable standards for ethical action in a context lacking political authority.

Equally irrelevant to the Hobbesian natural man's logic is the conventional claim that there is a tradeoff between rights and responsibilities. "You try vainly to tell me," Rousseau says, continuing to impersonate the role of Diderot's violent reasoner,

> that in renouncing the duties that natural law imposes on me I deprive myself at the same time of its rights and that my violence will justify every violence that others would like to use against me. I am all the more willing to agree because I fail to see how my moderation could protect me.

"Furthermore," and one can see the violent reasoner being brought inevitably back to the use of force, which he had tried for so long to avoid, "it will be my business to get the strong on my side, by sharing with them the spoils of the weak. This [i.e., force] would be better than justice for my own advantage, and for my security."[17]

With the argument that in a presocial state of anarchy the use of force will inevitably and irrevocably be perceived as being more effective for the "violent reasoner's" security than as an appeal to justice, Rousseau effectively undermines the attempt to derive a solution to the moral dilemma of a violent reasoner from an abstract concept of law that is somehow "natural" to human society. Having come to this point in his exploration of Diderot's argument, Rousseau proceeds to consider briefly whether religion can provide the basis for social justice and whether it is not possible to make "God's will intervene directly to bind the society of men." But, Rousseau argues (implicitly making a jab at Grotius's and others' attempts to find universally applicable standards of morality in "divine" law), the "sublime" concepts of a God who imposes laws of brotherhood and social virtues "will always escape the multitude"; instead of being a force for peace, popular religion usually takes the form of a religious fanaticism that serves only to perpetuate violence. "Let us therefore," says Rousseau, "set aside the sacred precepts of the various religions, whose abuse causes as many crimes as their use can avoid, and give back to the philosopher the examination of a question that the theologian has never dealt with except to the detriment of the human race."[18]

"But the philosopher," Rousseau goes on to say, clearly referring to Diderot,[19] "will send me back to the human race itself, which alone ought to decide because the greatest good of all is the only passion it has." Continuing to quote Diderot directly, Rousseau proceeds to summarize Diderot's claims for "a general will of the human race."

He will tell me that the individual should address himself to the general will in order to find out to what extent he should be man, citizen, subject, father, child, and when it is suitable for him to live and to die.[20]

But the violent reasoner, Rousseau finally points out, bringing his argument with Diderot to its culmination, would not be swayed by the claims for the morality of the general will.

"I admit that I see in this the rule that I can consult, but I do not yet see," our independent man will say, "the reason for subjecting myself to this rule."

"It is not a matter," Rousseau has him go on to say—and one is struck by the recollection of a similar request made by Glaucon and Adeimantus to Socrates in Book II of Plato's *Republic*—"of teaching me what justice is, but of showing me what interest I have in being just." Responding directly now to Diderot, Rousseau continues,

Indeed no one will deny that the general will in each individual is a pure act of the understanding. . . . But where is the man who can be so objective about himself . . . to look . . . at the species in general in order to impose on himself duties whose connection with his particular constitution is not evident to him?

Since the art of generalizing ideas in the way that Diderot had suggested with his notion of the general will of the human race is one of "the most difficult and belated exercises of human understanding," Rousseau asks further on, how can one expect the "average man" to derive his rules of conduct from this kind of abstract reasoning? "Don't the preceding objections still exist and doesn't it still remain to be seen how his personal interest requires his submission to the general will?"[21]

The implied answer to this last question is yes; it does still remain to be seen how personal interest requires a submission to the general will. Diderot may have shown that the general will is right, but he has not yet shown us the general will in a way that will effectively compel an allegiance to it. It is precisely this task—of showing a potential "violent reasoner" what interest he has in being just and of bringing a desire for such justice into his heart—that will be the central task of the *Social Contract*.

How will the *Social Contract* fulfill such a task? Again a comparison with Socrates's purposes can provide an apt analogy. Rousseau will hope to convert the violent reasoner not by stifling him by force, not by appeals to reason, to religion, or even to established customs, but by showing him the general will at work in a perfected society that the violent reasoner (much like Plato's Glaucon and Adeimantus) can "delight in for its own sake."[22] Just as Socrates used the creation of a desirable republic to develop justice in the "soul" of Glaucon and Adeimantus, so Rousseau will use the creation of a desirable social contract to develop the general will in the soul of Diderot's violent reasoner. This underlying Socratic purpose is luminously revealed in an extraordinary paragraph that Rousseau unfortunately did not include in his final version of the *Social Contract* but that I here take the liberty of quoting in full.

Rousseau begins with a recognition that the Hobbesian state of war does prevail in the human society that actually exists, but he then proceeds to envision the negation of that society and its replacement by "a better constituted order of things." "Although there is no natural and general society among men," the passage begins,

> although men may become unhappy and wicked in becoming sociable, although the laws of justice and equality mean nothing to those who both live in the freedom of the state of nature and are subject to the needs of the social state, far from thinking that there is neither virtue nor happiness for us and that heaven has abandoned us without resources to the depravation of the species, let us attempt to draw from the ill itself the remedy that should cure it.
>
> Let us use new associations to correct, if possible, the defect of the general association. Let our violent speaker himself judge of its success. Let us show him in perfected art the reparation of the ills that the beginnings of art caused to nature. Let us show him all the misery of the state he believed happy, all the falseness in the reasoning he believed solid. Let him see the value of good actions, the punishment of bad ones, and the sweet harmony of justice and happiness in a better constituted order of things. Let us enlighten his reason with new insights, warm his heart with new feelings; and let him learn to enlarge upon his being and his felicity by sharing them with his fellow men.
>
> If my zeal does not blind me in this undertaking, let us not doubt that with a strong soul and an upright mind, this enemy of the human race will at last abjure his hate along with his errors; that reason which led him astray will bring him back to humanity; and that he will learn to prefer his properly understood interest to his apparent interest; that he will become good, virtuous, sensitive, and finally—to sum it all up—rather than the ferocious brigand he wished to become, the most solid support of a well-ordered society.[23]

In his eloquent testimony to the power of "new associations" to correct the defect of the old, of "perfected art" to remedy the ills that the "beginnings of art" caused to nature, and of "new insights" and "new feelings" to transform a would-be "brigand" into a solid citizen, one is able to see firsthand the empowering optimism that permeates Rousseau's intentions in the *Social Contract*.[24] Although *de facto* civil society may indeed resemble the war of every man against every man that Hobbes described, says Rousseau at the end of the paragraph that directly precedes the above quotation, this does not mean that such violence is innate or necessary in man. Instead, and this is the resounding message of the passage quoted above, we must "draw from the ill itself the remedy that should cure it," for there is hope that by the use of "art" and the moral example of "new associations" humankind *can* create a different destiny for itself—one that avoids the war of every man against every man. Diderot's violent reasoner *can* be inspired to desire a different way of being in the world; the Hobbesian man *can* be brought to renounce his aggression and to prefer his real interest to his apparent interest.

But such a transformation will not result from applying the distant precepts of a general society of the human race. Instead, such a transformation must be self-consciously willed by active individuals who partake equally in the responsibility of upholding the laws of a small community. Although critics from the time of the French Revolution on have associated Rousseau's general will with the tyranny of the state,[25] when one looks at Rousseau's general will from the perspective of its origins in his dialogue with Diderot, a different reading comes into view. For what most clearly distinguishes Rousseau's general will from Diderot's is the former's recognition that the general will is not an abstraction sought for in a realm of pure understanding or a set of values that can be imposed from above. Instead, Rousseau's general will is the desire within each individual for the common good that is nurtured by social life itself. The view that a general will can be nurtured "from the inside out" has importance not only for Rousseau's domestic political principles but for his pedagogical theory and for his principles of international politics as well.

MAKING CITIZENS BEFORE
MAKING MEN

"It is only from the social order established among us that we derive ideas about the one we imagine," Rousseau explains in a passage in the "Geneva Manuscript" where he is challenging Diderot's claim that the general will is somehow "deposited" in the written principles of right and in the tacit conventions of civilized people:

> We conceive of the general society on the basis of our particular societies; the establishment of small republics makes us think about the large one; and we do not really begin to become men until after we have been citizens.

Rousseau ends this paragraph with a sharp put-down of anyone (and Rousseau may be implicitly referring to Diderot) who self-righteously places the cause of universal brotherhood above political concerns that are closer to home: "It is apparent from this what should be thought of those supposed cosmopolitans who, justifying their love of the homeland by means of their love of the human race, boast of loving everyone in order to have the right to love no one."[26]

Both passages point to the necessity of recognizing that a general will comes out of the life of a community, that it cannot be imposed on it, and that the consciousness of a general will must come from the experience of willing generally.[27] Since this aspect of Rousseau's political thought has often been misunderstood, it is important to take a brief look at how Rousseau presents the general will in the final version of the *Social Contract.*

In the final version of the *Social Contract* Rousseau reduces his entire argument with Diderot—his challenge to the notion that human justice can be based on a rational appraisal of a natural "general will of the human race"—into one brief statement: "This right [i.e., the right of social justice] does not come from nature; it is therefore based on conventions." Rousseau thus condenses not only the whole of the "Geneva Manuscript's" critique of Diderot's "natural right" and the second *Discourse*'s critique of Grotius's (and Pufendorf's) "natural law" but also his own conviction, which was touched upon at the end of Chapter 1, that right or legitimacy must be based on "convention," on deliberate political will. The problem that Rousseau focuses on in the *Social Contract* is "knowing what these conventions are."[28]

My earlier discussion of Rousseau's writings on war ended with his rigorous denunciation of all attempts to base political right on the "convention" of slavery. Since freedom is the essence of human nature ("Man is born free"), and since slavery denies that freedom, then, Rousseau argues, there is no way to reconcile human "right" and slavery: The two concepts are contradictory. But if one assumes that people have reached a point in their history where their very survival requires some collective efforts, then the problem becomes, as was pointed out in Chapter 1, to find a form of association that "defends and protects" each individual and at the same time enables each to "obey only himself."[29] In sum, the convention that needs to be found is one that enables modern man to find peace and yet to remain free.

The solution to the problem of simply coming together as equals without the use of force is provided by the convention of a social contract. For Rousseau, the social contract has nothing to do with "government"; the form of government is a later choice that will require specific legislation. Nor is the social contract a "deal" between "buyers" and "sellers" of human freedom. Instead, the social contract is "the act by which a people becomes a people."[30] It is this conscious and deliberate choice to associate with each other that constitutes the most legitimate and "true" basis of society.

But such an act of association must not be taken lightly. For along with the choice to participate in society comes the requirement to give up the total independence that characterizes life in the state of nature. In Book I of the *Social Contract* Rousseau says that choosing to become a people involves "the total alienation of each associate, with all his rights, to the whole community";[31] in Book II, however, he says that in reality the members have not actually "alienated" any rights;

> instead of an alienation they have only exchanged to their advantage an uncertain, precarious mode of existence for another that is better and safer; natural independence for freedom; the power to harm others for their personal safety; and their force, which [in the state of nature] others could overcome, for a right which the social union makes invincible.[32]

The crucial point is that "since the condition is equal for everyone, no one has an interest in making it burdensome for others." In contrast to the unequal contract between rulers and ruled put forth by Hobbes, and unlike the fraudulent social contract between rich and poor that Rousseau described in the *Discourse on the Origin of Inequality*, Rousseau's legitimate social contract is an association of equals: "As each gives himself to all, he gives himself to no one."[33] The "sovereign" or authority of the state then becomes identical with the assembled people, and the double dependencies of domination and servitude are overcome by the "convention" of individuals freely and equally contracting together to create a society. As I show in the next chapter, Rousseau attempted to apply the same principles of equal association to his *Project for Perpetual Peace* among states as he here applies to the *Social Contract* among individuals.

Once it is clearly understood that a healthy community is necessarily based on a self-conscious commitment to collective life on the part of all its members, then Rousseau's concept of the general will comes more clearly into view. As Rousseau describes it, the social contract can be reduced to the following terms: "Each of us puts his person and all his power in common under the supreme direction of the general will; and in a body we receive each member as an indivisible part of the whole." And with the change in the dimensions of life comes a necessary change in one's perception of what is right, for with a legitimate social contract comes not only increased security but also the birth of human morality and reason.

> This passage from the state of nature to the civil state produces a remarkable change in man, by substituting justice for instinct in his behavior and giving his actions the morality they previously lacked. Only then,

when the voice of duty replaces physical impulse and right replaces appetite, does man, who until that time only considered himself, find himself forced to act upon other principles and to consult his reason before heeding his inclinations.[34]

In other words, the act of association itself is based on an implicit choice to recognize the needs of the group as a whole. Like partners in a marriage who deliberate over which neighborhood, which school, or which job will best serve the interests of the family unit as a whole, so the members of a community who have consciously willed to belong to that community can be expected to make choices that promote the common good. As James Miller explains it in *Rousseau, Dreamer of Democracy*, "the general will . . . merely designates that part of our experience as individuals which moves each of us, in certain contexts, to say 'We,' and to act in accordance with that identification."[35]

Not only must some impulse to will for the common good be present at the forming of a community, but the impulse to will for the common good must guide the activity of making laws once that community has been formed, Rousseau points out at the beginning of Book II of the *Social Contract*. When individuals who have freely constituted a community for the sake of a common purpose make laws that have that common purpose as their object, such laws are by definition expressions of the general will. They represent the actions of an assembled people willing generally for its own common good.

Rousseau's discussion of legislation highlights the element of reciprocity that governs the relationship between the subject of lawmaking (the sovereign people) and the object of that activity (the laws themselves). A particular object, like the conferring of privileges on an individual citizen, can never become a law enacted by the general will of the people; only a general object, like the establishment of criteria for the conferring of privileges, can be acted on by the general will. The object of laws enacted by the general will must itself always be general.[36]

But the "willing" of the laws must be general also, and here one touches upon the most difficult part of the legislative process. For while one must assume that "the general will is always right and always tends toward the public utility, it does not follow that the people's deliberations always have the same rectitude."[37] Since each individual "can, as a man, have a private will contrary to or differing from the general will he has as a citizen," his private interest may at times "speak to him quite differently from the common interest."[38] In these situations, it is as if the "I want" becomes different from the "we should," and instead of a common will, what is expressed is merely an accumulation of personal wills—a "will of all" perhaps, but not an effective general will.

Given an adequately informed citizenry and a minimum of factionalism, such private interests will usually cancel each other out, leaving "the core of common interests" (as Miller expresses it) to prevail. But as Rousseau points out, "when factions, partial associations at the expense of the whole, are formed, the will of each of these associations becomes general with reference to its members and particular with reference to the state." [39]

The danger of "factions" blinding citizens' perceptions of the common good and arousing private passions at the expense of public judgments is a major concern for Rousseau, as it was for the writers of the *Federalist Papers* a generation later and as it is for those concerned about the future of the United Nations today. In the *Social Contract* Rousseau makes two proposals for mitigating the destructiveness of factions (or, as he sometimes calls them, "partial societies"): first, to try to multiply their number and prevent their inequality so that the society does not become split or polarized into two hostile camps; second, to hope for a "legislator" or moral leader like Moses or Lycurgus (or, in more recent history, perhaps like Abraham Lincoln or Gandhi or Martin Luther King, Jr.) who, instead of simply "writing laws," can help the people to verbalize their most basic "general will." Although Rousseau's assumption that new societies need a founder or a lawgiver who may personify near-mythical powers has often been criticized, in response one can argue that relatively few, if any, political societies have developed without a strong founder or spokesperson to voice the general will. In his writings on the *Project for Perpetual Peace* Rousseau even hints that any effective supranational peacekeeping structure would also require a "legislator" to bring it into being.

In describing the connection between the legislator and the general will, Rousseau says:

> The general will is always right, but the judgment that guides it is not always enlightened. It must be made to see objects as they are, or sometimes as they should appear to be; shown the good path it seeks; safeguarded against the seduction of private wills; shown how to assimilate considerations of time and place; taught to weigh the attraction of present, tangible advantages against the danger of remote, hidden ills. [40]

To help his young pupil "see objects as they are," to safeguard him against "the seduction of private wills," to show him how to "assimilate considerations of time and place," and to teach him to "weigh the attraction of present, tangible advantages against the danger of remote, hidden ills" will be the pedagogical tasks of the preceptor in the small body politic that Rousseau describes in *Emile*; but such lessons may also be thought of as the underlying message of the *Social Contract*. At moments Rousseau even saw himself as a kind of eighteenth-century legislator whose function it was to help his readers strengthen and broaden their notion of the general will.[41]

Having reviewed Rousseau's concept of the general will, we can now see how it differs from the "general will of the human race" that was put forth by Diderot in the article on "Natural Right." In response to Diderot's formal positing of a general will for the sake of reason, Rousseau elaborates the concept of a general will for the sake of social commitment; rather than a transcendent abstraction of justice, his general will is an indigenous expression of justice in a particular community. But at this point one might ask: Does Rousseau's localization of the general will mean that the general will must become a purely relative notion? Are there no absolute standards with which to judge the "generality" of each community's will? Does Rousseau's effort to make Diderot's general will more concrete put beyond reach all hopes for "universal" bonds of human morality that might provide a basis for international peace?

Rousseau himself confronted these questions in his article on "Political Economy," which appeared in the same volume of the *Encyclopédie* as Diderot's article on "Natural Right." After describing the general will in terms similar to those he would later use in the *Social Contract*, and after emphasizing that one's moral judgments of others must take account of what is legitimate for each particular community, Rousseau admits that what seems right for one community may not seem right to others:

> This rule of justice [i.e., the general will], infallible in relation to all citizens, can be defective with foreigners. . . . Then the will of the state, although general in relation to its members, is so no longer in relation to other states and their members, but becomes for them a private and individual will that has its rule of justice in the law of nature.

And here the reader may wonder if Rousseau is not coming surprisingly close to Diderot's and even Grotius's views:

> For then the large town of the world becomes the body politic, of which the law of nature is always the general will and the various states and peoples are merely individual members.[42]

The idea that a community's will is more valid to the extent that it is more general appears again a bit farther on in the article on "Political Economy" where Rousseau states that the norms of generality that affect decisions within small communities also can be applied to broader human associations.

> Since particular societies are always subordinate to those that contain them, one ought to obey the latter in preference to the former; the citi-

zen's duties take precedence over the senator's and the man's over the citizen's.

Rousseau continues this idea by acknowledging that "it is not impossible for a well-governed republic to wage an unjust war," just as it is not impossible for the council of a democracy to pass bad laws or to condemn innocent men. "But," he maintains,

> that will never happen unless the people is seduced by private interests that some wily men have been able to substitute for its own. Then the public deliberation will be one thing and the general will a completely different thing.[43]

Although Rousseau's use of "the law of nature" in the earlier quotation and his subsequent notion of particular societies being "subordinate to those that contain them" might make Rousseau's ideas in these passages seem identical to what Diderot was expressing in "Natural Right," a final look back at the "Geneva Manuscript" reveals the uniqueness of Rousseau's resolution of the question of the relationship between each community's general will and a possible general will for the human race. Having explained, as he did in the article on "Political Economy" and as he was to do in the *Social Contract*, that laws are properly considered as the expressions of the general will, Rousseau notes that "the specification of the actions that contribute to this greatest good, by means of a number of particular laws, is what constitutes right in the narrow, positive sense." The abstract notion of positive right, in other words, is built upon the laws that result from "willing generally." Most important, Rousseau acknowledges that such a concept of positive right can be extended to a supranational scale: "Extend this maxim to the general society of which the state gives us an idea," says Rousseau, perhaps hinting that the state presented in the *Social Contract* may have been intended to give readers the "idea" of a newly possible, more general society of relations among states:

> Protected by the society of which we are members or by the one in which we live, the natural repugnance to do evil is no longer counterbalanced in us by the fear of being wronged, and we are simultaneously moved by nature, by habit, and by reason to treat other men approximately as we do our fellow citizens.

After we gain a context of trust, Rousseau is saying here, it is possible that our concept of justice will extend to include others who do not happen to belong to our own community. For once our self-preservation is assured by the protection of the social contract, then our natural pity is no longer repressed by the fear of our neighbors, and we can feel free to be as civil to foreigners as we are to our compatriots.

Then our natural compassion and the habits of "willing generally" can come to the aid of reason to engender more universal conceptions of "right."

> From this disposition, transformed into actions, arise the rules of ratio-
> nal natural right, different from natural right properly so-called [i.e.,
> Diderot's presentation of natural right] for the latter is based only on a
> true but vague sentiment that is often stifled by love of ourselves.

To pinpoint the difference between what Rousseau calls "reasoned natural right" and Diderot's formulation, Rousseau states in the next sentence that "law comes before justice and not justice before law."[44] Only by participating in a legitimate political community governed by a will for the common good, in other words, can people form ideas of justice that could be applied to a more general society of the human race. A general will of the human race is not natural, Rousseau is telling us, but it may be creatable.

With the notion that the general will can be expanded outward to include those beyond one's national borders, Rousseau (without acknowledging it) seems to have come full-circle back to something resembling Grotius's faith in the "customary" laws that govern relations among states. Such a view provides an important glimmer of hope at the end of the tunnel of realist international relations theory.[45] For what is implied is that even if one assumes that relations among states resemble a Hobbesian state of war in which there is no basis for judging competing claims, there is the possibility that responsible political life within states can eventually lead to the development of more compassionate relations among them. In Part III we see that a similar confidence in the human capacity deliberately to nurture a political consciousness "from the inside out" characterizes Rousseau's writings on education; at this point, it is important to recognize that his underlying faith in the political institutions human beings can create for themselves also attracted Rousseau to the Abbé de Saint-Pierre's *Project for Perpetual Peace*, which is the focus of the next chapter.

4

POLITICAL MAN AND
PERPETUAL PEACE

A RESPONSE TO THE ABBÉ DE SAINT-PIERRE

Chapter 3 showed that in his debate with Diderot over the origin of the general will Rousseau argued against the notion that nature inscribes on human reason an easy means of bringing human beings together in peace. Human beings have no innate sentiments of sharing common interests with others, Rousseau maintained. The same needs that bring people into society also arouse feelings of dependency and resentment that tend to make them envious and hostile. Instead of being "natural," the sense of sharing a common humanity with others must be deliberately created; instead of being automatically "deposited" in human reason, the capacity for a general will can come only out of the habit of "willing generally" for a small community. "We conceive of the general society on the basis of our particular societies," Rousseau insisted. "The establishment of small republics makes us think about the large one, and we do not really begin to become men until after we have been citizens."[1]

Such a narrow view of the possibilities for stimulating sentiments of humanity and brotherhood have led many readers to believe that Rousseau was pessimistic about the possibility of promoting world peace. For what if the international context is dominated not by legitimately constituted and autonomous small republics like the one set forth in the *Social Contract*, one might well ask, but by large commercial empires, as Europe was beginning to be in the eighteenth century and as most of the world is today? Given the *de facto* "state of war" that Rousseau described in his critiques of Hobbes and Grotius, how can peace be achieved if the human feelings of identity with others are so limited? To begin to understand Rousseau's thinking about these questions, one needs to look closely at the seldom-studied responses that Rousseau wrote to a "project for perpetual peace" that had been drafted early in the 1700s by the Abbé de Saint-Pierre.

THE ABBÉ DE SAINT-PIERRE was an indefatigable humanitarian and re-former of the first half of the eighteenth century whose zeal for useful projects was often reputedly the object of ridicule among the King's ministers and royal bureaucrats to whom he was constantly petitioning for reforms. Although they were not of the same generation (Saint-Pierre having been born in 1658, Rousseau in 1712), Rousseau recalls in the *Confessions* that he had "occasionally seen the Abbé de Saint-Pierre in his old age," probably in the winter of 1742 at the brilliant salon of Mme. Dupin where the Abbé was a long-time intimate and Rousseau an awkward newcomer.[2] While recognizing the Abbé's shortcomings and noting certain excesses in his faith in reason, Rousseau always re-membered the Abbé with "respect," and in later years described the Abbé as a man who was "simple, honest, and true."[3]

In an anonymous biographical sketch of the Abbé de Saint-Pierre that is included in the Pléiade edition of Rousseau's works, there is even a slight indication of some similarities between the development of the Abbé's political consciousness and the development of Rousseau's. As a young man, the Abbé had come under the influence of Fontenelle and had gradually shifted the focus of his interest from physics and the other natural sciences to moral philosophy. As the Abbé matured, the sketch relates, in terms that resemble Rousseau's later account in the *Confessions* of his own intellectual development while he was in Venice, the study of moral philosophy led the Abbé to see "that the greatest part of the happiness and unhappiness of men come from good or bad laws. . . . It was this persuasion which determined him from now on to apply himself to the study of government: to try to discover the means of forming wise rules and promoting good organizations that would engage men's individual interests enough to work constantly and en-thusiastically for the public interest." Thus, the account continues, the Abbé became persuaded that "it was not moral philosophy but politics or the science of government that was most important for the happiness of man; and that a single wise law could make more men happy than a hundred good treatises on morality."[4]

While the anonymous biographical sketch of the Abbé de Saint-Pierre may point to certain similarities in the political interests of the two men, what is equally striking are the differences between them,

particularly the difference in their effectiveness as writers. Unlike Rousseau, who brought to his writings on "Political Institutions" the habits
of self-expression that had developed out of a natural ear for melody and
a youthful love of poetry and song, the Abbé de Saint-Pierre brought
to his political studies the rigorous training of a Jesuit education and an
early immersion in the Cartesian methodologies of physics and geometry. As a result, whereas Rousseau's writings were known for their
liveliness and rhythm, the Abbé's writings were notoriously convo-
luted and abstract, and so filled with tedious axioms and propositions
that they were almost impossible to read.

Because he had difficulty getting his work published commercially
while he was alive (what had been published of the Abbé's work was
done at his own expense), the bulk of the Abbé's prolific writings remained, after his death, in the form of manuscripts, notebooks, and
cartons of papers that had been passed on to his nephew, the Count
de Saint-Pierre. But by means of one of those chance contacts between
men of genius that were so often fortuitously (and, in view of subsequent history, perhaps ironically) facilitated by the petty aristocracy
and *haute bourgeoisie* of the eighteenth century, the Abbé's writings were
soon to be given a new life. Shortly after Rousseau's return from a
brief visit he made to Geneva in 1754, the Abbé de Mably—an old
friend of Rousseau's who knew of the existence of the Abbé de Saint-
Pierre's manuscripts—suggested to Mme. Dupin—who then made the
proposal to Rousseau—that Rousseau undertake the job of selecting
and editing the Abbé's writings so as to make them more useful to posterity. Motivated in part by curiosity, in part by a sense of indebtedness
to the Abbé de Mably and to Mme. Dupin, and in part by a lack of
any other specific project to engage his energies at the time (this being
shortly after he had completed the *Discourse on the Origin of Inequality*),
Rousseau agreed to take up the task.[5]

But little did Rousseau realize what he had committed himself to
when he accepted Mme. Dupin's assignment. Soon seventeen volumes
of the Abbé's writings plus six boxes and portfolios of notes and rough
drafts were delivered to Rousseau's door, and he found himself faced, as
he says in the *Confessions*, with "reading, considering, and selecting from
twenty-three diffuse and muddled volumes full of boring passages,
repetitions, and false or short-sighted views, out of which I had to fish
some few that were fine and great and would give courage to endure
this painful labour."[6] It was this work that Rousseau first undertook
when he went to live at l'Hermitage, a secluded cottage near Montmorency that had been lent to him by Mme. d'Épinay. In the six years
that Rousseau spent near Montmorency he would complete not only
his work on the Abbé de Saint-Pierre but also the three grand *oeuvres*

of his maturity—*La Nouvelle Héloise*, the *Social Contract*, and *Emile*—all of which were published between January 1761 and May 1762.

One of the first steps that Rousseau took to make his "painful labour" of selection more manageable was to draft a list of all the Abbé de Saint-Pierre's writings. A glance through this list, which is reprinted in the Pléiade edition of Rousseau's *Oeuvres complètes*, gives a hint of the extent of the Abbé's interests and helps one appreciate Rousseau's task. The list contains 83 published and 141 unpublished works, the large majority of which are either "Observations" or "Projects." The "Observations" range from observations on "Sobriety" and "the Ministry of War," to observations on "the Decrease of Evils and the Increase of Goods by means of Universal Reason" and "Judging Values Wisely." The "Projects," which are much more numerous, include everything from projects for "Women's Colleges," "Making Roads More Convenient in Winter," and "A Graduated Income Tax," to projects for "Perfecting Medicine," "Making Books More Highly Honored," and the Abbé's most often rewritten project, "A Project for Perpetual Peace."[7]

Having believed that the Abbé de Saint-Pierre's manuscripts would contain "treasures," Rousseau was at first put off by the superficiality and naiveté of many of the Abbé's proposals. The plans were "useful enough," Rousseau later wrote in the *Confessions*,

> but impracticable owing to one idea from which the author could never escape, that men are motivated by their intelligence rather than their passions. The high opinion he had of modern learning had led him into adopting a false belief in perfect wisdom which was the basis of all the institutions he proposed.[8]

Since Rousseau did not want his readers to confuse his own views about the possibilities of human reason with those of the Abbé de Saint-Pierre, the author of the *Discourse on the Sciences and Arts* finally decided that his editing of the Abbé's writings would have to result in two quite separate works, "one intended to display the author's various schemes . . . while in the other, which was not intended to appear until the first had had its effect, I should have delivered my own judgment on those same schemes." He first set about writing his "Summary" and his "Critique" of the Abbé de Saint-Pierre's *Project for Perpetual Peace* partly because, as he says in the *Confessions*, it was the most "considerable and most elaborate of all the works in [the] collection,"[9] but also undoubtedly because of his own interest in finding a solution to the contradiction between civil order and international anarchy that he had confronted in his *Discourse on the Origin of Inequality*.

The Abbé de Saint-Pierre's lifelong preoccupation with the cause of peace can easily be understood as a reaction to the turmoil of his times. The Treaty of Westphalia in 1648 had effectively put an end to the religious wars of the preceding century, but the balance-of-power politics on which the new configuration of sovereign states was based had not established any kind of lasting peace or stability. On the contrary, in the second half of the seventeenth century European states were buffeted by one war after another and finally succumbed in 1702 to the bloody War of the Spanish Succession that began when Louis XIV tried to unite the French monarchy with the crown of Spain. In 1713, shortly before the plenipotentiaries of Europe were to assemble at Utrecht to find a way to end the war, the Abbé de Saint-Pierre published his first *Projet pour rendre la paix perpétuelle en Europe*, the main argument of which was that the interests of sovereigns could much better be served by a grand alliance for peace than by temporary treaties or by the balance-of-power system that had been in effect since the Treaty of Westphalia.

Although it focused on ways to promote peace in Europe, the Abbé's plan has long been considered to be part of the history of international peacekeeping structures that began with Eméric Crucé's *Nouveau Cynée* in 1623 and evolved by way of Kant's *Perpetual Peace* to the twentieth-century proposals for the League of Nations and the United Nations.[10] It is thus on the basis of its significance as a representative model of international collective security rather than its relevance for Europe alone that the Abbé's plan and Rousseau's responses to it should be read today.

The Abbé de Saint-Pierre's main point was that by agreeing to organize themselves into a permanent league or union and by agreeing to settle their differences by peaceful negotiations rather than by war, the sovereigns of Europe could become much more secure in their power and could gain mutual protection against both invasions from without and uprisings from within. Addressing himself to the ruling monarchs of his time, the Abbé argued that by substituting a comprehensive league for the present insecure dynamics of power politics, ruling families would become more secure, commerce would be promoted, and with the money saved from military expenditures the arts and sciences would flourish. But such advantages, the Abbé made clear, could only come through some measure of restraint; any sovereign who either attacked the union or refused to accept its judgments or held back from joining it once it had been established by fourteen other states would be forced to do so by an army maintained by contributions from each member state. Unlike the present United Nations or its predecessor, the League of Nations, the Abbé's proposed association would thus be given the means actually to enforce peace. The decisions of the alliance's assembly, to be located permanently at Utrecht, would be made according to majority rule. As a way of persuading sovereigns that his plan was nothing radical or new, the Abbé took pains to point out that Henri IV, under the guidance of his wise minister Sully, had hoped to bring about a similar plan a century before. (What the good Abbé failed to realize, however, was that Sully's plan was at least as much a strategy of power politics for countering the domination of the Austrian Hapsburgs as it was an alliance for perpetual peace.)

As Rousseau would later observe, it was undoubtedly naive of the Abbé de Saint-Pierre to expect that sovereign rulers would ever agree to accept an overarching juridical power that might curtail their freedom. In any case, the obscurities of the Abbé's style of writing made it unlikely that the sovereigns would even bother to read the proposal in the first place. The *Projet de paix perpétuelle* eventually filled three substantial volumes, plus a 227-page "Abrégé" and a "Supplément" to the "Abrégé," and consisted of seven long "discourses" containing "propositions" to be proved, "articles" to be established, and "objections" to be refuted. The second volume, for example, which contained the sixth and seventh discourses, included no less than *seventy* possible objections to the plan, together with the Abbé's patient and painstaking "answers" to each objection.[11] Such a method was not likely to endear the Abbé to his readers; as Rousseau pointed out in a fragment that he wrote on the Abbé at this time, his writing style was basically counterproductive.

> [The Abbé de Saint-Pierre] once said that men are like children: you must repeat the same thing to them a hundred times before they hear it. But a child to whom you say the same thing twice yawns the second time and stops listening altogether unless he is forced to. So how do you force grown-up children to listen, except by the pleasure of reading? By neglecting to please his readers the Abbé was working against his own principles.[12]

Rousseau's editorial task, therefore, was to turn the Abbé's tiresome treatise into a proposal that would bring pleasure. Even more important, by transforming a dry formula into an intriguing challenge, he hoped to reach beyond the childlike yawning of power-hungry princes to the active minds of mature people ready to struggle for peace. In a few paragraphs that he wrote as an introduction to his summaries of the Abbé's projects Rousseau gives a sense of the spirit in which he hoped they would be read:

> It is a prejudice to scorn a project simply because it is new; it is even more ridiculous to scorn it because it hasn't been put into effect and to reject as impractical all that which has not been put into practice. . . . Although the things that are proposed here have not been put into effect, this is not to say that they cannot or should not be, nor that on the

contrary should this refusal indicate for them a favorable influence, nor
finally *that individuals cannot judge by them whether the government is right or
wrong*. Several of the projects summarized here were presented in their
time to the administration; they were all neglected. On that basis they
have been treated as fantasies and no one has read them. I have done my
best to put them in a condition to be read. It is for citizens to read them
in the same spirit as they were written and as they were edited; it is up
to the public to be their judge.[13]

As Rousseau makes explicit in this introduction, one of his main motives for editing the Abbé's writings on peace was to enable the public
"to judge by them whether the government is right or wrong." Like his
later assertion in Book V of *Emile* that the purpose of introducing his
pupil to the ideas of the *Social Contract* is to enable Emile "to know what
ought to be in order to judge soundly what is," Rousseau's introduction
to works on the Abbé de Saint-Pierre gives evidence of the extent to
which Rousseau saw his task as one of political education.

THE POSSIBILITY OF PEACE

As we see in Chapter 6 concerning the educational principles of Rousseau's *Emile*, one of the hallmarks of Rousseau's educational method-
ology is to begin his exposition of the pedagogy appropriate for each
stage of the child's life with a description of the natural physiological
and developmental characteristics of the child at that particular age.
Only by studying the *nature* of the child, he often repeats, can one discover the *art* of education. A similar assumption underlies Rousseau's
"Summary" of the Abbé de Saint-Pierre's *Project for Perpetual Peace*.

Rousseau begins with the natural ties among the different nations
of Europe and then explores how the artful creation of new political
forms can make the social bonds more secure. But first he introduces
his topic by pointing to the contradictions between civil life and international life that he had developed at greater length in the fragments
on "The State of War," and it is here that one can begin to appreciate
the seriousness with which Rousseau persisted in confronting the most
difficult issues of international relations. "If our social order were, as
it is claimed to be, the work of reason rather than of the passions," he
asks,

> would we have taken so long to see that as far as our well-being is con-
> cerned, we have accomplished either too much or too little; that each
> one of us being both in the civil state with his fellow citizens and in the
> state of nature with the rest of the world, we have prevented private wars
> only so as to set off public wars, which are a thousand times worse; and
> that by uniting with a few men we have really become the enemies of
> mankind?[14]

The questions asked in the above passage form a crucial link in the chain of Rousseau's reasoning about political institutions. For with his description of the contradiction between civil order and international violence and his speculation about whether in our political development we have not accomplished either "too much or too little," Rousseau is again asking, as he had asked in "The State of War" and will ask again in *Emile*, whether the destructiveness of war does not call into question the whole concept of national sovereignty—a concept that he held very dear. How can one preserve the integrity of the sovereign state, he implicitly asks, and yet also hope for more peaceful relations among states?

It is as a means of answering this question and overcoming the inherent contradiction between civil order and international war that Rousseau had earlier attempted to develop principles for the rights of war and that he will now elucidate the Abbé de Saint-Pierre's proposal of a confederation for peace. For if there is any way of removing the above contradiction, Rousseau says in his "Summary," it would only be by a form of "confederative government, which, by uniting nations with ties similar to those which unite individuals, submits each of them equally to the authority of laws." Just as the desire for lawful relations among individuals points to the need for a legitimate social contract, Rousseau is implying, so does the desire for lawful relations among states point to the need for a secure international confederation.[15]

Having provided the rationale for a confederation in theory, Rousseau goes beyond the Abbé's plan and proceeds to describe the nature of the territory on which such a confederation might be established. (Using a different metaphor, Rousseau wrote in a related fragment that "the Abbé drew the roof of an edifice whose foundation now needs to be outlined.")[16] He begins with a carefully compressed narrative of the gradual unification of Europe from the first isolated tribes of barbarians, to the Greeks, and finally to the Roman Empire, which by putting much of the then-known world under "the same yoke" formed a political and civil union among all its diverse members. He goes on to show that the land's evenly distributed fertility, its many rivers, its energetic peoples—all tend to bring people together and "make Europe not just an idealized collection of peoples who have only a name in common, like Asia or Africa, but a real society with its own religion, manners, customs, and even laws, from which no single nation composing it could withdraw without immediately causing problems for the others."

Once he has analyzed the underlying natural forces that make Europe a unified whole, Rousseau shifts the reader's attention to the actual state of violence that predominates in the relations among states. When one sees, he says, "the endless conflicts, violence, usurpations, revolts, wars, and murders" that continually disrupt this advanced culture, this "brilliant haven for the sciences and the arts," one hardly knows how to reconcile such contradictions. Then, Rousseau concludes bitterly, "the so-called fraternity of the peoples of Europe seems nothing more than a name of derision to express with irony their mutual hate."

And yet, in all this, Rousseau proceeds to point out, things are only following their natural course, since any society "without leaders or without laws, its union formed or maintained by chance, must necessarily degenerate into quarrels or dissension." In terms that recall his analysis of the natural conflict between states in "The State of War," Rousseau describes how the original ties between European peoples have been so infinitely complicated by overlays of cultural and economic interests that "their divisions are all the more deadly as their ties are more intimate; and their frequent quarrels have almost the same cruelty as civil wars."

Thus, "the relative state of the powers of Europe is properly speaking a state of war," Rousseau argues, which neither treaties nor the various attempts to formulate international law have been able to mitigate in any significant way. With no general principles or universally agreed upon guidelines about the justice of competing claims, reasoning in these matters always tends to favor the self-interest of individual sovereigns, and "war becomes inevitable even when each side would like to be just." Implied here is Rousseau's recognition of the futility of trying, as he himself had tried, to formulate a "rights of war" based not on "that which makes war advantageous to the one who wages it" but on "that which makes it legitimate," since without any overarching legal framework the whole concept of "legitimacy" becomes problematic. Rousseau's wording here also implies that without any guarantees for their own safety, states thus resemble Diderot's "violent reasoner" in a premoral state of nature. Each state's intimations of its own aggressive passions prevents it from trusting the passions of others, no matter how much one might preach the advantages of adhering to international law.

Once the causes of war are known, however, "they are sufficient to indicate a remedy, if one exists," Rousseau goes on to say. The remedy in this situation would have to be some coercive force that could build upon the natural bonds of unity in Europe and ensure the maintenance of peace.

> Everyone can see that society is formed by common interests; that discord arises out of opposing ones; that since a thousand fortuitous events can change and modify these interests, then once there is a society it is necessary to have a coercive force to organize and coordinate the movements of its members so that the common interests and reciprocal ties are given the solidity that they would not be able to have by themselves.

By stating that "once there is a society it is necessary to have a coercive force to organize and coordinate the movements of its members," Rousseau is touching on a question that has always evoked fear and scepticism in the search for peace, namely, the question of whether such a "coercive" force would jeopardize the sovereignty of the confederation's member states. Rousseau answers this question later in the "Summary"; at this point he introduces an important assertion. "It would be a great error, however," he says, "to hope that the violent state of things could ever change simply by the force of circumstances and without the help of art," that is, without the deliberate creation of new political structures. Similar to the argument that appears at the beginning of the *Social Contract* that political society is established not by "nature" but by "convention" (and somewhat similar also to the argument at the beginning of *Emile* that to form a natural man there is very much that one must *do*), Rousseau is underscoring the fact that legitimate political societies can only be the result of self-conscious human will.

By insisting on the "artificial" nature of the project, Rousseau is setting himself apart not only from Grotius's earlier assumption that the "customary" laws of nation-states could be relied on to bring about peace but also from Adam Smith's and Kant's later assumption that international trade or the increasing destructiveness of wars could eventually lead to peace. Indeed, according to Rousseau, trade is part of the problem, since it serves to complicate and extend the ties of international dependency and envy that are the cause of war in the first place. In contrast to the internationalist and liberal pacifist traditions, Rousseau saw no "hidden hand" that would bring a natural or automatic improvement in the relations among states.[17] And to emphasize this point more fully, Rousseau proceeds to show that when left to themselves the sovereign states of Europe will tend to fall into precisely the kind of vacillating and tumultuous fluctuations of victory and defeat that characterized the balance-of-power politics of Europe since the Treaty of Westphalia.

Rousseau's description of the European balance-of-power system has a double purpose. On the one hand, he points out that the politics of European "equilibrium" are based on a natural condition of equality and that the tendencies of the various states to resist domination by one another has the effect of preventing a universal hegemony of any kind. On the other hand, he makes clear that with nothing governing such interactions, the constant attempts to upset or restore the equilibrium make for a more or less constant state of war. By emphasizing these two points, Rousseau seems to be trying to convince his readers of the need for a confederation at the same time as he is reassuring them that such a confederation need not jeopardize the equality of sovereign states. "If I have insisted on the equal distribution of power that results in Europe from its present situation," he says, "it was to point to a consequence that is important for the establishment of any more general association."

> For in order to form a solid and durable confederation, it would be necessary to put all the members in such a mutual dependence not only that no one singly would be in a condition to resist all the others, but also that particular associations that might be harmful to the whole would meet in it obstacles sufficient to prevent their execution.

In its stress on the equality of states, Rousseau's "Summary" again anticipates a central teaching of the *Social Contract*. "Rather than destroying natural equality," he will argue in Book I, "the fundamental compact on the contrary substitutes a moral and legitimate equality for whatever physical inequality nature may have placed between men, and . . . although they may be unequal in force or in genius, they all become equal through convention and by right."[18] In the *Social Contract*, the natural equality among men provides the basis for the mutual dependence necessary to make a republic legitimate and secure; here, in the *Project for Perpetual Peace*, a natural equality among European states provides the basis for the mutual dependence necessary to make a confederation legitimate and secure. Given the extremes of natural inequality that exist among sovereign states today, this aspect of Rousseau's "Summary" of a European *Project for Perpetual Peace* is admittedly difficult to apply to a more universal plan for collective security. Nevertheless, it is an important principle to aim for and underlies the provision for the equal representation of member states in the United Nations General Assembly.

At the same time, Rousseau emphasizes that the proposed association "would not consist simply of futile deliberations that each participant could ignore at will; instead, it would give rise to an effective power, capable of forcing ambitious men to keep within the limits of the general treaty." Specifying the requirements of such a body, he insists that to be effective it would be necessary that the confederation "be so general that no considerable power could refuse it; that it have a judiciary tribunal to establish laws that would be binding on all the members; [and] that it have a compulsory and coercive force to constrain each state to submit to the common deliberations." Rousseau's language clearly indicates that the proposed confederation would go well beyond the present United Nations in its comprehensiveness and power.

In words that might remind the reader of his eloquent appeal, in the "Geneva Manuscript," to "draw from the ill itself the remedy that should cure it" and to "use new associations to correct, if possible, the defect of the general association," Rousseau ends this section of his "Summary" with a call for a radical transformation. By undertaking the difficult but necessary task of confederation, he says, "all of its members could draw their happiness from that which presently causes their misery and could change into an eternal peace the state of war that now reigns amongst them."

The wording of the last phrase is significant. By referring to the possibility of changing the "state of war" into an "eternal peace," Rousseau is opening his readers' minds to the possibility of solving the international dilemma. Contrary to Stanley Hoffmann's and other commentators' assumptions that Rousseau's writings on the Abbé de Saint-Pierre's project were overshadowed by the pessimistic implications of "The State of War," this phrase makes it very plausible to see Rousseau's "Summary" as a tentatively hopeful alternative to his depressing description of *de facto* international violence. And yet, as will be evident in his "Critique" of the *Project for Perpetual Peace*, Rousseau's solution is in many respects very different from the Abbé de Saint-Pierre's, for by acknowledging that the project will never be accepted by "princes," Rousseau throws the responsibility for bringing about peace back to the people themselves.

AS A WAY of leading his readers into the practical question of how a confederation for peace might be established, Rousseau asks, "Now let us see how this great work, begun by chance, could be achieved by reason, and how, by taking on the force and the solidity of a true body politic, the free and voluntary society that unites all the European states could change into a real Confederation." This brings Rousseau to speculate about the initial impetus for confederation. But while faithfully following Saint-Pierre's argument that such a confederation might evolve out of a peace congress or international conference of sovereigns similar to the Council of Utrecht, Rousseau reveals his skepticism about such a possibility by taking on an ironic tone. This passage may also remind us of more recent attempts by sovereign powers to discuss the mechanisms for promoting peace.

> From time to time there occurs among us various general assemblies called Congresses to which envoys are solemnly sent from all parts of Europe only to return just as they went, . . . where they deliberate about whether the table should be round or square, whether the room will have more or fewer exits, whether such and such a dignitary will have his back or his front facing the window . . . and about a thousand other questions of equal importance that have been uselessly stirred up for the

past three centuries and that are assuredly worthy of preoccupying our
own statesmen today.

It could happen, however, that the members of one of these assemblies
might at some point be gifted with common sense, nor is it impossible
that they might sincerely wish for the welfare of the public, nor . . . is it
inconceivable that . . . the delegates . . . could receive orders from their
respective sovereigns to sign the general Confederation.

Later in his "Critique," Rousseau acknowledges that given the apparent
self-interest of "princes" who control the political fate of Europe, the
establishment of a confederation would probably require nothing less
than a revolution. But in the "Summary" he skips over this difficult
issue and moves on to a discussion of the articles of confederation that
could establish peace.

Rather than follow the Abbé's original version, which contained
twelve "Fundamental Articles," eight "Important Articles" and eight
more "Useful Articles," Rousseau follows the outline of the Abbé's
"Abrégé" of the *Projet* and reduces the twenty-eight articles to five.
The first article focuses on the original act by which the contracting
sovereigns would establish a permanent assembly that would have the
purpose of settling conflicts by means of arbitration; the second article specifies the number of sovereigns that would be represented, how
the presidency of the assembly would rotate, and the relative contributions of each member to the common expenses; the third article assures
each member state of its present possessions; the fourth article indicates
what would constitute a crime against the alliance and when the use
of force against a hostile state would be justified; and finally, the fifth
article provides guidelines for the deliberations of the assembly. Like
Saint-Pierre's original proposal, Rousseau's version argues for a form
of association that would be more than a simple alliance or assembly.
While allowing for national autonomy in domestic affairs, the confederation would have the power actually to enforce peace between the
confederated states.

After having introduced the five articles, Rousseau admits that they
may be "subject to a thousand minor difficulties, some of which would
require long clarification." Right now, however, "it is a question of
whether, in the nature of things the enterprise is possible or not . . .
[and] it will be sufficient to show that it can be done." As Rousseau had
pointed out at the beginning of the "Summary," the speculative aspect
of the project may be inherent in the subject matter: "I am not sure
whether in [the case of a project for perpetual peace] the dreams of a
truly human heart, whose own zeal makes everything seem easy, are not
to be preferred to that cold and calculating reason which always finds

in its indifference for the public good the first obstacle to everything that might benefit it."

In summarizing the Abbé de Saint-Pierre's arguments in favor of the *Project for Perpetual Peace*, Rousseau first shows how all the possible motives that cause princes to take up arms would be eliminated by the proposed system. The desire to invade another state, to defend oneself, to weaken a too-powerful neighbor, to punish another for a perceived injury, or to fulfill the responsibilities of a treaty—all these motives for war would disappear if there were a permanent peace-enforcing agency to maintain order and enable potential conflicts to be settled juridically. "It would thus be impossible . . . that the objective of perpetual peace would not be perfectly fulfilled by carrying out the proposed system," he argues.

From the "general usefulness" of the plan Rousseau turns to what he calls its "particular usefulness," and it is here that Rousseau finally confronts the difficult question of whether the Abbé's *Project* would jeopardize sovereignty. The issue of sovereignty is an important part of any discussion of the search for peace, but it is particularly significant in the hands of the author of the *Social Contract*, since the *Social Contract* has often been assumed to contain the most clearly stated expression of the inviolability of the national state. The body politic, or the sovereign, Rousseau says in the chapter of Book I titled "On the Sovereign," "deriving its being solely from the sanctity of the contract, can never obligate itself, even toward another, to do anything that violates that original act, such as to alienate some part of itself or to submit itself to another sovereign." Yet, in the same context, Rousseau argues that "this does not mean that this body cannot perfectly well enter an engagement toward another with respect to things that do not violate this contract. For with reference to the foreigner, it becomes a simple being or individual." [19]

Later in the *Social Contract* Rousseau asserts firmly that sovereignty is both "inalienable" and "indivisible," but once again he reminds the reader that the sovereign is a "collective being." As a part of the sovereign's indivisibility, Rousseau mentions that the specific acts of declaring war and making peace should not be considered separate acts of sovereignty but "applications" of the more general law that is the expression of the general will. [20]

In his "Summary" of the *Project for Perpetual Peace*, Rousseau approaches the question of sovereignty from a very different angle. Addressing the question whether the international confederation would be in the interest of sovereign "princes," Rousseau begins by saying, "It is obvious that it would be futile to speak of public self-interest to the detriment of private self-interest. Proving that peace is in general preferable to war says nothing to someone who believes he has reasons to prefer war over peace." But what such a person in effect will be arguing, Rousseau continues, is that the plan will take away the sovereigns' right to determine justice for themselves, that is, "their precious right to be unjust as they please."

> You are taking away their power to grow at the expense of their neighbors; you are making them give up the apparatus of power and terror with which they love to frighten the world—that glory of conquest from which they derive their honor; finally you are forcing them to be equitable and peaceful.

"How will they be compensated," Rousseau asks with cutting sarcasm, "for such cruel deprivations?"

The sarcasm that Rousseau expresses in this passage has far-reaching implications. For what his tone suggests is that while the limitation of a state's arbitrary use of external power might threaten the "particular" or individual interests of "princes," it would not threaten the more "general" interests of a legitimate sovereignty that included the people themselves. By ridiculing the notion that sovereignty would be threatened by a plan for peace, Rousseau seems to be both broadening the notion of sovereignty and implying that peace would be the object of the general will. Indeed, one could argue that since the original purpose of a legitimate social contract, according to Rousseau, is to "defend and protect the person and goods of each associate," then a legal framework that promised to enhance each individual's protection and security could not possibly be perceived as a violation of the contract.[21] It should be recalled at this point that in the *Social Contract* itself Rousseau suggests that confederations might provide a way for small states to avoid being subjugated by large ones—another indication that he saw no inherent contradiction between collective security and sovereignty.[22]

The remainder of the "Summary" has the relationship between sovereignty and peace as its underlying message. While appearing to address the "self-interest" of "princes," Rousseau's rhetoric is also aimed at showing the extent to which the Abbé's *Project* would be in accordance with the general will of a sovereign people. These intentions are especially evident when Rousseau explicitly sets himself apart from the Abbé de Saint-Pierre's faith in the benevolence of "enlightened" monarchs. "Here I would not dare to reply, as the Abbé de Saint-Pierre does," Rousseau says, "that the true glory of princes consists in procuring the happiness of their subjects" and that the most certain way that a king can stand out among his peers would be "to work for the welfare of the public." In the offices of the kings' ministers, Rousseau observes, such naive assumptions on the part of Saint-Pierre were met only with ridicule. He himself will avoid such naiveté, he says, for he knows that one has a chance to be listened to by princes only if one speaks "in terms of their own self-interest." Rousseau's language in this passage contains a hidden meaning, for in the guise of appealing to the reasoning of rulers, he is actually collaborating with his readers against them. In spite of this deliberate subterfuge, the knowing winks that Rousseau tried to bury in these phrases did not get past the suspicious eyes of the royal censors.[23]

Rousseau's argument that a peace confederation would be in a sovereign's "self-interest" (whether that sovereign be a prince or a people) takes several different forms, most of which are familiar to those attempting to promote new peacekeeping structures in the world today. First he emphasizes the element of risk that is inherent in the free-for-all system of balance of power. Since there is no real consensus about what constitutes "right" in the international domain, or any competent arbiter for conflicts, the whole effort to rectify claims by means of force depends essentially on chance, and "simple common sense" should forbid us to risk our present possessions for uncertain future gain—an argument that is perhaps even more relevant to the present age of complex and unpredictable nuclear technologies than it was to the eighteenth century. In equally relevant terms, Rousseau next points to the financial drain of a war economy. His main point is that even a victor suffers financially from a war, and that "being always weaker after a war than he was before, his only consolation is to see the defeated suffering even more than himself." In connection with the question of "economy," Rousseau also inserts a double-edged comment regarding the size of states; in general, he argues, "a prince who, to extend his frontiers, loses as many subjects as he acquires new ones, thus becomes weaker through his desire to grow." This leads Rousseau to point out that one can gain more by setting a good example than by taking up arms.

> It is by means of good laws, wise policies, and economic foresight that a judicious sovereign, without leaving anything to chance, can thus add to his strength. The real victories that he will gain over his neighbors will be whatever beneficial institutions he develops in his own states.

The internal policies of a state, Rousseau is saying, are more important for its long-term security than military exploits; it is more in the sovereign's interest to perfect institutions at home than to expand the sovereign's power abroad.

With a passing criticism of the apparent need that some princes have for military parades and displays of weaponry (they are nothing but a kind of "infantile game" and "kings are not supposed to play with toys"), Rousseau again takes up the tricky question whether the proposed European confederation would jeopardize absolute sovereignty. Although later in his "Critique" he argues that "princes" would probably not accept the Abbé's plan because it might force them to treat their own citizens as justly as they treat foreigners, here in his "Summary" Rousseau follows the Abbé's reasoning quite closely and argues that the mutual dependence on the common tribunal would in no way diminish the rights of sovereignty, "but on the contrary would strengthen them." Each sovereign would be guaranteed not only "his security against any foreign invasion but also his authority in respect to any internal rebellion." Moreover, by submitting their quarrels to the judgment of the assembly and by depriving themselves of the dangerous power of seizing the property of others, "they would only assure themselves of their real rights and renounce those that they do not have." In terms that bring to mind the basic assumptions about equality in the *Social Contract*, here in his "Summary" of the Abbé de Saint-Pierre's *Project for Perpetual Peace*, Rousseau argues that in the proposed confederation "each [sovereign] is responsible for the guarantees that would assure his own liberty. This liberty might be alienated in the hands of a master, but it is strengthened in the hands of one's peers."[24] Thus, in both the social contract and the international confederation, the absolute equality of the participants transforms liberty and responsibility into two aspects of the same relationship. The similarity in the kind of commitment that the popular association and the international assembly require demonstrates that Rousseau's reflections on Saint-Pierre's writings about peace were as important a step in the development of the political principles of the *Social Contract* as were his reflections on Grotius's and Hobbes's writings about war.

Toward the end of his "Summary," Rousseau finally shifts to the commercial advantages of peace. Introducing the subject with a deft verbal cut that indicates that increasing a nation's wealth is not his priority, Rousseau says, "To all these considerations is added another which is much more important for people who are as avid for money as princes always are. That is, the great facility of gaining additional wealth," both from the advantages of peace and from the "excessive expense that would be spared by the reforming of the military state." With such savings, commerce, agriculture, the arts, and "useful institutions" could be developed, "and the state would thus have a much more perfect security than that which it could gain from armies and from the whole apparatus of war, which never ceases to weaken it, even in times of peace." Once again, this argument, originally put forth by the Abbé de Saint-Pierre in 1713 but transmitted to us with the help of Rousseau in 1761, continues in our own day to be an essential component of all efforts to convince "princes" of the need to find alternatives to war.

In his final weighing of the disadvantages of the present state of war and the advantages that would be gained by a confederation for peace, Rousseau emphasizes the lack of security in the present situation and the potential assurance of security that would result from establishing the confederation. "I leave to the judgment of my readers," he says, reminding us of the intentions expressed in his introduction, "both the examination of all these articles [of confederation] and the comparison of the state of peace that would result from the Confederation with the state of war that results from European anarchy." It is very obvious, here at the end of the "Summary," which side Rousseau himself is on.

But having appealed to his readers' judgment, Rousseau ends the "Summary" with an implicitly revolutionary statement: "If we have reasoned well in the exposition of this project, it is demonstrated firstly that the establishment of perpetual peace depends solely on the consent of sovereigns and presents no difficulty other than their resistance." Reiterating the fact that he had not portrayed princes "as they ought to be"—that is, good, generous, and with humanitarian concerns—but only "such as they are"—that is, unjust, greedy, and looking to their own self-interest above all else, Rousseau emphasizes dramatically that there is no valid reason except their own blindness that should prevent princes from adopting the plan. "If, despite all of this," he concludes, "the project remains unfulfilled, it is not therefore because it is too idealistic; rather, it is because men are insane, and because it is a sort of folly to remain wise in the midst of those who are mad."

THE REALITY OF POWER

When Rousseau had completed his "Summary" of the Abbé de Saint-Pierre's *Project for Perpetual Peace*, he sent a copy of it to Mme. Dupin for her to look over, and if necessary, to edit. There is no existing copy of her response, but a note from Rousseau shortly afterward gives a sense of what her reaction probably was. "In revising the *Abrégé* [of the *Projet de paix perpétuelle*]," Rousseau wrote, "I knew that the project was impractical and that, even if it had not been so on its own, it would become so in the form that I gave it. But I was writing for the public and not for the ministers of state. I hope never in my life to have to write for men of that sort." [25]

Rousseau's insistence on writing "for the public and not for the ministers," caused some problems when it became a question of getting the "Summary" of the *Project for Perpetual Peace* published. In 1760 Jean-

François Bastide, the editor of a new periodical to be titled *Le monde comme il est*, was badgering Rousseau for a piece of writing to include in the first issue of the periodical, and "for lack of anything better" at that time (*La Nouvelle Héloise* had already been promised to Rey and *Emile* was far from finished), Rousseau sent him his "Summary." When Bastide read the manuscript he saw that Rousseau's scarcely veiled attacks on "princes" might cause problems with the erratic but touchy French censors, and he took the dual precautions of getting the usually liberal Malesherbes to be the examiner and suggesting that Rousseau change some of the more inflammatory passages. Rousseau firmly re-sisted most of Bastide's suggestions, however, and this caused Bastide to decide that, rather than print Rousseau's "Summary" as an article in Paris, he would publish it as a separate book safely across the border in Amsterdam.[26]

Unlike some other peace plans of the eighteenth century, Rousseau's "Summary" of the Abbé de Saint-Pierre's *Project for Perpetual Peace* was widely read.[27] Although Voltaire joked about Rousseau wanting "to govern Europe himself the way he governed the house of Mme. Wol-mar" (the Julie of *La Nouvelle Héloise*), and Grimm snidely commented in a letter to Frederick the Great (who was then engaged in the Seven Years War) that the *Project for Perpetual Peace* was even more "absurd" in Rousseau's hands than it had been in the hands of its author, others, like Alexandre Delayre, the librarian for the Duke of Parma, praised the work and wrote to Rousseau to thank him for speaking "in the name of the human race."[28]

More important than these immediate reactions in France, however, were the long-term influences that Rousseau's work on the *Project for Perpetual Peace* would have throughout the Western world. The "Sum-mary" was translated into English and published in London in 1761 and 1767, and it may have influenced Jeremy Bentham, whose own *Principles of International Law* incorporated a project for perpetual peace similar to the Abbé's, and Thomas Paine, who in his *Common Sense Addressed to the Inhabitants of America* declared boldly that it was monar-chies that caused the wars that perennially afflicted Europe, while "the republics of Europe are all . . . in peace."[29]

Most important, perhaps, was the influence of Rousseau's "Sum-mary" on Immanuel Kant. Kant always acknowledged a spiritual in-debtedness to Rousseau, and in his two great political writings, the *Idea for a Universal History with a Cosmopolitan Purpose* and *Perpetual Peace*, Rousseau and the Abbé de Saint-Pierre are very much present. A com-parison of Rousseau's and Kant's conceptions of war and peace would require a separate chapter (or more likely a whole book); suffice it to say that whereas Kant believed that political structures for peace would arise naturally out of the historical process of ever more destructive wars, Rousseau believed firmly that peace among nation-states would not come naturally but could arise only out of a deliberate act of political will.[30] Despite this important difference, Rousseau and Kant are similar in their understanding of the necessary link between domestic politics and international politics.

In the period between the 1899 Peace Conference at the Hague and the outbreak of the World War II, many commentators perceived in Rousseau's "Summary" a precursor of the peace plans of the early twentieth century, and by making this connection, they implicitly gave Rousseau a role in the movement for international peace.[31] More recent "cold war" analysts, such as F. H. Hinsley and Stanley Hoffmann, have criticized this interpretation, and instead have stressed the skepticism about the *Project for Perpetual Peace* that Rousseau expresses in his "Critique," which was published posthumously in 1782 and which Kant, for example, probably never saw. In order to evaluate the crucial question whether Rousseau was an idealist or a skeptic about the possibility of peace, one must turn to the "Critique" of the Abbé de Saint-Pierre's *Project for Perpetual Peace*, which, according to the *Confessions*, Rousseau wrote at approximately the same time as he wrote the "Summary."

Rousseau begins his "Critique" with a rather loaded observation about the total lack of "self-interest" with which the Abbé de Saint-Pierre dedicated himself to the cause of peace. After commenting on the sense of commitment that made the Abbé persist in promoting his project "despite the obvious impossibility of its success" and despite the ridicule and humility he was continually made to endure because of it, Rousseau goes on to say: "It seems that this humane soul was so single-mindedly focused on the public good that he measured the efforts that he gave things solely on the basis of their usefulness, without ever letting himself be discouraged by obstacles and without ever thinking about his personal self-interest."[32]

Using the Abbé de Saint-Pierre's unselfish concern for peace as a counterpoint, Rousseau directs most of his "Critique" at the perversely excessive selfishness of princes. First he takes up the same argument with which he ended the "Summary": "If ever a moral truth has been demonstrated, it seems to me that it is the general and the specific usefulness of this project." Indeed, he continues, "so much would the experience allow each individual to gain from the common good, that to realize the European Republic for one day would be enough to make it last forever." "However," he then says, in an apparently sudden turnabout, "these same princes who would defend the European Republic with all their might once it existed would now be opposed even to its being set up, and they would invariably prevent it from being established with just as much energy as they would prevent it from being destroyed."

How can one explain this contradiction? Rousseau responds by stating that the result of an excess of *amour propre*, the competitive instinct that makes one envious of others, "is usually forever to resort to the means that abuse it." An excess of a princely honor or pride, in other words, tends to result in aggressiveness and bellicosity. In *Considerations on the Government of Poland* and in *Emile*, Rousseau focuses on pedagogical methods for channeling *amour propre* toward more constructive goals; in the *Project for Perpetual Peace*, he says simply that we must distinguish, in politics as well as in morality, "real self-interest from apparent self-interest." Real self-interest is to be found in perpetual peace —"that," Rousseau maintains, "has been demonstrated in the *Project*." Apparent self-interest, in contrast, is found in the present situation of anarchic independence, where sovereigns are tempted away from the rule of law by the attractions of the rule of chance, "like a mad sailor who, in order to show off his knowledge and intimidate his crew, would prefer to drift dangerously among reefs during a storm than to secure his ship with an anchor."

Rousseau's account of how their apparent self-interest would tend to make monarchs reject the *Project for Perpetual Peace* is blunt and hard hitting. The sole preoccupation of kings, Rousseau asserts, or of those to whom they delegate their duties, is to "extend their domination outside their borders and make it more absolute within." Any other objectives, like "public well-being, the happiness of the people, the glory of the nation," are simply pretexts for the overriding desires to conquer and control—as is proven, Rousseau says, by the fact that such noble-sounding phrases are never mentioned in "official circles" and are always greeted by the people as a sign of impending bad news.

Given their needs for both external and internal domination, princes would naturally tend to react negatively to a proposal that "strikes directly at the first and is hardly favorable to the second." For according to the proposed confederation, "the government of each state would be just as clearly defined as its borders," and "princes could not be guaranteed their security from the revolts of their subjects without at the same time guaranteeing to subjects their security from the tyranny of princes . . . otherwise the institution could not survive." Rousseau is pointing to the probability that most sovereigns would be reluctant to join any international structure that had the means to enforce what we today refer to as basic "human rights." The Abbé's proposal, Rousseau implies, would never be accepted by princes because by becoming a member of a larger juridical entity they would be forced to apply the law as equitably toward their own subjects as they would have to apply it toward foreigners, and this they could not tolerate. But again, there is a hint at an alternative solution in these words: It is likely that Rousseau hoped that his readers would speculate that if the sovereigns were the people themselves, rather than "princes," there would be much less resistance to the Abbé's plan.

A similar *double entendre* is suggested in the next section where Rousseau argues that not only would sovereign princes' apparent interests be threatened by the prospect of perpetual peace but such interests are actually supported by the state of war. Here Rousseau gives an acute analysis of the circular self-reinforcing relationship between war and tyranny that has relevance for our own age as well. War can serve as a pretext for imposing high taxes and maintaining large armies, both of which have the effect of keeping the people oppressed; at the same time, oppressed people usually can be relied on to allow money and men to be extorted for the purpose of subduing others. "Anyone can see," Rousseau says firmly, "that aggressive princes make at least as much war against their own people as against their enemies."

There are other reasons why it is likely that princes would never accept the Abbé de Saint-Pierre's plan. How can one expect, Rousseau asks, that men "who dare boast that their power comes only from their swords and would not pay their respects even to God except that he is in heaven" would deign to submit to the judgment of a tribunal? To argue for the proposed confederation by pointing to the risks involved in any act of aggression is similarly futile, Rousseau argues, because the *amour propre* of princes tends to cause them to pay less attention to the risks than to the possible advantages of war: A prince "fears fortune far less than he hopes to profit from his own skill." Moreover, war provides a useful way to stifle internal complaints and clamp down on political agitators. A clever politican even knows how to take advantage of his own wartime losses. Once again, the link between aggression abroad and repression at home is made very clear.

"Ceaselessly deceived by the appearance of things," Rousseau concludes, "princes will therefore reject this peace when judging it by their own self-interest." So just think, he adds with obvious sarcasm, "what will happen when they leave such judgments to their ministers." Ministers have absolutely no interest in bringing about peace; in fact, they "need war to make themselves necessary." The public keeps demanding why, if it is possible, the Abbé de Saint-Pierre's plan has not been adopted. "They fail to see," says Rousseau, "that there is nothing impossible about the project except its adoption"; ministers will respond to it as they always have done—"they will turn it to ridicule."

Rousseau's observation is apt and prophetic: Ridicule has in fact almost always been the response of state officials to proposals for peace, from the Abbé de Saint-Pierre's and Rousseau's time up to our own. By anticipating this response, however, could Rousseau perhaps be urging his readers to think of other strategies that might force ministers to take peace proposals more seriously? Certain statements in his next paragraph make such an interpretation plausible. In discussing the difficulty of finding a ripe moment for putting the project into effect, Rousseau mentions that it would require "a convergence of aims among so many different interests that one could hardly hope to get the happy agreement . . . simply by chance," and then he procedes to make a surprisingly radical statement:

> The only way to make up for the failure of this agreement to come about by chance would be to make it come about by force. Then it would no longer be a question of persuading but of compelling, and then what would be needed is not to write books but to levy troops.

With the above words, one is brought to the final section of the "Critique" where Rousseau seems to be opening up the possibility of using force to bring about peace. Although such a notion contrasts sharply with the *Social Contract*'s fundamental argument that legitimate political society cannot be based on force but must arise out of the free will of the people, here one must remember that Rousseau is discussing not an ideal association of citizens for the sake of civil order but a *de facto* collection of self-interested princes in a "state of war" with one another. The possible relationships between force and law in such a context may be different. As long as power is assumed to be in the hands of princes blinded by the excesses of *amour propre*, it may be necessary to assume, as Hobbes does, that peace can come about through conquest. This is indeed the implication of Rousseau's decision to insert, toward the end of the "Critique," a summary of the plan for European peace that Sully wrote in the name of Henri IV.

The Abbé de Saint-Pierre had uncritically extolled Henri IV for being the originator of the idea of a European league for peace. Rousseau tells us a somewhat different story. By presenting a detailed description of the international rivalries and political maneuvers leading up to the plan, Rousseau reveals the extent to which the "good" Henri's intentions (and those of his faithful minister Sully) were guided not only by ideals of peace but also by a deliberate strategy aimed at giving the French monarchy strong allies against her old enemy, the house of Austria. "What helped this general movement [i.e., the fulfillment of Sully's plan] along?" asks Rousseau toward the end of the "Critique."

> Was it perpetual peace, which no one foresaw and few even cared about? Was it public concern, which is never any private person's concern? The

Abbé de Saint-Pierre might have thought so! But in fact each one worked only with regard to his own individual self-interest, which Henri had the ingenuity to show them all in a very attractive guise.

At this point in his account Rousseau seems to be implying that Henri IV could have been a kind of founding father or "legislator" for the confederation.[33] Unfortunately, because of a freak event, Henri IV's plan was never realized; the king was assassinated, and Europe was plunged "back into eternal wars that she can scarcely hope see come to an end." Nevertheless, says Rousseau, "those were the elements that Henri IV brought together to form the same enterprise that the Abbé de Saint-Pierre claimed to create with a book."

Having confronted the Abbé de Saint-Pierre's illusion that the desire for peace alone might motivate princes to form a confederation, Rousseau ends the "Critique" with a hint of militancy that is generally absent from the rest of his political writings:

> We may not say, therefore, that if [the Abbé de Saint-Pierre's] system has not been adopted it is because it was not good; on the contrary we must say that it was too good to be adopted. *For evil and abuse, which so many men profit from, happen by themselves, but whatever is useful to the public must be brought about by force*—seeing as special interests are almost always opposed to it. Doubtless perpetual peace is at present a project that seems absurd; but were we to be given a Henri IV and a Sully, perpetual peace might become a project that once again would seem reasonable.[34]

Rousseau's meaning is clear: Unlike the convention of free will that he later describes as the basis of the ideal "social contract," in a real situation dominated by *amour propre* and apparent self-interest, the possible methods used to establish political order may include the use of force.[35]

But having acknowledged the inevitable conclusion that follows from the rigor of his own logic, Rousseau, at the very end of the "Critique," steps back from the abyss and leaves the reader with an equivocation: The war to end all wars may not be worth the risk.

> We will not see federative leagues establishing themselves except by revolution, and, on this principle, who would dare say whether this European league is to be desired or feared? It would perhaps cause more harm in one moment than it could prevent for centuries to come.

In a context dominated by the rule of narrow self-interest, Rousseau implies, the pursuit of reason inevitably must lead to revolution; but who can guess, given the uncertain outcome of such an event, whether the revolution would eventually negate or affirm the spirit of rationality that produced it? In this passage one sees Rousseau wrestling with the same questions about the relationship between reason and revolution

that would perplex those later historians of the future who would seek
to understand the upheavals of his century.

"TO KNOW WHAT OUGHT TO BE IN ORDER TO JUDGE SOUNDLY WHAT IS"

Not surprisingly, Rousseau's "Critique" of the Abbé de Saint-Pierre's
Project for Perpetual Peace was never published during Rousseau's life-
time. Having met with some censorship of the "Summary," which was
ostensibly only a presentation of the Abbé's views, Rousseau drew back
even from trying to publish his own, more blatantly antimonarchist
"Critique," and in the *Confessions* he wrote that he was not sure whether
it would ever be published.[36] In a *nota bene* that appears at the end of
his manuscript for the "Critique," however, there is a hint that Rousseau had hoped it would someday become an acknowledged part of his
work; the note also, I must add, should make one somewhat wary of
trying to interpret in any simple or conclusive way Rousseau's underlying convictions about the possibilities of peace. "Take care," the note
says, "to have the final copy of this made by someone who is very intelligent, very precise, but who won't meddle with trying to guess what
it means."[37]

Notwithstanding these humbling words, one is nevertheless driven
forward by Rousseau's compelling prose to consult other writings that
might help to clarify what his response to the Abbé de Saint-Pierre
means. After completing his work on the *Project for Perpetual Peace*,
Rousseau went on to draft a "Summary" and "Critique" of another of
the Abbé de Saint-Pierre's more significant political tracts, his *Polysynodie*. The *Polysynodie* was a proposal for a plurality of councils that
would both counterbalance and supplement the centralized power of
the French monarchy. Unlike the labyrinthine tangle of his works on
perpetual peace, the Abbé's proposal for a plurality of councils was
fairly straightforward; as Rousseau mentions with a smile in his "Critique" of it, "This piece of writing was just a sketch which he claimed
to have not had the chance to abridge, but which in effect he didn't
have the time to spoil by wanting to say everything. May God spare
impatient readers from the kind of abridgements that he wrote!"[38] As
a result of the Abbé's relative brevity, the "Summary" of the *Polysynodie* required less input from Rousseau than the "Summary" of the
Project for Perpetual Peace had, and the final product was a fairly faithful
recapitulation of the Abbé's ideas.

In his "Critique" of the *Polysynodie*, however, Rousseau's own views
come to the fore, and in this seldom-mentioned work one finds ideas
that cannot help but reawaken some of the same questions that one is

left with at the end of the "Critique" of the *Project for Perpetual Peace*. Rousseau's main contention is that while the Abbé had claimed that his proposed councils were so close to the existing system that it would require only a simple reforming of the *status quo* to bring them into effect, in fact the changes that he proposed, while subtle, were so fundamental that the actual realization of them "would require nothing less than a revolution."[39]

But again, at the same time as he recognizes that to change permanently the locus of power from the monarchy to an aristocracy of merit would require starting completely anew, Rousseau expresses profound doubts about the desirability of taking such a risk. "No one can ignore," he prophetically warns, "how dangerous, in a large state, is that moment of anarchy and crisis that necessarily precedes the establishment of a new system. . . . Just think of the danger of once arousing the enormous masses which make up the French monarchy!"

> Who could manage the resulting upheaval or foresee the effects that it could produce? Even when all the advantages of the new plan were indisputable, what man of good sense would dare begin abolishing old customs, changing ancient maxims, and giving a new form to a state which a history of three hundred years has given us?[40]

Thus one is left with the same ambivalence that was apparent at the end of the writings on the *Project for Perpetual Peace*. On the one hand, in the "Summary," Rousseau presents convincing reasons why a more rational reorganization of social life is necessary; on the other hand, in the "Critique," he presents equally convincing reasons why, given the apparent self-interest of princes, such change could not come about except by means of a revolution that might cause more harm than it would prevent. Confronted by such a contradiction, one cannot help asking, *why, if Rousseau really thought the Abbé de Saint-Pierre's proposals were so dangerous, did he take such pains to have them read?*

That Rousseau very much feared violence and anarchy is indisputable. Not only in his works on the Abbé de Saint-Pierre but in other writings as well, he repeatedly expresses a deep aversion to the prospect of the political and social chaos that would result if the *ancien régime* were indeed turned upside down.[41] Rousseau seems to have wanted history to remember him as a lawgiver or political educator rather than as a revolutionary; as he stated in the beginning paragraphs of his fragments on "The State of War," he intended to "limit" himself to "examining human institutions by means of their principles; to correcting, if possible, the false ideas given about them by self-interested authors; and, at the very least, to insuring that injustice and violence don't shamelessly take on the names of right and equity."

Despite his own reluctance to take on a revolutionary role, there are many indications in his political writings that Rousseau saw a future revolution as inevitable and even necessary. In *Emile*, for example, he emphasizes the need to raise his young pupil to be ready to meet any unforeseen circumstances in his adult life: "Given the unsettled and restless spirit of this age which upsets everything in each generation, can one conceive of a method more senseless than raising a child as though . . . he were going to be constantly surrounded by his servants?"; and later in the same work he states emphatically that "we are approaching a state of crisis and the age of revolutions."[42] In the *Discourse on the Origin of Inequality* one finds other provocative statements: In a passage in which he is describing the stage of "nascent government" but where the wording is somewhat similar to his later description of the balance-of-power system in the "Summary" of the *Project for Perpetual Peace*, Rousseau says,

> Despite all the labors of the wisest legislators, the political state remained ever imperfect because it was almost the work of chance, and because, as it began badly, time in discovering faults and suggesting remedies could never repair the vices of the constitution. People incessantly mended, whereas it would have been necessary to begin by clearing the area and setting aside all the old materials."[43]

Farther on in the second *Discourse* Rousseau makes another reference to revolution: The final state of inequality, he says, "the stage of master and slave," will continue "until new revolutions dissolve the government altogether or bring it closer to its legitimate institution."[44]

Thus while it is certain that Rousseau himself consistently shied away from advocating radical social change, it is also evident that he sensed such change coming. Furthermore, it is hard to believe that he was not aware, on some level, of the revolutionary import of his own writings. For as his introduction to his collection of the Abbé de Saint-Pierre's projects asserts, his purpose in making the Abbé's idealistic schemes available to the public was to enable people to "judge by them whether the government is right or wrong." Similarly, he states in *Emile* that the purpose of introducing his pupil to a summary of both the *Social Contract* and his own writings on war and peace is to enable his pupil "to know what ought to be in order to judge soundly what is." Given his familiarity with the life and teachings of Socrates, Rousseau could not have been blind to the fact that helping people to "judge" their political institutions is a form of political activism that can be as threatening to the *status quo* as any direct call for revolution.[45]

At this point it might be useful to recall the eccentric Count d'Antraigues's perception of a dangerous similarity between the *Social Contract* and a manuscript supposedly given to him by Rousseau that showed "the means by which small states could coexist with great powers by forming confederations." As was pointed out in the Introduction, d'Antraigues claimed to have destroyed the manuscript because it, like the *Social Contract*, might be used by the French revolutionaries in ways that could threaten "the authority of the King." Although recent research has indicated that the manuscript on confederations allegedly destroyed by d'Antraigues was probably nothing more than a figment of his imagination, the Count's fears echo the same truth that Rousseau had confronted in his own responses to the *Project for Perpetual Peace* of the Abbé de Saint-Pierre. Both Rousseau and the Count fully understood that a proposal for a confederation limiting the independent rights of princes to make war on one another was as potentially revolutionary as a proposal for a social contract that would base political sovereignty on the will of the people.

But while the Count d'Antraigues reacted to the revolutionary implications of Rousseau's writings on peace by imagining that he himself had destroyed them, Jean-Jacques Rousseau took care that his writings on peace were preserved. In 1764, when he was corresponding with Du Peyrou about what was to be included in the first edition of his complete works, Rousseau listed his writings on the Abbé de Saint-Pierre in the table of contents of the first volume, right after the *Social Contract*. As pointed out by Sven Stelling-Michaud, the Pléiade editor of Rousseau's works on Saint-Pierre, this choice indicates that Rousseau saw his writings on Saint-Pierre as a homogeneous unit and that they were very important to him.[46] The evident concern on the part of Rousseau to keep questions about international peace alive is also supported by his firm comment, at the beginning of the "Critique" of the *Project for Perpetual Peace*, that while some readers may say that the Abbé's *Project* "seems like nothing but vain speculation," in fact it is "a solid and sensible" piece of writing, and "it is very important that it exists."

AFTER he had completed his "Summaries" and "Critiques" of the Abbé de Saint-Pierre's *Project for Perpetual Peace* and *Polysynodie* in 1759, it appears that Rousseau felt ready to go on with the study of "Political Institutions" that he had started fifteen years earlier in Venice. At this point he put aside the works on Saint-Pierre, giving as an excuse that the Abbé's "critical observations upon certain features of the government" might get him into trouble with the authorities, but probably more likely because the close attention that he had given to Saint-Pierre's reforms had provided him with enough stimulating reflections to develop, more concretely than he would previously have been able to do, the part of "Political Institutions" that would soon appear as the *Social Contract*.

As one can easily see in the above examination of the "Summary" and "Critique" of the Abbé de Saint-Pierre's *Project for Perpetual Peace*, Rousseau's confrontation with the problem of finding a way for free and equal sovereign states to come together in a confederation for international peace undoubtedly helped him formulate ideas about how free and equal individuals might come together in a social contract for civil order. Both the *Project for Perpetual Peace* and the *Social Contract* call for new forms of political association that are instituted by deliberate agreement, that are maintained by equal participation and mutual interdependence, and that are finally justified in terms of their ability to ensure human security. More important, both works demonstrate that while to reconcile the conflicting ideals of peace and freedom may not be an easy task, neither is it an impossible one.

But just as important as the stimulation that his writings on war and peace during this period gave to Rousseau's thinking about political institutions was the stimulation that such writing gave to his thinking about education. For what Rousseau's anguished dialogue with the Abbé de Saint-Pierre brought to the fore was the fundamental moral corruption that, in both individuals and states, arises out of a blind adherence to apparent self-interest and excessive *amour propre*. In an effort to suggest ways to go beyond external institutional change, Rousseau would show in the great educational writings of his later life that any attempt to create new forms of political order based on real self-interest rather than apparent self-interest would require new forms of education based on *amour de soi* rather than *amour propre*. It is to this effort that I turn in the next section.

For to be fully understood, Rousseau's writings on politics must be read in conjunction with his writings on education. Rousseau was a political educator both in the sense that he educated his readers about the possibilities of politics and in the sense that he saw different political contexts requiring different methods of education. Convinced since his early years in Venice that people are largely "what they are made to be" by the social institutions surrounding them, he clearly perceived that politics and education are intimately related and that educational choices should be made on the basis of an informed and self-conscious assessment of the political context within which the educational process takes place.

A brief summary may be in order. As Chapters 3 and 4 have shown, Rousseau's attempt to find alternatives to the *de facto* state of anarchy and violence that he had confronted in the *Discourse on the Origin of Inequality* and in his fragments on "The State of War" led him to explore the possibility of peace from two rather different angles. First, in his dialogue with Diderot over the origin of the general will, Rousseau argued that a common concern for others grows out of the experience of "willing generally" in a small, legitimately constituted community. By developing the habit of thinking in terms of public concerns rather than in terms of personal concerns, he maintained, a sense of humanity can gradually be extended to include those who dwell beyond one's national borders. In the same period in which he carried on his dialogue with Diderot, however, Rousseau also committed himself to editing, evaluating, and publicizing the *Project for Perpetual Peace* of the Abbé de Saint-Pierre. Taking as its frame of reference a political world dominated not by small, legitimately constituted republics but by large commercial empires, Rousseau argued in his "Summary" of the *Project* that the contradiction between civil order and international anarchy might be resolved by an international peacekeeping structure that would effectively limit the rights of sovereign states to make war on one another. Instead of giving priority to the freedom of citizens in a small young state, Rousseau now was giving priority to the protection of subjects in a large and expansive one; instead of looking back to ancient autonomous republics as he had in his formulation of the general will, he was looking forward to modern international relations in ways that are very relevant to the developed world today.

With these contrasting contexts in mind, it is not surprising to find that parallel in many respects to the two solutions to the challenge of peace in Rousseau's political writings are two solutions to the challenge of peace in his educational writings. In the chapters that follow it is evident that Rousseau's educational proposals are put forth not as abstract formulations but as the specific means of mediating the individual's relationship to two very different political environments.

PART III

POLITICAL EDUCATION FOR PEACE

5

CIVIC EDUCATION AND NATIONAL DEFENSE

A RESPONSE TO THE PATRIOTS OF POLAND

In the present chapter the word *response* has a somewhat different meaning from the one it has in other chapters of this book. In general I have used (and continue to use in the next chapter) *response* to refer to the stimulation of Rousseau's thinking that resulted from his reading of other political theorists of his time. As has been shown in the preceding chapters, both classic writers such as Hobbes and Grotius and contemporaries such as Diderot and Saint-Pierre can be considered the springboards or pushing-off points for many of Rousseau's most insightful contributions to political theory. Here, however, his "response" to the patriots of Poland was not a reflection on something the Poles had written; instead, it was a direct answer to their call for his advice. Although the topical aspect of Rousseau's *Considerations on the Government of Poland* has generally made the work less influential than the *Social Contract*, the specific challenge of providing advice to a developing nation threatened by greedy superpowers gave Rousseau an opportunity to explore the relationships among education, economics, and national defense in ways that can provoke useful thinking about our own age as well as Rousseau's.

SQUEEZED in between the borders of Prussia to the west, the Hapsburg and Ottoman empires to the south, and Russia to the east, Poland in the eighteenth century was in an extremely precarious position. As at other moments in the nation's history, the Polish people in the 1760s were divided into two rival factions whose main source of contention was Poland's relationship with Russia.[1] The Czartoryski faction, which favored a close relationship with Russia, put, as C. E. Vaughan describes it, "reform before independence" whereas an opposing group, the Potocki, put "independence before reform"—differences in approach that would shape much of Rousseau's advice to Poland and that can still be seen in Polish politics today. The balance between the two groups shifted significantly in 1764 when Stanislas Poniatowski, a member of the Czartoryski family and a former lover of Catherine the Great, was elected to the throne. In the following years Poland came more and more under the influence of Russia.

Then as now, however, the perception of growing foreign encroachment had the effect of stiffening the Poles' resistance, and a number of landowners in Poldonia banded together into a group called the Confederation of Bar, which had as its purpose to free Poland from Russian interference. In the meantime, Catherine became distracted by a war against Turkey, and her hold over Poland seemed to begin to weaken. This gave the Confederates hope, and although Catherine denounced them as "rebels" and engaged Cossacks to undertake brutal attacks on them, the Confederates' influence grew, and in 1769 they were able to convene an assembly of representatives from almost every part of Poland. One of the resolutions of the assembly directed that a number of leading political theorists of the day be asked to provide the Confederates with advice on a new constitution for Poland in the event that its hoped-for independence were won. Among those who answered the patriots' call were several Physiocrats, Rousseau's long-time friend the Abbé de Mably, and Rousseau himself.

When Count Wielhorski, the member of the Confederation who was made responsible for contacting Rousseau, appealed to him in 1771, Rousseau was in a mood of discouragement and exhaustion that at first made him skeptical about his ability to undertake the enormous task of proposing a new form of government for the vulnerable and chaotic Polish state. The period following the burning of *Emile* in 1763 and the issuance of a warrant for its author's arrest had been the worst period of Rousseau's life. Pursued by public officials and consumed by private fears, he had fled from Paris to Yverdon, from there to Môtiers, to the Île de Saint-Pierre, then to Strasbourg, Berlin, and to David Hume's estate in England; then back to Europe again to Amiens, Lyon, Grenoble, and finally to Paris.[2] Seven years of continuous flight and uncertainty had left Rousseau with little taste for political controversy, and he had planned to spend his final days copying music, studying botany, and living quietly with Thérèse in his old apartment on the rue Plâtrière.

Wielhorski apparently persisted in his request, however, and supplied Rousseau both with information about the history of Poland and with the proposals for reform that had already been drafted by Mably and several important Physiocrats, including Mirabeau, Dupont de Nemours, Quesnay, and others.[3] Soon Rousseau's interest in the matter was aroused, and the challenge of testing the extent to which the principles of political right that he had set forth nearly a decade earlier in the *Social Contract* might be applied to an actual historical context summoned reserves of energy and insight that the sixty-year-old man scarcely knew he had. As he reported to Wielhorsky, he worked continually on his *Poland* for six months, taking time off from it only for the music-copying jobs by which he supported himself and Thérèse.[4]

Although the path toward peace that Rousseau recommends for a newly independent state will look very different from the path toward peace that he recommended for Europe's *anciens régimes*, in the opening section of his *Considerations on the Government of Poland* Rousseau lays down the same general principle with which he began his "Summary" of the *Project for Perpetual Peace*, namely, that one must be thoroughly familiar with the nature of a people or a situation before undertaking the work of perfecting it. This comment at first leads Rousseau both to belittle his own or any other foreigner's ability to do more than "offer some general observations" and to stress that "good institutions for Poland can only be the work of Poles," since they alone have sufficient knowledge of their nation.[5] But as one reads his carefully thought out suggestions, Rousseau's own appreciation of the historical resilience of the Polish people becomes apparent, and one can easily see why he became energized by the prospect of having a role in their political future.

What his preliminary studies of Poland would have revealed to Rousseau was a people who, ever since the founding of Poland in 963, had had to struggle for their identity against the encroachment of more powerful neighbors, who had retained from the early years of their history a unique system of local representative councils or diets, and who engaged in the practice, rare in Europe during the eighteenth century, of electing their king instead of following the usual practice of letting the monarchy become hereditary. These manifestations of the Poles' native political energies gave Rousseau great hope for them. In fact, at the beginning of his *Considerations* he says that, of all the people now living, the Poles are the "least separated" from the heroes of the ancient Holy Land, Sparta, and Rome.[6] It is perhaps not so surprising, therefore, that in his proposals for reform Rousseau often seems to caution *against* any major change that might dampen the Polish people's political zeal.[7]

At the beginning of the treatise Rousseau describes with robust irony the contradictory aspects of Poland's historical situation. "While reading the history of the government of Poland," he observes, "it is hard to understand how a state so strangely constituted has been able to survive so long."

> A large body made up of a large number of dead members . . . a body which exerts itself greatly to accomplish nothing . . . which falls into dissolution five or six times a century . . . and which, in spite of all this lives and maintains its vigour; that, in my opinion, is one of the most singular spectacles ever to challenge a rational being.

Rousseau's admiration for a people who can so defy their circumstances becomes especially evident in the passage that follows. While the other states of Europe are "rushing to their ruin," he says, while "all these fine governments, for all their prudent checks and balances, have grown decrepit and threaten soon to die," Poland, a depopulated and oppressed region, "still shows all the fire of youth; she dares to ask for a government and for laws as if she were newly born. She . . . feels in herself the kind of force that the forces of tyranny cannot overcome."[8]

It is this last quality—the Poles' passionate sense of the power of their own identity—that Rousseau cautions the Poles to be sure not to jeopardize by undertaking an abrupt or radical change in their constitution. "Worthy Poles," he says, addressing them warmly,

> Beware lest, in your eagerness to improve, you may worsen your condition. In thinking what you wish to gain, do not forget what you may lose. Correct, if possible, the abuses of your constitution; but do not despise that constitution which has made you what you are.[9]

Two possible meanings of the word "constitution" are brought deftly into his readers' consciousness by Rousseau's careful phrasing: The Poles may think that they need a new constitution—a set of laws written on paper; at the same time they should be careful that the paper constitution does not undermine their native constitution—the qualities of pride and passion that have enabled them to survive so long.

Rousseau warns that the desire for peace and order may even contradict, in some essential way, the need for independence and freedom. "Wearied by the troubles of your [homeland]," he tells them, "you are sighing for tranquility. That can, I think, be easily won; but to preserve it along with liberty, that is what I find difficult." The patriots who have saved Poland from oppression, he says, "would like to combine the peace of despotism with the sweets of liberty. I fear they may be seeking contradictory things."[10]

Here in the opening chapter of his *Considerations on the Government of*

Poland Rousseau is pointing to a dynamic relationship between political energy and historical change that, as J. G. A. Pocock's *The Machiavellian Moment* helps one to appreciate, underlies much of the tradition of classical republican thought from Aristotle and Boethius onward and appears most revealingly in the complex interplay between *virtù* and *fortuna* in the political writings of Niccolò Machiavelli. For Machiavelli and his predecessors, virtue became the name for the capacities of civic responsibility, military valor, and political commitment that could be called forth by certain sets of unpredictable circumstances in the social order and that were thus necessarily based on contingency, chance, and change. In Pocock's words, *"virtus* was that by which the good man imposed form on his *fortuna."* [11]

Because Machiavelli's notion of *fortuna* included contingency in a republic's foreign relations, the notion of civic virtue also came to be linked with the ability to control a republic's external environment, and in Machiavelli's writings the concept was used to justify expansionary as well as purely defensive military actions.[12] I discuss Rousseau's reworking of this aspect of the Machiavellian tradition more closely in the section on "Defense without Threat"; here the focus is on Rousseau's Machiavellian understanding of Poland's internal political prospects.

As Pocock makes clear, the relationship between civic virtue and historical contingency becomes especially problematical when one desires to try to make virtue permanent in time. For, obviously, if one succeeds too well in achieving a stable constitution, one may risk losing the openness to fortune that was perceived to be the basis for virtue in the first place. In a passage of the *Discourses* that Rousseau may have had in mind when he wrote his *Considerations on the Government of Poland*, Machiavelli had argued, for example, that "those who blame the quarrels of the Senate and the people of Rome condemn that which was the very origin of liberty"; later on, he adds, "nor can we regard a republic as disorderly where so many virtues were seen to shine."[13] This same understanding of the danger of too much "order" underlies Rousseau's admonition to the Poles that their political forms "must be touched only with extreme circumspection."

Grounded in his Machiavellian understanding of the fragility of political commitment, particularly in a state as large as Poland, Rousseau's advice for reform focuses on encouraging those institutions that allow for the frequent exercise of popular will. Among his concrete proposals is the strengthening of the dietines, the smallest units of local self-government. "I observe," he says, "that the Poles are not sufficiently aware of the importance of their dietines, of all they owe to them, nor of all they might get from them by extending their authority and by regulating their form. I myself am convinced that . . . the die-

tines . . . are the true palladium of liberty."[14] Rousseau recommends
that the dietines should be given responsibility for the election of members to the central diet; that, for the sake of maintaining the sovereignty
of the legislative power, the central diet itself should meet very frequently; and that the representatives should be bound strictly to follow
the policy deliberations at the local level. At the same time as he spells
out these representative procedures in detail, however, Rousseau also
cautions against trying to systematize too much. After suggesting a way
of determining who should vote in the dietines, Rousseau says that it
might be possible to find a better system of discipline for the diets and
dietines, but he warns against seeking two contradictory things at the
same time. "Discipline is good," he says, "but liberty is better."[15]

Another means that Rousseau proposes for keeping the spirit of civic
participation alive is to make sure that the crown never becomes hereditary. Based on his conviction (explained in the *Social Contract*) that larger
states need a more centralized administration than smaller ones, Rousseau believes that Poland does need a king, but he recommends that the
king be deprived of the power of appointing senators and that the office
never become hereditary. "I assure you that the moment that law is
adopted," he says, referring to the adoption of an hereditary monarchy,
"Poland can say good-bye forever to her freedom."[16]

Rousseau bases his stand against hereditary monarchy not only on
the familiar arguments about the tendency of hereditary rule to become
corrupt and selfish but also on the more unusual observation that there
is positive benefit to be gained from periodic political change. "Poland
is free," he maintains, "because each reign is preceded by an interval
when the nation, renewing all its rights and regaining new vigour, cuts
off the progress of abuses and usurpations, when the law revives and re-
covers its original power."[17] Here again, he is very close to Machiavelli:
"I say," Machiavelli had stated in Book III of the *Discourses*, "that those
changes are beneficial that bring [mixed bodies, such as republics] back
to their original principles. And those are the best constituted bodies,
and have the longest existence, which possess the intrinsic means of
frequently renewing themselves."[18]

I have thus far been focusing on the similarities between Rousseau's
and Machiavelli's reactions to political disorder; it is at this point interesting to compare their reactions with that of Hobbes. As we saw in
Chapter 1, Hobbes instinctively sought to counter chaos with repression; his response to the prospect of disorder and civil war was to argue
for a centralized power that would "keep men all in awe." In contrast
to Hobbes, both Rousseau and Machiavelli recognize the possible dangers inherent in trying to stifle popular unrest; as Rousseau pointed out,
"discipline is good but liberty is better."

This is not to say that Rousseau was by any means advocating full political democracy for the Poles. In two areas in particular, his proposals seem to go against the respect for democratic responsibility that one often associates with the ideal of the sovereignty of the people. Most salient in this regard is his advice against immediately granting freedom to the Polish serfs. "To free the common people of Poland would be a great and worthy enterprise, but bold, perilous, and not to be attempted lightly." Since liberty is "a food easy to eat, but hard to digest," and since in many ways the laws of freedom are "more austere . . . than the yoke of tyrants is heavy," it would be necessary first to make the serfs who are to be freed "worthy of liberty and capable of enduring it." "Do not free their bodies," he counsels, "until after you have freed their souls." [19] In a later section, in which he describes a "Plan for a Sequence of Promotions Embracing all Members of the Government" (and which in its spirit may recall the plan for a rotation of offices in Harrington's *Oceana*),[20] Rousseau explains how peasants distinguished by "good conduct, education, and morals" could gradually be selected by the dietines for manumission.[21] From the author of the argument in the *Social Contract* that slavery and "right" are contradictory notions and that it is the condition of being in chains that makes a man servile, Rousseau's caution in recommending the freeing of Poland's serfs may be somewhat surprising.

Another recommendation that seems to conflict with Rousseau's concern for political responsibility is the one regarding the perpetuation of the Confederation of Bar, the political cadre that took the initiative for Polish independence and reform. Unlike Mably, who had recommended its dissolution, Rousseau maintained that the Confederation should remain on the sidelines, ready to assume power in any emergency. As with Rousseau's provisions for granting emergency powers to a single leader in the *Social Contract*,[22] one questions why Rousseau did not see that the existence of such potential rescuers might encourage the very apathy and political dependency that his other recommendations were designed to prevent.

One way to understand Rousseau's occasional equivocations about allowing virtue to be free to respond to fortune is to remember the international context in which he saw Poland in the eighteenth century. His close study of "The State of War" and his summary of the Abbé de Saint-Pierre's *Project for Perpetual Peace* had made Rousseau fully aware of the precariousness of national security within the European balance-of-power system and the tendency for weak states like Poland to become pawns in the internecine power struggles of their more highly organized neighbors. In the war of every *state* against every *state* it is security as well as liberty that must be paid attention to, and in such situations one cannot afford to take too many risks. "No matter what plan is adopted," Rousseau warns in his conclusion to the *Considerations*,

> you should not forget what I have said in the *Social Contract* regarding the state of weakness and anarchy in which a nation finds itself as soon as it establishes or reforms its constitution. In the moment of disorder and effervescence, it is incapable of putting up any sort of resistance, and the slightest shock is capable of upsetting everything.[23]

In a double sense, then, Rousseau's recommendations for Poland aim at preserving Poland rather than reforming it. In the first place, he wanted to preserve the natural political energies of the Polish people; in the second place, he wanted to preserve the identity of the Polish state in Europe. In bringing together these dual objectives, Rousseau, like the Potocki faction ten years before, was essentially arguing for putting "independence before reform." "You will never be free as long as a single Russian soldier remains in Poland," Rousseau says toward the end of his *Considerations*, and "you will always be in danger of losing your freedom as long as Russia interferes in your affairs."[24] This overriding concern for Poland's survival in the context of an implicit "state of war" influenced his advice against freeing the serfs and doing away with a potentially dictatorial revolutionary faction. This same overriding concern for national security also shaped his proposals regarding Poland's education, economics, and national defense.

Before going on, it is important to acknowledge that in the course of exploring these topics it often appears that Rousseau's proposals for Poland are diametrically opposed to what he had advocated in his "Summary" of the Abbé de Saint-Pierre's *Project for Perpetual Peace*. Certainly the aims of the two texts are different: In the "Summary" Rousseau was seeking to limit the destructive capacities of large and expansionary empires for the sake of international security; in the *Considerations* he is seeking to promote the political energies of an oppressed and backward people for the sake of civil freedom. Is there any contradiction here? Is the need for peace among old states compatible with the desire for freedom in young ones?

To reconcile the divergent aims of peace and freedom it is important to remember Rousseau's important teaching about the origin of the general will. As he demonstrated in his argument with Diderot, concepts of universal or international justice do not appear naturally but must first be nurtured within the context of a small and relatively circumscribed political community. "We conceive of the general society on the basis of our particular societies," he wrote in the first draft of the *Social Contract*; "the establishment of small republics makes us think about the large one; and we do not really begin to become men until after we have been citizens." In reviewing Rousseau's recommendations for Poland it must be kept in mind that experiences of intense patriotism thus do not necessarily preclude an eventual confederation for peace, but such experiences may necessarily precede one.

EDUCATION FOR CIVIC SOLIDARITY

In discussing the origins of war in the first chapter, I suggested that Rousseau's understanding of the *de facto* relations among states could be put in terms of a manifestation on a national scale of the developmental relationship between *amour de soi* and *amour propre* that he had first put forth in his *Discourse on the Origin of Inequality*. With none of the natural limits to its self-esteem that an individual has (an individual's "years are numbered, his pleasures have their measure, his heart too its natural confines"), a nation's *amour de soi*, or basic instincts of self-preservation, tend easily to become dominated by *amour propre* —the competitive need to feel superior to one's neighbor. The state "can always expand, and yet it always feels weak as long as there are other states that are stronger than itself," Rousseau explained in his unfinished manuscript on "The State of War." "Its power being purely relative, the political body is forced ceaselessly to compare itself in order to know itself."[25]

As we saw in the earlier discussions of Rousseau's analysis of the war system, what feeds external competition is the internal need of the state to counter the centrifugal forces of the individuals and factions that compose it with an excess of political passion vis-à-vis its potential enemies. "It is necessary, therefore, for the state to survive, that the intensity of its passions supplement the intensity of its actions and that its will become animated to the extent that its strength becomes slack."[26] When such compensatory passions are directed outward, war comes to be viewed as the "health" of the state. In his "Summary" of the Abbé de Saint-Pierre's *Project for Perpetual Peace*, Rousseau elaborated on this dynamic by showing in more detail how princes blinded by "apparent self-interest" try to maintain control over their subjects at home by engaging in foreign conquest and aggression abroad.

The predominance of *amour propre* in the international arena thus perpetuates a weblike economic and military system in which the people of Europe, as Rousseau explained in his "Summary," "have complicated their interests and rights in a thousand ways" and in which "their divisions are all the more deadly as their ties are intimate." In his *Considerations on the Government of Poland* Rousseau warns that in such a context a vulnerable and chaotic state like Poland is doomed.

Poland is a large state surrounded by even more considerable states which, by reason of their despotism and military discipline, have great offensive power. Herself weakened by anarchy, she is, in spite of Polish valour, exposed to all their insults. . . . No economic organisation; few or no troops; no military discipline, no order, no subordination; ever divided within, ever menaced from without, she has no intrinsic stability, and depends on the caprice of her neighbors.[27]

How, then, might Poland survive? One way out of "the state of war" generated by excessive national *amour propre* is, as we have seen in Rousseau's response to the Abbé de Saint-Pierre, a confederation for peace "which, by uniting nations with ties similar to those which unite individuals would submit each of them to the equal authority of the laws." But for the young state of Poland, Rousseau proposes a very different path. Instead of attempting to join the international "system," Poland must separate itself from it altogether; unable to compete effectively in an arena dominated by excessive *amour propre*, Poland must redirect its social passions so that they serve its *amour de soi*.

"I can see only one way to give [Poland] the stability she lacks," Rousseau says near the beginning of his *Considerations*: "It is to establish the Republic so firmly in the hearts of the Poles that she will maintain her existence there in spite of all the efforts of her oppressors."

You may not prevent them from swallowing you up; see to it that at least they will not be able to digest you. . . . The virtue of her citizens, their patriotic zeal, the particular way in which national institutions may be able to form their souls, this is the only rampart which will always stand ready to defend her, and which no army will ever be able to breach.

"If you see to it that no Pole can ever become a Russian," Rousseau sums up, "I guarantee that Russia will not subjugate Poland."[28]

And what are the means of such a transformation? "How is it possible to move the hearts of men, and to make them love the [homeland] and its laws?" Rousseau asks. "Dare I say it? Through children's games; through institutions which seem idle and frivolous to superficial men, but which form cherished habits and invincible attachments."[29] Poland's national security will thus be based not on a threatening military posture but on the civic solidarity of its people. Nurtured by participation in patriotic festivals and games and by public education, Poland's political virtue must be formed in such a way that it strengthens the nation's self-sufficiency and self-love. If Poland depends only on itself for the satisfaction of its passions, it will be less in need of reaching beyond its borders for the stimulation of its political will. Patriotic solidarity, not war, must become the health of the state.

That the cultivation of a secure identity for Poland will therefore require withdrawing from a larger international culture is very clear from the beginning of Rousseau's *Considerations*. Making an observation similar to one he had made in *Emile* about the bourgeois "man of our time" being a "nothing," Rousseau says that there are "no longer Frenchmen, Germans, Spaniards or even Englishmen" but simply "rascals" who "wish to be as rich as Croesus,"[30] and he counsels firmly: "Incline the passions of the Poles in a different direction." Instead of letting Poles be coopted into the international system, "give their souls a national physiognomy which will distinguish them from other peoples, which will prevent them from mixing, from feeling at ease with those peoples, from allying themselves with them."[31]

The precepts that follow such principles often sound extreme to twentieth-century readers. Rousseau's recommendation of national ceremonies and celebrations, his advocacy of rewarding patriotic virtues with honors and public awards, his praise for public games, spectacles, and solemnities—all of these may strike modern cosmopolitans as trivial; and his advice to "arrange things so that every citizen will feel himself to be constantly under the public eye" may even sound dangerous. But it is necessary to remember that it was precisely modern cosmopolitanism that Rousseau was trying to prevent in Poland; he praises Poland for having customs and even a national dress that are "peculiar to itself," and scorns "the general European tendency to adopt the tastes and manners of the French."[32] At this point, Rousseau is as far as he could be along the axis that separates his views from Diderot's regarding the efficacy of a "general will of the human race" as the basis for peace and social justice. Poles need, first of all, to learn the art of "willing generally" for Poland. As Rousseau explains in *Emile* (perhaps with his argument with Diderot still fesh in his mind),

> Every particular society, when it is narrow and unified, is estranged from the all-encompassing society. Every patriot is harsh to foreigners. They are only men. They are nothing in his eyes. This is a drawback, inevitable but not compelling. The essential thing is to be good to the people with whom one lives. . . . Distrust those cosmopolitans who go to great length in their books to discover duties they do not deign to fulfill around them. A philosopher loves the Tartars so as to be spared having to love his neighbors.[33]

At the same time, it is necessary to understand that for all his approval of customs and practices that stimulate patriotic zeal and foster a "repugnance of mingling with foreigners," Rousseau is careful not to support forms of xenophobia that might turn into belligerence or aggression; the patriotism that he wishes to encourage in the Poles is zealous but nonthreatening. At the ceremony celebrating the Confederates' successes, for example, a monument should be raised, eulogies be given, and the families of the dead be honored, but no "invectives against the Russians, or even any mention of them, be permitted at these solemnities . . . you must despise them too much to hate them."[34]

From his discussion of the games and ceremonies that can stimulate patriotism, Rousseau turns to the more specific topic of public education. He may have first become aware of the political significance of education while he was writing the article on "Political Economy" for the *Encyclopédie* in 1755: the lead-in to its discussion of "training citizens" states that "I end this part of public economy where I ought to have started it."[35] Sixteen years later, in his *Considerations on the Government of Poland*, he avoids his previous mistake and near the beginning of his treatise acknowledges the close connection between politics and education: "This is the important question. It is education that must give souls a national formation and direct their opinions and tastes in such a way that they will be patriotic by inclination, by passion, by necessity."[36]

Rousseau gives a definition of public education in *Emile* that can illuminate his actual proposals for it in *Considerations on the Government of Poland*. He begins with the kind of human being that the institution aims to shape. Unlike natural man, the focus of the educational context described in *Emile*, who is "entirely for himself . . . a numerical unity, the absolute whole which is relative only to itself or its kind," civil man, the patriotic citizen of a closely knit republic, should be considered "only a fractional unity dependent on the denominator; his value is determined by his relation to the whole, which is the social body."

> Good social institutions are those that best know how to denature man, to take his absolute existence from him in order to give him a relative one and transport the *I* into the common unity, with the result that each individual believes himself no longer one but a part of the unity and no longer feels except within the whole.[37]

Poland's system of education thus needs to transform the natural "absolute existence" of the child into a "relative" one. This purpose is evident in the first paragraph of the section on education in the *Considerations*. "When first he opens his eyes," Rousseau says, pointing to the importance of the family in civic education, "an infant ought to see the [homeland] and up to the day of his death he ought never to see anything else. Every true republican has drunk in love of country, that is to say love of law and liberty, along with his mother's milk. This love is his whole existence." Rousseau then asserts, "At twenty, a Pole ought not to be a man of any other sort; he ought to be a Pole."[38]

Based as they are on the understanding that the more closely bound the members of the body politic feel to one another, the less the state will need to reach beyond its borders to compensate for internal weakness, Rousseau's proposals for civic education are thus integrally linked with his concern for the survival of small states in a context of balance of power politics. This understanding, at least as much as any nostalgia for the vigorous closely knit communities of Sparta and Rome, must be seen as underlying the specific educational recommendations in *Considerations on the Government of Poland*.

The curriculum that Rousseau proposes for Polish schools aims to solidify the young child's preoccupation with Poland, and Polish history and institutions will be the main focus of his formal studies:

> I wish that, when he learns to read, he should read about his own land; that at the age of ten he should be familiar with all its products, at twelve with all its provinces, highways, and towns; that at fifteen he should know its whole history, at sixteen all its laws, and in all Poland there should be no great action or famous man of which his heart and memory are not full, and of which he cannot give an account at a moment's notice.[39]

In his article on "Political Economy" Rousseau had recommended that, unlike domestic education, which should be undertaken by a child's father, public education should be the function of a public official, a magistrate. In his *Considerations*, Rousseau's advice is more specific: Rather than the responsibility of "foreigners and priests," Polish children "ought to have only Poles for teachers." (Emile's education, in contrast, will be entirely the responsibility of a "foreigner," Rousseau himself.) Moreover, in order to avoid the development of factionalism or "particular wills" that might jeopardize a citizen's perception of the general will, teaching should never be allowed to become a profession with its own standards and aims; instead, it should be considered as an important step or "testing place" on the ladder of a worthy citizen's career in public service. Teachers should be chosen for their moral character and civic attainments, and after having performed their service well, should be able to look forward to other employments "less arduous and more brilliant."[40]

Another important aspect of the system of public education proposed by Rousseau for Poland is that it be free of charge. "All, being equal under the constitution of the state, ought to be educated together and in the same fashion," he says firmly. But if it should not be possible to make education completely free, Rousseau proposes that scholarships be offered to those who cannot afford to pay for their schooling. Such scholarships should be given, Rousseau argues, "not as an act of charity but as a reward for the merit of the father"—thus producing the double advantage of equalizing education and encouraging the civic virtue of fathers.

As one might expect, an important role is to be given in Poland's schools to physical education. Rousseau recommends that in every school there should be a gymnasium or special place for physical exercise and that school coaches should be eligible, like other teachers, for higher positions in the state depending on the "zeal and vigilance" with which they perform their function in the schools. As Rousseau sees it, physical education has a moral as well as a physical purpose; not only does it build healthy and robust bodies but it actively distracts children from corrupting influences and bad habits. "I can never sufficiently repeat that good education ought to be negative," he says, restating a principle that he had developed fully in *Emile*; "Prevent vices from arising, and you will have done enough for virtue." Instead of giving children lectures about morality and boring them with studies "of which they understand nothing and which they hate simply because they are forced to sit still," keep them alert and actively engaged in healthful exercises that give them pleasure.[41]

Rousseau goes on to argue that Polish children (again unlike the young Emile) should not be allowed to play alone "as their fancy dictates," but "all together and in public, so that there will always be a common goal toward which they all aspire, and which will excite competition and emulation." Here one can see that in Rousseau's eyes, physical education has a political as well as a physical and moral purpose; public games and competitions accustom children at an early age "to rules, to equality, to fraternity, to competition, to living under the eyes of their fellow citizens and to desiring public approbation."[42] Certainly this is patriotic education in its most explicit form, but in evaluating its principles one must remember that they derive from the foreign policy requirements of a young and threatened state.

Rousseau's description of the competitive games to be encouraged among Polish youth makes it clear that in his desire to channel Poland's energies into forms that will bolster its autonomy, he is far from suggesting that Poland try to eliminate *amour propre* completely. For, as Terrence Cook explains in "Rousseau: Education and Politics," "a man having only the minimal desires of *amour de soi* without *amour propre* would be naturally lazy," like the presocial natural man of the *Discourse on the Origin of Inequality*.[43] *Amour propre* provides an energizing force; it arouses a fresh dimension of passions relative to others that a solitary individual does not naturally have. Since "a man who had no passions would certainly be a very bad citizen,"[44] the concern in Rousseau's *Poland* is not to quench *amour propre* but to channel its passions into patriotism. "By combining the force of [*amour propre*] with all the beauty of virtue, [patriotism] gains an energy which, without disfiguring it, makes it the most heroic of all the passions."[45]

Accordingly, the Poles will be encouraged to compete, but only against each other; and they will be taught to become highly sensitive to public opinion, but this is good when their own political institutions have allowed public opinion to be good. In contrast with Rousseau's refusal to give public opinion any educative role within the politically corrupt context of *Emile*, in a politically legitimate society public opinion is respected.[46] Rousseau's implicit trust in the ability of sound political institutions to channel *amour propre* into life-sustaining forms can be seen in his suggestion that the prizes and rewards of the winners "should not be distributed arbitrarily by the games-coaches or by the school officials, but by the acclamation and judgment of the spectators; and you can be sure that these judgments will always be just, above all if care is taken to make the games attractive to the public."[47]

Rousseau ends his specific proposals for Poland's educational system with an intriguing comment about a "Mock State" that was set up in Berne as a means to acquaint young people with the challenges of self-government. "It is a copy in miniature of everything that goes to make up the political life of the Republic," explains Rousseau admiringly, "a senate, chief magistrates, officers, bailiffs, orators, lawsuits, judgments, solemnities. . . . This institution . . . is the nursery of the statesmen who will one day direct public affairs in the same employments which at first they exercised only in play."[48]

To have helped his readers understand that the knowledge of civic responsibility could come only from the experience of it is perhaps the most important lesson of Rousseau's *Considerations on the Government of Poland*.

THE POLITICAL ECONOMY OF A NONALIGNED STATE

Rousseau begins the section of his *Considerations* titled "The Economic System" by stating that Poland's choice of an economic system depends on "the purposes she has in view in reforming her constitution."[49] Poland's economy, in other words, needs to be chosen to suit its political aims. In making such a statement Rousseau is highlighting two points often stressed by political economists of development today. First, instead of thinking of it as a natural "given," people should consider the economy, like the social contract, as a creation of deliberate human will; second, the economic system must be shaped to serve political goals rather than subvert them.[50]

Having recognized the need to make basic economic choices, Rous-

seau explains to his readers in clear and morally challenging terms
exactly what Poland's economic choices are. "If your only wish is to
become noisy, brilliant, and fearsome," he argues, "and to influence
the other peoples of Europe, their example lies before you; devote
yourselves to following it."

> Cultivate the arts and sciences, commerce and industry; have profes-
> sional soldiers, fortresses, and academies; above all have a good system
> of public finance which will make money circulate rapidly, and thereby
> multiply its effectiveness to your great profit; try to make money very
> necessary, in order to keep the people in a condition of great dependence;
> and with that end in view, encourage material luxury, and the luxury of
> the spirit, which is inseparable from it.

"In this way," Rousseau goes on to say with a sharp edge to his tone,
"you will create a scheming, ardent, avid, ambitious, servile and knav-
ish people, like all the rest," a people divided by extremes of "opulence
and misery, of licence and slavery, with nothing in-between."
He continues,

> But you will be counted as one of the great powers of Europe. You
> will be included in all diplomatic combinations; in all negotiations your
> alliance will be courted; you will be bound by treaties; and there will
> be no war in Europe into which you will not have the honor of being
> plunged.[51]

The implications of Rousseau's logic are provocative: To choose to be
"brilliant" means to lose one's political integrity; to choose the path
of what we might today call "first world" economic development is
to choose at the same time a potentially disastrous involvement in the
international war system.

But such consequences are not inevitable, since Poland—and, by in-
ference, any nation with sufficient political will—can make a different
choice. Indeed, Rousseau proceeds to present an alternative possible
future for Poland in language that implies that even though this will
not be the easiest path to take, in the long run it may be the most
satisfying one. "If, by chance," he says knowingly, "you would prefer
to create a free, wise, and peaceful nation [rather than a "noisy, brilliant, and fearsome" one], one which has no fear or need of anyone,
but is self-sufficient and happy, then you must adopt wholly different
methods";

> you must preserve and revive among your people simple customs and
> wholesome tastes, and a warlike spirit devoid of ambition; you must
> . . . devote your people to agriculture and to the most necessary arts
> and crafts; you must make money contemptible and, if possible useless,

seeking and finding more powerful and reliable motives for the accomplishment of great deeds.

"I admit," Rousseau goes on to say, "that, in following this path, you will not fill the news-sheets with the noise of your celebrations, negotiations, and exploits; . . . you will not be much talked about in Europe. But," he says,

> you will live in true prosperity, justice and liberty; no one will try to pick a quarrel with you; people will fear you without admitting it; and I guarantee that neither the Russians nor anyone else will ever again come to rule over you, or that if, to their own misfortune they do come, they will leave even more hurriedly.

Rousseau ends the passage with a stern warning: "Above all," he says, "beware of trying to combine these two objectives, for they are too incompatible; and if you try to divide your forces and march toward both, you are condemning yourselves to a double failure. Choose then," he urges, but he makes his own stand completely clear: "If you prefer the first, stop reading me. For all my remaining proposals are directed exclusively to the second."[52]

Having made clear his own conviction that Poland must disassociate itself from the international financial network and develop frugal and relatively autonomous economic forms of its own, Rousseau outlines some of the specific precepts that should guide its policy decisions. The dominant theme of this part of his advice to Poland is the harmfulness of relying on money to motivate human behavior. He had already argued in his opening paragraphs that "you must make money contemptible and, if possible, useless, seeking and finding more powerful and reliable motives for the accomplishment of great deeds"; farther on, he says, "Money at best is a supplement to men, and the supplement is never worth as much as the thing itself." Since men desire money only as a means, or as a medium, for satisfying other passions (such as greed, ambition, and vanity), it is those passions that must be addressed, not their substitute. "Learn how to foment and satisfy them directly," Rousseau advises, "and money will soon lose all its value."[53]

Because of the negative side effects of pecuniary compensation, Rousseau urges the Poles to rely whenever possible on payment "in kind," and he praises the system of paying public officials in tithes of wine and wood and of using required public service, or *corvées*, to accomplish state needs (building roads, bridges, public buildings, etc.). If the recipients of public compensation are very rich, as the magnates of Poland tend to be, Rousseau says, they should be compensated for their services with "authority, honors, and exalted positions" rather than monetary rewards. Such a system would give the implicit message that it is not enough to be "rich and nothing more"; by these means you "sap the strength of wealth and . . . create men who are not for sale." "I lay great emphasis on this point," Rousseau says, "for I am sure that your neighbors, particularly the Russians, will spare no efforts to corrupt your officials, and that the great problem of your government is to strive to make them incorruptible."[54] Today, when the ideological and political allegiance of third-world countries is being courted by both the Soviet Union and the United States, Rousseau's advice is perhaps more relevant than ever.

From his discussion of the dangers of money, Rousseau moves to a discussion of the benefits of agriculture. Underlying Rousseau's linkage of the two topics is his awareness of the debate between the Mercantilists and the Physiocrats, which aroused a good deal of controversy during the second half of the eighteenth century. Analogous in some ways perhaps to those contemporary political economists who argue that developing nations should build up their agricultural sector before devoting resources to industry, the Physiocrats argued that it was not the accumulation of bullion that made a country rich but its ability to feed its people. Although Rousseau did not by any means agree with all of the Physiocrats' theories ("the fault I find with them is that [even] they are more favorable to wealth than to prosperity"), it is probably his sympathy with many of their views that led Rousseau to stress that "pecuniary wealth is only relative," that "it is not the token but the thing it represents that ought to be multiplied," and that agriculture needs to be the backbone of the economy. "Encourage agriculture and the useful arts," Rousseau advises, "not by enriching the farmers, which would only incite them to leave their calling, but by making that calling pleasant and honorable." "The prevailing spirit of your economic system, if I had my way," he sums up later, "would be as follows: pay little attention to foreign countries, give little heed to commerce; but multiply as far as possible your domestic production and consumption of foodstuffs."[55]

Rousseau was not blind to the need for a certain degree of division of labor in the world economic context, however, and he conceded that Poland's ability to produce a surplus of wheat for export would enable the country to import those commodities such as oil and wine that it could not produce itself. But "apart from this necessary and certain produce," he advises, "you will be poor as long as you want more; and as soon as you learn how to get along without more, you will be rich."[56] As a contemporary third-world leader has put it, developing nations must aim to "raise consciousness, not stimulate appetites."[57]

Toward the end of his recommendations for Poland's economy, Rousseau finally confronts the difficult subject of taxes. In the spirit of his earlier advice against depending on money, Rousseau again argues for paying for state services with one's "person" rather than one's "purse"; but when taxes are absolutely necessary, they should be made as equitable as possible. Rousseau runs through the different methods of taxation from per capita taxes, taxes on property, and stamp taxes ("Experience shows that the stamp taxes are especially hard on the poor"), to a proportional property tax, as had been suggested by both Marshal de Vauban, an early Physiocrat, and the Abbé de Saint-Pierre. Rousseau argues that this latter is "the best and most natural tax . . . for after all, it is that which produces that ought to pay," but proposes that the tax be levied not on the land directly but on its products, and that payment be made in kind.[58]

Since one of the main reasons for levying taxes is to pay for the national defense, the section titled "The Military System" follows directly after the section on "The Economic System." Here, too, it is evident that Rousseau's main concern is to strengthen Poland's *amour de soi* from within and to give the Poles the sense that Poland should rely on itself, not on anyone else. "Only then" he emphasizes, "will she be all she is capable of becoming."[59]

DEFENSE WITHOUT THREAT

"The word 'strength' has two rather different meanings that are not always clearly distinguished," argues Dietrich Fischer, a contemporary analyst of international security issues and author of *Preventing War in the Nuclear Age*. "Strength can mean the capability to harm others and to threaten them; it can also mean the capability to resist harm intended by others and to be immune against threats." Fischer distinguishes between the strength that threatens and the strength that resists in order to argue for a shift in the military policies of the United States away from an offensive to a more strictly defensive military posture in the world today, but his general conceptual framework provides an appropriate starting point for an examination of the military system that Rousseau recommended for Poland over two hundred years ago.[60]

Fischer's distinction between the strength that resists and the strength that threatens is similar to Rousseau's distinction between *amour de soi* and *amour propre*, and it can similarly be applied both to individuals and to states. Making an analogy between personal security and national security, Fischer points out that just as individuals who are overly sensitive and quick to offend others are the most difficult people to get along with, and those who do not get hurt easily and are tolerant of others are relatively easy to get along with, so, too, states that are both vulnerable and aggressive tend most often to become involved in war, whereas those that are relatively invulnerable and nonaggressive tend to contribute the most to world peace. In *Emile*, Rousseau demonstrates how to create in the individual the capacity for resisting harm without threatening others, but in *Considerations on the Government of Poland* he proposes principles for creating a similar form of nonthreatening strength in the state.

Throughout the section on "The Military System," Rousseau stresses repeatedly that although Poland needs to develop a robust and unique military identity, it must completely renounce offensive aggression and foreign conquest. Poland must have the strength to turn away its enemies, but it would be folly for the state to try to invade them; Poland's stance vis-à-vis other states should be purely defensive. In his insistence on a defensive military posture for Poland, Rousseau is firmly separating himself from that part of the tradition of "armed civic virtue" that glorifies empire building and military expansion. "To want to make conquests and to acquire offensive power . . . is incompatible with the form of your government," Rousseau argues. "Anyone who wants to be free ought not to want to be a conqueror." Later on, he reiterates the necessary connection between freedom and nonaggression by warning that if the nation were to allow itself to become "beguiled by plans of conquest," he would "no longer answer for anything. Whoever wants to deprive others of their freedom," he says firmly, "almost always ends by losing his own."[61] Here Rousseau is obviously disassociating himself from Machiavelli's admiration for the military history of imperial Rome.[62]

In his recommendations on how Poland should defend itself, however, Rousseau does follow Machiavelli, for closely tied to his understanding that an offensive military stance is incompatible with a nation's freedom is Rousseau's long-standing contempt for professional armies and his desire to return the responsibility for national defense to citizens themselves. It was pointed out in Chapter 2 that in the *Discourse on the Sciences and Arts* Rousseau had included a sharp attack on "modern" professional military tactics, and in *Considerations on the Government of Poland* he again counsels firmly against imitating such methods: "Regular troops, the plague and depopulators of Europe, are good for two purposes only, to attack and conquer neighbors or to bind and enslave citizens. Both of these ends are equally foreign to you; renounce then, the means which lead to them." Rousseau agrees that "the state should not remain without its defenders"; but, he says, "its true defenders are its members. Each soldier should be a soldier by duty, none by profession."[63]

In the specific proposals that follow, Rousseau reveals that what he has in mind for Poland's system of defense is a civilian-based militia somewhat like that of Switzerland. In the eighteenth century, just as today, Switzerland's system of armed neutrality was based on the assumption that a certain period of military service each year was part of the responsibility of citizenship, and that being prepared to defend one's country in case of an attack should be part of a people's everyday life. Rousseau describes how in Switzerland each citizen is furnished with a uniform ("which becomes his festive dress"), a rifle, and the equipment of a foot soldier, and how each citizen–soldier is expected to enroll in the company of his district. During the summer, on Sundays and holidays the citizen–soldiers engage in training and drills, and regularly are required to spend somewhat longer periods of time in the country, where they camp out and are drilled in more complicated maneuvers. One of the principal advantages of such a system, Rousseau points out, is that it costs so little. While they are living at home and are thus not interrupted from their work, the members of the militia receive little pay; during their period of service in the country, they receive rations and are paid by the state. Rousseau also stresses that "no one is allowed to send another in his place, in order that each may receive training and that all may see service."[64]

"Why not, then," argues Rousseau, "instead of regular troops, a hundred times more burdensome than useful to any people uninterested in conquests, establish a genuine militia in Poland exactly as in Switzerland, where every inhabitant is a soldier, but only when necessary?" Rousseau acknowledges that it would be unwise to arm the Polish serfs before they are freed ("arms in servile hands will always be more dangerous than useful to the state"), but he sees in the inhabitants of the cities plenty of potential defenders for Poland. On a more fundamental level, he acknowledges also that the transition from a professional army to a citizen militia would require a change in "public opinion." A soldier must come to be looked at not "as a bandit who, in order to live, sells himself for five cents a day," but "as a citizen who is doing his duty in the service of his country." One way to transform public opinion about military service would be to make promotions in the militia just and equitable. In the choice of officers, for example, promotions should be made not at all according to one's rank in society but solely according to experience and talent.[65]

Although he refers to the Swiss system as a model, Rousseau repeatedly stresses that Poland must develop defense capabilities that are uniquely its own. Noting those qualities that distinguish Poland from other European nations, he recommends extending the concept of a civilian-based defense to the Polish equestrian order—the class of noble landowners that dominated Poland's political life throughout most of its history. Given the Polish nobility's renowned skills of horsemanship,

Rousseau says, each provincial area should build up its own cavalry corps, in which all the nobles would be enrolled, and which would meet regularly to drill and develop tactics. In his description of such drills, Rousseau allows his military imagination free rein, and in his use of the term "guerrilla warfare" one can see how close the spirit of Rousseau's recommendations to eighteenth-century Polish nobles is to the concerns of developing nations trying to establish an identity today.

> Let these brave noblemen learn how to drill in formation, to perform all sorts of movements . . . I should like them to evolve tactics of their own . . . to practice for lightness and speed, learning how to break off, disperse and regroup without difficulty or confusion; to excel in what is called guerrilla warfare, in all the manoeuvres appropriate to light troops, in the art of inundating [a terrain] like a torrent, of striking everywhere without ever being struck, of continuing to act in concert though separated, of cutting communicatons, of intercepting envoys, of charging rear-guards, of capturing vanguards, of surprising detachments, of harassing large bodies of troops marching and camping together.[66]

Again, however, it must be remembered that the purpose of such drilling is purely defensive. Given the openness of Poland's borders, "you will never be able to make it difficult for neighbors to enter your territory; but you can make it difficult for them to withdraw with impunity."[67]

IN THE conclusion to his *Considerations on the Government of Poland* Rousseau emphasizes once again that "a state of liberty deprives a people of offensive power, and that in following my plan you should renounce all hope of conquest. But," he continues,

> twenty years from now, when your work has been done, if the Russians try to overrun you, they will learn what sort of soldiers in defence of their hearths are these men of peace who do not know how to attack the hearths of others, and who have forgotten the value of money.[68]

Unfortunately, the Poles did not have twenty years in which to implement Rousseau's advice. In February 1772, at the very time that Rousseau was completing his *Considerations*, a secret Treaty of Partition was being signed by Catherine the Great of Russia, Frederick the Great of Prussia, and Maria Theresa of Austria. This first partition, which did not become public until shortly after Rousseau had finished his work, was followed by a second in 1793, and by a third in 1795, at which point Poland was swept from the map of Europe altogether and did not regain an independent national identity until after World War I.

One might recall such events and conclude that Rousseau's faith in

Poland's political spirit was a naive illusion and that his *Considerations* were a waste of time. Alternatively, one might take the view that much of Polish history demonstrates that Rousseau's *Considerations* contained understanding and foresight. For although Poland's enemies have frequently "swallowed her up," they have not been able to "digest" her; although Poland may have periodically been erased as a state, Polish patriotism has remained alive in the hearts of Polish people.[69] Had the Poles been given more time to listen to Rousseau's advice about reforming their public education, economy, and system of defense, it is possible that Poland could have experienced a different fate.

Rousseau's recommendations for Poland enable us to appreciate how closely linked Rousseau saw politics and education to be. Rejecting the notion of education as a separate concern with limited vocational aims, Rousseau conceived of education in its broad classical sense, as a lifelong shaping of character for political and social life. Is the polity a republic, or an empire? Is it legitimate, or not? Only after having answered these political questions, Rousseau implies, can one make the difficult pedagogical choices between "public" education and "private" education, between socialization and self-development, between making a "citizen" and making a "man." As we have seen, Rousseau's assessment of Poland's political needs prompted him to recommend a system of civic or patriotic education that would encourage the Polish people to unify as a nation and become a free and independent state. In *Emile*, which is the focus of the next chapter, Rousseau's educational recommendations are very different. Assuming a context similar to the decadent and aggressive monarchy that France had become during the *ancien régime*, Rousseau develops a method of natural education that aims to cultivate the pupil's humanitarianism and his individual moral conscience. Unlike the Polish patriot educated to defend his country, Emile is educated to become a man of peace.

The one element that both of Rousseau's educational models have in common, however, is the need to strengthen the harmless human instincts of *amour de soi* and to limit or at least sublimate the destructive social instincts of *amour propre*. In order to resist being corrupted by the competitiveness of imperialism and international trade within Europe as a whole, the new Poland would have had to develop a national *amour de soi*, whereas Emile, in order to resist being corrupted by the competitiveness and materialism within his own country, must develop his individual *amour de soi*. The contexts are very different, but the desire to promote peace through the nurture of nonthreatening forms of human strength is the same.

6

NATURAL EDUCATION AND GEOPOLITICAL VIRTUE

A RESPONSE TO LOCKE

When one turns to Rousseau's most monumental work, *Emile: or On Education*, one enters a world that is very different from the context of the *Considerations on the Government of Poland* but similar in many ways to the context of the *Project for Perpetual Peace*. Instead of a self-contained, vigorous republic whose participatory politics are perceived as a worthwhile means of carrying out one's public responsibility, the setting one encounters is a decadent and expansionist monarchy whose claims on the individual are perceived only as the repressive demands of arbitrary authority.[1] In such a setting civic education "no longer exists and can no longer exist, because where there is no longer a [homeland] there can no longer be citizens," Rousseau observes near the beginning of Book I.[2] Rather than evoke the tradition of civic virtue that arose out of the Greek city-states, Rousseau now evokes the tradition of Stoicism that appeared during the decline of the Roman Empire. To develop human integrity in such a context requires an education that identifies the pupil not with his compatriots but with humanity as a whole, and to preserve peace in such a context requires a defense without threat that relies not on the military system of the state but on the instincts of *amour de soi* preserved in each individual heart.

Although many scholars have pointed to the close connection between the educational program that Rousseau describes in *Considerations on the Government of Poland* and the political principles of the *Social Contract*, few have acknowledged the parallel relationship between the pedagogy of Rousseau's *Emile* and his arguments for a *Project for Perpetual Peace*. The purpose of this chapter is to show that far from focusing solely on forms of socialization that aim to bolster the integrity of the nation-state, Rousseau's educational ideals also include a fully developed understanding of the methods that might be used to create citizens of the world. Rousseau admits in his preface that the "greater or lesser facility of execution" of any educational plan "depends on countless circumstances" that vary from place to place and from one social class to another, but that his purpose is to offer normative principles, not practical applications:

> All these particular applications, not being essential to my subject, do not enter into my plan. . . . It is enough for me that whenever men are born, what I propose can be done with them; and that, having done with them what I propose, what is best both for themselves and for others will have been done.[3]

As in his *Project for Perpetual Peace*, Rousseau's aim in *Emile* is to expand his readers' visions of human possibility.

ALTHOUGH the setting chosen for *Emile* was meant by Rousseau to refer to France during the late eighteenth century, the setting also exhibits many of the characteristics associated with modern life. The social corruption of the city, the insidious pervasiveness of self-serving bureaucracies, a gross inequality between the rich and the poor, the stifling division of labor, unsettling changes in religion and the family, and, in the relations among states a continual threat of war—these recognizable aspects of modernity form the dark background against which and opposed to which the young Emile's natural education is set in luminous relief. One soon comes to realize that Rousseau's bold new pedagogical principles are as relevant to contemporary industrial societies as they were to the *ancien régime*.

Perhaps even more familiar than the setting of *Emile*, however, is the conflicted and insecure "your pupil" whom Rousseau contrasts with his own imaginary Emile at every stage of his development. Raised according to conventional pedagogical practices that are ambivalent about whether to foster sentiment or social mores in the child, "swept along in contrary routes by nature and by men," "your pupil" is a divided being, overly sensitive to prejudice but insensitive to human needs, always "appearing to relate everything to others and never relating anything except to himself alone." Most of all, "your pupil" is consumed by the passions of *amour propre*, for conflict within the individual, like factionalism within the state, causes one to seek outside oneself for the satisfaction of one's passions. In "your pupil" we see the vulnerable, narcissistic, and aggressive modern being in whom we recognize ourselves.[4]

Rousseau makes clear from the beginning of *Emile* that the divided quality of modern consciousness is a direct result of the contradictions inherent in modern education. For when one tries to combine the full development of individual sensibilities with a rigorous adherence to social norms—a dual purpose that characterizes most modern educational practices—one is attempting to follow contradictory aims. "One must choose between making a man or making a citizen," Rousseau contends, "for one cannot make both at the same time."

> He who in the civil order wants to preserve the primacy of the sentiments of nature does not know what he wants. Always in contradiction with himself, always floating between his inclinations and his duties, he will never be either man or citizen. He will be one of these men of our days: a Frenchman, an Englishman, a bourgeois. He will be nothing.[5]

In his reference to one "who in the civil order wants to preserve the primacy of the sentiments," Rousseau was referring to the educational aims of John Locke, whose *Some Thoughts Concerning Education* had appeared at the end of the seventeenth century. Locke had laid the foundations for modern progressive education by arguing for a more tolerant, humane, and enlightened approach to childrearing. But in his attempt to "preserve the primacy of the sentiments" and at the same time to follow the dictates of the "social order," Locke can be seen as the catalyst for Rousseau's desire to provide an alternative educational vision for modern man. In place of the "bourgeois" nonentity that he perceived to be the product of Locke's dual purposes, Rousseau's aim was to create a new, entirely "natural" human being, one who would be distinguished not by dividedness but by wholeness, not by bellicosity but by a love of peace, not by a competitive anxiety to follow public opinion but by a serene commitment to follow his private conscience.[6]

There was undoubtedly much in Locke's proposals for a new method of childrearing that Rousseau admired, and it is not without significance that Rousseau made an analogy between Locke's book and his own on the first page of *Emile*. Locke's recommendations for simplicity in the choice of a child's diet and clothing, his criticisms of being overly protective or spoiling children by "humouring and cockering" them, his advice that children should be permitted "the foolish and childish Actions suitable to their Years," his understanding that knowledge should begin with "the Things that fall under the Senses" rather than in "abstract Notions of Logick and Metaphysicks," and finally his frequent counsel that one needs to begin the educational process by observing the child and looking to see "what are his predominant Passions and prevailing Inclinations"—these elements of Locke's educational method Rousseau agreed with and fully incorporated into *Emile*.[7]

But a close reading of Locke's *Thoughts* also reveals a number of ambiguities and contradictions that Rousseau could not have failed to notice. The most obvious, as has been pointed out by Locke's commentators, is his contradictory advice regarding physical punishment. In one part of his book, for example, Locke states that "the usual lazy and short way [of punishment] by Chastisement and the Rod . . . is the most unfit of any to be used in Education"; but then, several pages later, he states with equal conviction that "Stubbornness and obstinate Disobedience must be mastered with Force and Blows."[8] There are other, more subtle ambiguities, some of which can be found within a single sentence. "He that is not used to submit his Will to the Reason of Others when he is Young," Locke asserts, "will scarce harken to submit to his own Reason when he is of an Age to make use of it"— a statement that Rousseau will later counter with the argument that a child cannot be expected to develop his own reasoning as an adult if he is always expected to follow the reasoning of others as a child. Given Rousseau's distrust of fear as a motivating force, he also may have found somewhat problematical Locke's assertion that "Fear and Awe ought to give you the first Power over their Minds, and Love and Friendship in riper Years to hold it," especially since Locke never makes clear how he expects the child's love to ripen out of fear.[9]

Rousseau probably became aware of what he perceived to be the developmental contradictions in Locke's *Thoughts Concerning Education* when he reflected upon his own disastrous failure as a tutor for M. de Mably's sons, a job he had undertaken in 1740 with Locke's book fresh in his mind if not firmly in his hand. The "Project for the Education of M. de Sainte-Marie" that Rousseau wrote at the time outlining his aims for his young student reflects both in tone and in content a close familiarity with Locke.[10] But what may have provided the most important seedbed for Rousseau's *Emile* was Locke's problematic assertion, at the end of a section on discipline, that the final pedagogical authority in the governance of a child ought to be what Locke refers to as "Reputation" or public approval. While reputation may not be "the true Principle and Measure of Vertue (for that is the Knowledge of a Man's Duty and the satisfaction it is to obey his Maker)," Locke admits, "yet it is that which comes nearest to it; And being the Testimony and Applause that other People's Reason . . . gives to vertuous and well-ordered Actions, it is the proper Guide and Encouragement of Children til they grow able to judge for themselves."[11]

Here Locke's and Rousseau's pedagogical principles radically diverge. To count on "reputation" as the standard by which to guide behavior might be valid in a legitimately constituted small republic like ancient Sparta or a young patriotic state like Poland, Rousseau believes; but in a large, amorphous empire where true citizenship is impossible and public opinion has been corrupted—in part by material progress and possessive individualism (forces that in many ways had been given ideological sanction by the writings of Locke himself)—to give "reputation" any weight in a young boy's education is simply to create a divided consciousness dominated by the competitive and aggressive instincts of *amour propre*.[12]

Given the fact that Emile's world does not constitute a meaningful political community, the conflicting claims of the social order will be deliberately avoided. The imaginary pupil will be educated not as a patriotic citizen, nor even as Locke's "gentleman," but only as a human being. "On leaving my hands he will," Rousseau admits, "be neither magistrate nor soldier nor priest. He will, in the first place, be a man." The education that Rousseau will offer Emile aims to prevent the development of *amour propre*—the tendencies toward both domination and servitude that arise when the self senses itself to be divided; and it aims to promote the development of *amour de soi*—the instincts of freedom and self-preservation that the self senses when it senses itself to be whole. "But what will a man raised uniquely for himself be for others?" we may ask. To this question, Rousseau slyly answers that to judge of this we must wait to see the young Emile "wholly formed."[13]

NATURE, NECESSITY, AND NEGATIVE EDUCATION

"Everything is good as it leaves the hands of the Author of things; everything degenerates in the hands of man," Rousseau ringingly proclaims in the opening paragraph of *Emile*. "He forces one soil to nourish the products of another, one tree to bear the fruit of another. He mixes and confuses the climates, the elements, the seasons." Making an implicit comparison between the mutilation of the natural environment that results from technological progress and the mutilation of human nature that results from modern education, Rousseau goes on to state that man "disfigures everything." "He wants nothing as nature made it, not even man; for him, man must be trained like a school horse; man must be fashioned in keeping with his fancy like a tree in his garden." Implicit in these opening analogies is a powerful exhortation for modern man to respect both the natural environment and the nature of the child.

The analogy between the child's nature and a tree is continued a paragraph later as Rousseau entreats mothers to shelter and cultivate the child's nature instead of pruning and distorting it. From the child's earliest life, he says, mothers should be responsible for "keeping the

The five books that make up *Emile* correspond to the five stages of early life—infancy, childhood, youth, adolescence, and marriage—and the "education of things" that predominates until adolescence is prepared for even in Book I, which covers the first stage of infancy.

To begin to comprehend fully Rousseau's complex and profound principles concerning the "education of things," one needs, first of all, to review Rousseau's understanding of what constitutes human happiness. As mentioned in Chapter 1, Rousseau perceives happiness not as a dynamic "progress of the desire from one object to another," as Hobbes had described it, but as a relative balance between desires and powers. Our unhappiness consists, Rousseau argues, not in the absence of desirable objects in any absolute sense, but in "the disproportion between our desires and our faculties." It is in "putting power and will in perfect equality" that "the soul will . . . remain peaceful and man . . . will be well ordered."[16] This equilibration of desires and faculties, power and will, provides the basis for Emile's eventual capacity to live in peace both with his natural environment and with his fellow human beings.

At each stage of the child's development the relative balance between powers and needs provides the physiological foundation for Rousseau's pedagogical principles. The most fundamental biological fact about infancy and early childhood, he observes in Book I, is the child's physical weakness. At the same time, however, the rapid development of the senses at this stage causes everything in the external world to become a desirable object for the child; wanting to taste, see, and touch everything, his reach is constantly exceeding his grasp. Children's powers being completely insufficient to their needs, they therefore often feel unhappy, and as their only sign for unhappiness is crying, "they cry a lot."[17]

What are the necessary teachings at this time? It is a crucial moment, for "from these tears that we might think so little worthy of attention is born man's relation to all that surrounds him; here is formed the first link in that long chain of which the social order is formed." Rousseau's account of how the "chains" of society originate in the way one responds to the infant's first frustrations is vivid and revealing, and the recurrence of the words "empire" and "domination" makes it clear from the start that Rousseau's aims for Emile are not strictly cognitive and intellectual but rather are ethical and political.

> A child cries at birth; the first part of his childhood is spent crying. At one time we bustle about, we caress him in order to pacify him; at another, we threaten him, we strike him in order to make him keep quiet. Either we do what pleases him, or we exact from him what pleases us.

nascent shrub away from the highway and securing it from the im
of human opinions." In contrast to the "civic" mother whose fun
it is to form a tight bond between the young citizen and the vir†
state, the function of a "natural" mother is to isolate the child
corrupted public opinion. "Cultivate and water the young plant,"
seau advises, but also "form an enclosure around your child's sou
early age."[14]

The metaphor of the tree helps to clarify what Rousseau me
a child's "nature." Like an individual tree, each child has his o
dividual form or constitution, his own dispositions and inclir
which are prior to the influences of external shaping. But childr
trees, also have certain principles of growth or stages of devel
that are characteristic of their species. Not all the particular te
that Rousseau will give Emile would be suitable for every ch
Rousseau will continually remind the reader to observe his or
children for their individual tendencies. The more general p
of Rousseau's pedagogy, however, are derived from the capac
needs that are generic to the biological commonalities of ⟨
species lives, and those principles should be able to be appli
education of all children. What will be stressed in Emile's edu
thus the qualities that signify his distinctly human nature, th⟨
that enable him to identify, without dependency or resentm
the other members of his species.

But Rousseau acknowledges that nature is not the only
human development. A child allowed to grow to adulthoc
teaching from the external world would become "an imbe⟨
tomaton." To become a fully developed human being capat
life a child also needs the education that comes from his
the education that comes from his physical surroundings.
comes to us from nature, or from men, or from things," R
serves.[15] But since nature is the basic "given" of the educatio
since it is the force that is most beyond our control, th
to make a whole human being, it is the education of na
which the education of society and the education of thing⟨
directed.

Because Emile lives in a world that has no political legit
which public opinion, one of the sources of the educatior
been corrupted, Emile's social education, unlike that of ⌡
will be delayed as long as possible—until, that is, he h⟨
stage of his biological development when it becomes nat⟨
seek out a mate and establish a family. Until then, the di
his learning will be "things," the concrete sense objects ⟨

Either we submit to his whims, or we submit him to ours. No middle ground; he must give orders or receive them. Thus his first ideas are formed of domination and servitude.

"Thus," Rousseau reiterates farther on, "from their own weakness, which is in the first place the source of the feeling of their dependence, is subsequently born the idea of empire and domination." [18] While questions of international security are never referred to directly in this part of *Emile*, it is possible that Rousseau's concern about the origins of human aggression was in part inspired by his writings on war and peace in the previous decade. Implied in Rousseau's overriding concern to create a child who will be neither a "tyrant" nor a "slave" is the recognition that a more just and peaceful world can be sought for not only in the deliberate extension of the system of international relations and in the reform of particular states but also in the way that individual children are nurtured and socialized.

In the first cries of children, then, is the initial seed for "your pupil's" tendencies to become a human being who is not able simply to live but only to command or to obey, a being whose fear and aggressiveness give rise to "our deploring human miseries and perversity." How can one avoid this destructive development of *amour propre*, this tendency toward either domination or servitude that makes the child into either a "tyrant" or a "slave"?

Rousseau summarizes his childrearing principles for Emile's infancy in four maxims, each of which he explains more fully in other parts of Book I. "Far from having superfluous strength, children do not even have enough for everything that nature asks of them," Rousseau points out in his first maxim. "One must, therefore, let them have all the strength that nature gives them—a strength they would not know how to abuse." [19] Because of their natural weakness, instead of swaddling infants, for example, and binding their limbs, which only prevents them from developing their full strength, one should provide them with padded cradles that permit them to stretch their limbs and move about. Likewise, Rousseau says, one should not spoil or pamper children with overprotectiveness—raising children "delicately" only weakens them; instead, one should "harden their bodies" against extremes of hot and cold, hard and soft, wet and dry. When a mother "makes an idol of her child," he warns, "she preserves him for a moment from a few discomforts without thinking how many mishaps and perils she is thereby accumulating for him to bear later." [20]

The same principle is extended into the second stage of childhood when Emile begins to walk and run. Unlike "your pupil," who will be raised in carpeted drawing rooms amid the sedentary comforts of the city, Emile will be raised in the countryside. "Instead of letting him stagnate in the stale air of a room, let him be taken to the middle of a field."

> There let him run and frisk about; let him fall a hundred times a day. So much the better. That way he will learn how to get up sooner. The well-being of freedom makes up for many wounds. My pupil will often have bruises. But, in compensation, he will always be gay. If your pupils have fewer bruises, they are always hindered, always enchained, always sad.[21]

The second maxim of Rousseau's principles for the earliest stages of childhood aims at the other side of the relation between powers and needs. Since there are very definite limits to the child's powers at this age, even a child who has been allowed to develop his maximum capacities will still be unable to satisfy all his natural needs himself and will require deliberate assistance. Hence the second maxim is "One must aid [children] and supplement what is lacking to them, whether in intelligence or strength, in all that is connected with physical need."[22] The child must be fed when hungry, cared for when sick, clothed and sheltered and kept away from seriously harmful objects. The satisfaction of basic needs must be prompt, consistent, and unconditional.

The third and fourth maxims may be combined, and they are the most difficult but the most important to follow. "One must," Rousseau advises, "in the help one gives, limit oneself solely to the really useful, without granting anything to whim or," and he here gives a brief definition of whim, "to desire without reason." Whim is the contrary of natural need—it is the arbitrary desire to cause others to serve oneself. One must observe children closely to see by their language and their signs which desires come from "nature" (i.e., from what they truly *need*) and which ones come from "opinion" (i.e., what they merely whimsically *want*) so that one can react appropriately to each demand. "The spirit of these rules," Rousseau goes on to say, "is to accord children more true freedom and less dominion, to let them do more by themselves and exact less from others. Thus, accustomed early to limiting their desires to their strength they will feel little the privation of what is not going to be in their power." One can see that far from advocating the kind of pedagogical permissiveness that encourages self-gratification and consumerism, Rousseau's purpose is to offer a way for human beings to learn to live with limitation—a pedagogical purpose that has ecological as well as political implications.[23]

How can one put such aims into practice? It is at this point that one can begin to understand the "natural education" or "education of things" put forth in Book II. For what encourages manipulative behavior on the part of the child, what encourages behavior that eventually develops his habits of domination, is the child's perception that the pedagogical authority is in fact manipulable, that it is based not on an inflexible natural necessity but on arbitrary human will. To counter this tendency the child must experience the resistance to his impulses as the necessity of "things" rather than as the capriciousness of "wills." "As long as children find resistence only in things and never in wills, they will become neither rebellious nor irascible and will preserve their health better." "Dependence on things, since it has no morality, is in no way detrimental to freedom and engenders no vices. Dependence on men, since it is without order, engenders all the vices, and by it master and slave are mutually corrupted."[24]

After making an analogy between the authority of necessity in the educational context of *Emile* and the authority of law in the ideal political context of the *Social Contract*, Rousseau continues, "Never present to the child's undiscriminating will anything but physical obstacles or punishments which stem from the actions themselves . . . your child ought to . . . do things not out of obedience but only out of necessity."[25] With these principles, Rousseau is very far from the mixed messages of Locke's attempt to encourage self-reliance in the child and at the same time to enforce strict submission to the father. Far from the dictates of the "civil order," the child is deliberately and consistently enabled to experience the freedom once permitted by the necessity of nature.

The education of things does not mean that the teacher can thus leave education to chance. On the contrary, he must be very much and continually in control. But his job is to control the child's circumstance, not the child himself. If the child wants to plant bean seeds in a neighboring farmer's well-cultivated garden, arrange it so that the plants the child's bean seeds replace are melon plants intended by the gardener to grow into fine melons for the child himself. If the child in a fit of temper breaks the windows of his room, let him shiver day and night from the consequences, and do not worry about whether he will catch cold, "for it is better that he have a cold than be crazy." In those rare cases when it is impossible to make "things" the pedagogical authority, the teacher must take on a thing-like resistance of his own: "Let your 'no,' once pronounced, be a wall of bronze" that the child can never bend or push over, Rousseau counsels firmly. Above all, never reason with a young child. "To reason with children was Locke's great maxim," the author of *Emile* points out in the middle of Book II. But since of all the faculties reason develops last, to reason with children at an early age teaches them only "to show off with words"—to become verbal manipulators. Emile will get his lessons "from nature and not from men."[26]

"Thus the first education ought to be purely negative," Rousseau insists. "It consists not at all in teaching virtue or truth but in securing the heart from vice and the mind from error." Rather than pour information into the child, put the child into circumstances that inform him. And closely linked to the notion of negative education is the crucial principle of letting learning happen at its own pace. "Dare I expose the greatest, the most important, the most useful rule of all education?" Rousseau asks, and the word "dare" is appropriate here, for the precept is as daring today as it was two hundred years ago: "It is not to gain time but to lose it." One should let the child exercise his body, his organs, his strength, Rousseau says, recalling the intention to develop the child's faculties and powers so that they are in a better balance with his desires and needs, "but keep his soul as idle as possible. . . . let childhood ripen in children."[27]

In the rest of Book II the reader is presented with a richly textured description of the curriculum that will "ripen" Emile, and here the principles of nature, necessity, and negative education become realized in practice. It will be a curriculum absorbed not in a closed classroom but in the open countryside, not through books but through concrete objects of the senses, not according to a schedule set by a teacher but according to the timing of Emile's own developmental clock. In his argument against imposing book learning on children at this age (foreign languages and history are to be avoided at least until adolescence), Rousseau gives an extended critique of the mixed moral messages embedded in a fable of La Fontaine. Again one can see that Rousseau is deliberately providing us with an alternative to the views of Locke, for not only had Locke recommended the reading of fables for young children but had edited a special translation of Aesop's fables to be used in schools.

But beyond his specific criticism of fables is a more general criticism of any unnecessary stimulation of the child's imagination. In direct opposition to the frenzied creation of new desires and wants in children promoted by today's culture, Rousseau counsels a firm restriction of what children should be exposed to. "The real world has its limits; the imaginary world is infinite. Unable to enlarge the one, let us restrict the other, for it is from the difference between the two alone that is born all the pain which makes us truly unhappy." Instead of "taking your pupil's mind far away," Rousseau adds later, keep him "always within himself and attentive to what touches him immediately."[28] Emile will learn to read not by being introduced to a fantasy world but by receiving letters addressed to him that he will be eager to discover the contents of; he will learn to draw not by inspiration from artistic masterpieces but by closely observing the natural forms around him.

While Emile's imagination of the "there" and "then" is limited at this age, the experience of the "here" and "now" is savored in all its fullness. In contrast to the rather somber picture one gets of the courses of instruction for young children described in Locke's book, the second half of Book II of *Emile* explodes with energy, color, texture, movement, sights, smells, and sounds. Within a context of simple country objects —trees, stones, a stream, paintbrushes, boxes, a rope, a lever, and a ladder from the barn—the reader is taken on a kaleidoscopic journey that allows him or her to peep in with delight at scenes of Emile swimming, running, playing games in the dark, jumping, climbing, touching, singing, measuring, balancing, and tasting his way through a full range of sense experiences. It is a journey that one envies, for teacher and student alike. Again it should be remembered, however, that Emile's education of the senses is not aimed at cultivating self-gratification or sophisticated "taste"; instead, its purpose is to strengthen Emile's *amour de soi* and prevent the development of dependencies that degenerate into envy, belligerency, and distrust.

As one takes leave of Emile at the end of Book II one sees a healthy and alert twelve-year-old boy who is completely free of both fear and pretension. His step is firm, his voice is clear, and if one asks him a question, he answers simply but truthfully. "His ideas are limited but distinct," Rousseau maintains. "If he knows nothing by heart, he knows much by experience." He will not understand a command, and yet "you see by the way in which he makes a request that he is aware that he is owed nothing." The young Emile is neither servile nor domineering. Most important, and at a time in which technological means so often run counter to human ends, one is struck by the significance of Rousseau's words, "his means are always appropriate to his designs."[29]

THE USE OF SCIENCE

At the beginning of Book III Rousseau makes it clear that he understands human strength in the same terms that he understands human happiness. Strength, like happiness, is a relative quality that has to do with the balance between powers and desires. "From where does man's weakness come?" Rousseau asks. "From the inequality between his strength and his desires. It is our passions that make us weak, because to satisfy them we would need more strength than nature gives us. Therefore diminish desires, and you will increase strength."[30] The nurturing of Emile's intellectual and moral strengths—strengths that will free him from the need to inflict harm on others—thus requires a careful attention to the child's own capacities at each stage of his development.

There is a period between childhood and adolescence, Rousseau explains—the stage between the ages of twelve and fifteen that one might call youth—when "the growth of strength has passed that of need, and the growing animal, still weak absolutely, becomes strong relatively." The youth's muscles and coordination are well developed, but he has yet to experience the violent and all-consuming passions that will appear at adolescence. At this stage he is thus quite self-sufficient; indeed, and it is the only time in his life that this will be true, he has strength beyond what he needs to preserve himself. It is thus a period that must not be wasted, a period when he should use his surplus energy in ways which "can be of profit to him" later on. By nature's own indications, it is thus a time "of labors, of instruction, of study." Unlike the previous stages of learning, there is now no time to lose.[31]

At this point in *Emile*, it becomes evident that the careful sequencing of Rousseau's pedagogical principles is as much an attempt to rectify the ambiguities and omissions of Locke's *Essay Concerning Human Understanding* as it is to go beyond Locke's *Some Thoughts Concerning Education*. In his *Essay* Locke had made provocative suggestions about the ways in which the mind develops the ability to form abstract intellectual concepts out of the material furnished by the data of the sense impressions, but his exposition failed to show exactly how this process takes place; nor does Locke provide any full analysis of the genesis of *moral* ideas.[32] Except for a brief statement that "that we call Good which is apt to raise or increase our Pleasure. . . . And . . . we call that Evil which is apt to produce or increase any Pain," and in Book IV a brief proof of the existence of God, the human ability to formulate and adhere to abstract moral principles is never fully explained.[33]

It is precisely the need to develop the human mind's capacity to make the transition from simple sense experience to complex moral judgments that underlies the educational principles of Books III and IV of Rousseau's *Emile*. "Let us transform our sensations into ideas but not leap all of a sudden from objects of sense to intellectual objects," Rousseau counsels near the beginning of Book III, undoubtedly with Locke's *Essay* in mind.[34] Between the stage of sense experience and the stage of formal thought there needs to be an intermediate step enabling Emile to extend his expanding powers into the world beyond the one he can see but at the same time keeping him firmly grounded in what is most important for his own self-preservation. Once again, Rousseau's concern to develop a foundation for human morality that is rooted firmly in Emile's own natural capacities has important implications for moral education today. For underlying the hope of educating future citizens of the world for what one might call "geopolitical virtue" is the need to find principles of moral development that are based on the most concrete commonalities of human life.[35]

The guiding principle for this stage of Emile's development will thus be not the law of necessity, which governed his earlier years, nor will it be Locke's hedonistic pleasure principle, for that would serve only to stimulate the passions. Instead, the guiding concept will be the law of utility. The "useful" natural sciences and social studies will form the basis of Emile's curriculum, and the question that will indicate the direction of his explorations will be, what is it useful for? "Up to now [i.e., in Books I and II] we have known no other law than that of necessity," Rousseau explains as he and Emile begin a study of geometry prompted by the need to find a square equal to a given rectangle. "Now [i.e., here in Book III] we are dealing with what is useful. We shall soon [but not until Book IV] get to what is suitable and good."[36]

Rousseau's introduction to the subject matter of Emile's curriculum provides an interesting corollary to the *Discourse on the Sciences and Arts*, for it shows that Rousseau (or at least the mature Rousseau) was not adverse to scientific progress per se but only to scientific progress pursued with no sense of caution regarding its possibly harmful consequences. In three intriguing paragraphs Rousseau "narrows down" the whole sphere of scientific knowledge to the small circle of knowledge that is suitable for Emile to study. From the "inexhaustible" number of possible truths, one must separate out the limited number that human intelligence is capable of knowing; and from that number one must separate out the false, useless, or pride-engendering truths. "The small number of those which really contribute to our well-being is alone worthy of the wise man," Rousseau says, but even from that number one must remove those requiring either speculative capacities or experiences that make them unsuitable for children. "Thus we are reduced to a very small circle relative to the existence of things." Still one must approach such knowledge with extreme caution. In this part of Book III, Rousseau's intimation of the potential dangers of scientific progress—an intimation that perhaps can be fully appreciated only by late-twentieth-century readers—pours passionately forth.

> But what an immense sphere for the scope of a child this circle still forms! Darkness of human understanding, what reckless hand dares to touch your veil? What abysses I see opened up around this young unfortunate by our vain sciences! Oh tremble, you who are going to lead him in these perilous paths and raise nature's sacred curtain before his eyes. Be sure, in the first place, of his balance and your's; . . . Fear the specious attraction of lies and the intoxicating vapors of pride. Remember, remember constantly that ignorance never did any harm, that error alone is fatal, and that one is misled not by what one does not know but by what one believes he knows.[37]

Having issued this profound warning, Rousseau proceeds to give his reader glimpses of the busy Emile as he gains a rudimentary but well-founded knowledge of the basic principles of geometry, geography, astronomy, and physics—all of which are instrumental both for the immediate goal of helping him find his way around the countryside in which he lives and for the more distant goal of showing him his place in the broader universe. As in Book II, however, the teacher's role in all this learning is not to instill facts or precepts but to create the context for discovery. "Let him know something not because you told it to him but because he has understood it himself," Rousseau advises, repeating a principle that he voices frequently in this book. "Let him not learn science but discover it."[38] A seemingly chance walk up a hill from which one can view the far horizon on one day at sunset and then on another day at sunrise provides the starting point for Emile's exploration of geography; taking a stone and feigning to place it in the air, letting it drop, and asking, "Why did this stone fall?" initiates the boy into the fundamentals of physics; going on a hike just before lunch and getting lost in the forest gives a stimulus to the study of astronomy.

Use value becomes the guiding principle not only for Emile's study of the natural sciences, which is described in the first half of the book, but also for Emile's introduction to what one might call "social studies," which is described in the second half. "It is by their palpable relation to his utility, his security, his preservation and his well-being that he ought to appraise all the bodies of nature and all the works of man," Rousseau observes.[39] The transition between the natural sciences curriculum and the social studies curriculum is bridged by Rousseau's discussion of the first book to which Emile is exposed, which is neither Aristotle nor Pliny nor Buffon but *Robinson Crusoe*, "the most felicitous treatise on natural education." The story of how a man stranded on an island, with only a few of the tools of civilization, might nevertheless manage to provide for his subsistence, his preservation, even for "a kind of well-being," can serve both as a stimulus and as a model for Emile's own thinking about what is most essential to human life. "This state [the solitary subsistence of Robinson Crusoe on his deserted island], I agree, is not that of social man," Rousseau admits. "Very likely it is not going to be that of Emile."

> But it is on the basis of this very state that he ought to appraise all the others. The surest way of raising oneself above prejudices and ordering one's judgments about the true relations of things is to put oneself in the place of an isolated man and to judge everything as this man ought to judge of it with respect to his own utility.[40]

Just as Rousseau's political purpose in the *Discourse on the Origin of Inequality* was to enable us "to separate out what is original from what is artificial in the present nature of man" so as to "judge our present state correctly,"[41] so his pedagogical purpose in *Emile* is to enable his student to "put [him]self in the place of an isolated men" so as to "[order] [his] judgments about the true relations of things." Unlike the emphasis on group activities and competitive games that characterized the educational system recommended for the youths of Poland, Emile's education at this point stresses what is significant for himself alone.

Robinson Crusoe's story encourages Emile to explore and evaluate "the natural arts"—those activities "for which a single man suffices" before moving on to the study of "the arts of industry"—agriculture, metallurgy, construction—which require "the coordination of many hands" and the division of labor. Again Emile is at a crucial juncture in his education, for although it is appropriate for him to begin to understand the functional relationships between various social occupations, it is not yet time for him to be introduced to the moral questions that might be involved in such relationships. One's greatest care ought to be to keep away from the pupil's mind "all notions of social relations which are not within his reach," Rousseau asserts. In order to keep Emile's judgment free from the warping effect of public opinion, "with all things it is important that the uses be well presented before the abuses are shown."[42]

Thus as Emile becomes aware of the workings of trade, of government, and the circulation of money, the "real material relations" between things must always be kept in view. One of Emile's most important lessons, for example, might simply be to reflect upon the full sequence of activities that goes into the production of a single meal in a rich man's house.

> We go to dine in an opulent home. We find the preparations for a feast —many people, many lackeys, many dishes, an elegant and fine table service. All this apparatus of pleasure and festivity has something intoxicating about it which goes to the head when one is not accustomed to it. I have a presentiment of the effect of all this on my young pupil. While the meal continues, while the courses follow one another, . . . I lean toward his ear and say, "Through how many hands would you estimate that all you see on this table has passed before getting here?" What a crowd of ideas I awaken in his brain with these few words! Instantly, all the vapors of the delirium are dispelled. He dreams, he reflects, he calculates, he worries. While the philosophers, cheered by the wine, . . . prate and act like children, he is all alone philosophizing for himself in his corner. . . . He gets impatient; he forgets to eat and drink; he burns to get away from the table to discuss with me at his ease. What an object for his curiosity! What a text for his instruction! With a healthy judgment that nothing has been able to corrupt, what will he think of this luxury when he finds that every region of the world has been made to contribute; that perhaps twenty million hands have worked for a long

time; that it has cost the lives of perhaps thousands of men, and all this
to present to him with pomp at noon what he is going to deposit in his
toilet at night?[43]

In Rousseau's subsequent discussion of the banquet lesson, he makes
it clear that this teaching might not be suitable for all children but
only for those whose "healthy judgment" has not yet been corrupted
by *amour propre*. A less innocent child than Emile might look at such
expensive preparations with vanity or pride. For Emile, such invidious
comparisons are unknown, and the lesson will serve only to make him
all the more clear about preferring a simple repast in a peasant's home
to the elaborate banquet at the rich man's house. At the same time, the
experience of reflecting on the complexity of economic interrelation-
ships can serve as a significant basis for Emile's later, more sophisticated
study of the "political institutions" of his times.

Having surveyed the interrelated sciences and productive activities
of men, it is now time for Emile to choose his own way to become a
part of the economic life of his community. No one can remain in the
self-sufficient state of nature once others have left that state; the division of labor is a given aspect of Emile's world, and in order to justify
his existence in it he also must contribute to it. "Outside of society
isolated man, owing nothing to anyone, has a right to live as he pleases.
But in society, where he necessarily lives at the expense of others, he
owes them the price of his keep in work." Furthermore, because "the
present order of society . . . is subject to inevitable revolutions," Rousseau prophetically warns, in which "the noble become commoners, the
rich become poor, and the monarch becomes a subject," Emile should
not be raised to assume that he will always be able to live off his in-
heritance. Though the son of an aristocrat, Emile must have a trade.[44]
But given the corruptions of the large impersonal society that Emile
was born into, it is not easy to find a trade that is free from the falsify-
ing influences of public opinion. In contrast to Locke's pupil, who was
to learn the skills of embroidering, gilding, or varnishing, Rousseau's
Emile will learn the skills of carpentry—a type of work that is both
useful and clean and that is relatively independent of the vagaries of
social whim or fashion.

At this point, Emile is ready "to stop being a child" and to enter
the adult world as a fully developed individual. "After having begun
by exercising his body and his senses, we have exercised his mind and
his judgment." Now, in order to "complete" this man, it remains only
"to make a loving and feeling being—that is to say, to perfect reason
by sentiment."[45] This final task, of making Emile's reason more perfect
and humane through the development of his sentiment, is the focus of
Books IV and V.

EMILE AS A MAN OF PEACE

Book IV of *Emile* opens with Rousseau's description of the tempestuous changes brought about by a youth's coming into adolescence, an event that, Rousseau says, is so momentous that it can be thought of as a kind of "second birth." "As the roaring of the sea precedes a tempest from afar," Rousseau begins, "this stormy revolution is proclaimed by the murmur of nascent passions." In addition to the signs of change in the adolescent's humor are noticeable changes in his looks: The fuzz on his lower jaw darkens and gains consistency, his voice begins to change, his eyes take on a new "fire," and he begins to sense that "they can say too much." "It is now," Rousseau explains, "that man is truly born to life and now that nothing human is foreign to him," for with the birth of his sexuality comes the birth also of his ties with the rest of his species. "As soon as a man has need of a companion, he is no longer an isolated being. . . . All his relations with his species, all the affections of his soul are born with this one." It is therefore time to change one's method. To study only his relations with things is no longer sufficient; now is the time for Emile to begin to study his relations with other human beings.[46]

Along with the adolescent's need to find a mate and become a responsible member of society, however, comes the inevitable danger of arousing his *amour propre*—the socially generated instinct to compare oneself with others that leads to vanity and aggressiveness. Until now Emile's natural instinct of self-preservation, his *amour de soi*, has been allowed to develop in a context that was deliberately free from the seductive stimulation of *amour propre*. Removed from the inequities of city life, ignorant of conventional morality and public opinion, never encouraged to compete with others, and prevented from being tempted to dominate them, Emile has reached adolescence with no conflicting claims on his natural integrity. Now, however, the educational milieu must be changed, and Emile will be confronted by all the divisive influences of a decadent society. How can his integrity be preserved?

The passions that draw Emile into society cannot be eliminated— that Rousseau makes clear—but they can be channeled and guided. The pedagogical challenge for the teacher of an adolescent child is to guide his learning in such a way that the natural passions of *amour de soi* are strengthened by what he learns about others at the same time as the socially stimulated new passions of *amour propre* are sublimated—at least until he has developed the reason and inner conscience to control them. As Rousseau admits toward the end of Book IV, "One must use a great deal of art to prevent social man from being totally artificial."[47]

Rousseau sums up the pedagogical challenge of nurturing *amour de soi* and sublimating *amour propre* in a passage I quote in full because it illuminates the conceptual foundations of Rousseau's educational and political psychology.

> [*Amour de soi*], which regards only ourselves, is contented when our true needs are satisfied. But *amour propre*, which makes comparisons, is never content and never could be, because this sentiment, preferring ourselves to others, also demands others to prefer us to themselves, which is impossible. This is how the gentle and affectionate passions are born of [*amour de soi*] and how the hateful and irascible passions are born of *amour propre*. Thus what makes man essentially good is to have few needs and to compare himself little to others; what makes him essentially wicked is to have many needs and to depend very much on opinion. On the basis of this principle it is easy to see how all the passions of children and men can be directed to good or bad. It is true that since they are not able always to live alone, it will be difficult for them always to be good. This same difficulty will necessarily increase with their relations; and this, above all, is why the dangers of society make art and care all the more indispensable for us to forestall in the human heart the depravity born of their new needs.[48]

In Rousseau's recognition of the need deliberately to counter the "wickedness" engendered by the dependencies of social life one finds a theme that unites Rousseau's educational theory with his political theory and his theory of international relations. In all three contexts— the educational milieu, the political milieu, and the international milieu —the condition of solitude or self-sufficient autonomy is the condition most conducive to harmlessness and goodness: A man alone is a man who is limited to preserving himself and who does not hurt others, just as a state that withdraws from the war system has the greatest chance to remain at peace. But once one wishes to associate with others— whether as an individual for the sake of propagating one's species or as a community for the sake of mutual protection or as a group of states for the sake of culture and commerce—then much "art and care" are necessary to prevent or at least forestall "the depravity born of [the] new needs" that automatically arise out of human contact and the temptation to compare and compete. As Rousseau explained in the *Social Contract*, the process of coming together as a society is a process that is "conventional," not "natural," and thus it is a process that must be undertaken deliberately and willfully. This is as true of both interpersonal and supranational forms of association as it is of national forms of association.

The pedagogy of art and care that Emile's teacher provides for him at this stage of Emile's development consists of what might be thought of as five long "courses," each of which aims to channel Emile's sexual passions in a way that will preserve his natural integrity in the face of the falseness and divisiveness of modern society. Beginning with the development of Emile's instincts of pity and peace-loving compassion for others, the "education of men" moves on to courses in spiritual reasoning, aesthetic judgment, and romantic love, finally culminating in the course on "political institutions" that includes the study of an ideal social contract and a plan for perpetual peace. In many ways Emile's entire education can thus be seen as a means of preparing him to judge soundly the political institutions of his time.

The final stages of Emile's education will also bring out fully the basic differences between the education proposed for Emile and the education proposed for the young citizens of Poland. Because of Poland's need to defend itself against expansive and aggressive monarchies, Rousseau urged the Poles to turn inward and to cultivate a narrow and focused collective will. In contrast, because Emile lives in a decadent and already too-powerful empire, Rousseau encourages him to reach out beyond the narrow interests of his family, town, and country and to feel compassion for those who live beyond his national borders. Emile's education does not deny him citizenship, but his is a citizenship that will be humanitarian rather than patriotic. Whereas the Polish youth can only be citizens of Poland, Emile will eventually be able to feel and act like a citizen of the world.

The first "course" in the profound and challenging curriculum that fills Books IV and V of *Emile* has as its purpose the nurturing of Emile's feelings of compassion for others. A prerequisite for the success of this enterprise, however, is to shelter Emile as much as possible from artificial stimulations of his sexuality; he needs to have time to develop an affection for humanity before he gets caught up in romantic love. "The first act of his nascent imagination is to teach him that he has fellows; and the species affects him before the female sex."[49]

The primary means of developing Emile's feelings for humanity is through his natural pity—a form of *amour de soi* that Rousseau had pointed to in the *Discourse on the Origin of Inequality* as being one of the aspects of human nature neglected by Hobbes. Here, in Book IV of *Emile*, Rousseau once again emphasizes this elemental form of altruism that is natural to human beings' species life. Pity, he tells us, is "the first relative sentiment which touches the human heart according to the order of nature." Rousseau's explanation of the origin of this sentiment is interesting. "It is man's weakness which makes him sociable," he says, recalling the stage in the *Discourse on the Origin of Inequality* when human beings first left their solitary autonomous existence to join with others for the sake of shelter and protection from natural calamities. "We are attached to our fellows less by the sentiment of their pleasures than by the sentiment of their pains, for we see far better in the latter the identity of our natures with theirs and the guarantees of their attachment to us." The sight of a happy person only makes us feel envious and dissatisfied with ourselves, while the sight of an unhappy person draws us toward that person and at the same time makes us feel glad that we are not suffering as he is.[50]

Being a relatively weak sentiment, however, pity needs to be deliberately cultivated if it is to offset the competing tendencies of envy. Once again, Rousseau provides pedagogical maxims for the successful guiding of this stage of Emile's development. In order to "incline a young man to humanity," instead of making him admire the brilliant circumstance of others he should be shown the "sad sides" of human life; he should also be made to understand that "the fate of these unhappy men can be his"; and perhaps most important, he should be encouraged to "do things in such a way that he puts himself in no [social] class but finds his bearings in all."[51]

But Rousseau recognizes that the effort to stimulate Emile's pity and to offer him "objects which swell the heart, which extend it to other beings, which make it find itself everywhere outside of itself"—can be overdone; by seeing too much death and suffering, Rousseau asserts, "priests and doctors become pitiless." He also recognizes that the extension of Emile's humanitarian instincts will take time: "In directing his nascent sensibility to his species, do not believe that it will at the outset embrace all men, and that the word 'mankind' will signify anything to him," Rousseau warns, in words reminiscent of his argument with Diderot over the origin of the general will.

> No, this sensibility will in the first place be limited to his fellows . . . those with whom he has relations, those whom habit has made dear or necessary to him, those whom he observes to have ways of thinking and feeling clearly in common with him, those whom he sees exposed to the pains he has suffered and sensitive to the pleasures he has tasted, those, in a word, whose nature has a more manifest identity with his own and thus make him more disposed to love himself.

Unlike those phony cosmopolitans who, as Rousseau described them in the "Geneva Manuscript," "boast of loving everyone in order to have the right to love no one," Emile will begin by loving those who are closest to him. "It will be only after having cultivated his nature in countless ways, after many reflections on his own sentiments and on those he observes in others," Rousseau explains, "that he will be able to get to the point of generalizing his individual notions under the abstract idea of humanity and to join in his particular affections those which can make him identify with his species."[52]

In Rousseau's statement that Emile can "get to the point of generalizing his individual notions under the abstract idea of humanity" only *after* having "cultivated his nature in countless ways," one can see a clear parallel with Rousseau's account of the genesis of the general will in the "Geneva Manuscript." As shown in Chapter 3, Rousseau argued, in opposition to Diderot, that human beings have no innate or "natural" sense of their identity with the whole human race; instead, the sense of a general will that goes beyond one's own private self-interest can be developed only through regular and self-conscious participation in a political community. In *Emile*, Rousseau puts forth an alternative means to the same end. In a context that does not offer the kind of meaningful political participation idealized in the *Social Contract*, an individual's awareness of the larger claims of humanity must be nurtured not so much by political participation as by the art and care of a deliberate and farsighted pedagogy.

Having been made to feel a sense of identity with others and to appreciate the commonalities that unite humankind into one species, Emile is now ready to understand the inequalities and differences between people that are imposed by society; he is now ready to understand the moral aspect of social relationships that was carefully kept out of his sight in Book III. "Let him know that man is naturally good; let him feel it; let him judge his neighbor by himself. But let him see that society depraves and perverts men; let him find in their prejudices the source of all their vices." How will Emile gain such knowledge of the human heart "without spoiling his own"? At this point in his education he is ready to learn history—not the kind of history that tries to interpret everything, and not the kind of history that focuses only on wars, but history that encourages "the study of the human heart." Emile's first history book will be Plutarch's *Lives*. Because he is still free of prejudice and *amour propre*, Emile will see in the stories of famous men that it is not conquests and external successes that makes one happy but only the balanced harmony within one's heart. He will pity the Emperor Augustus, for example, as an unfortunate man who wanted to govern the world and yet did not even know how to govern his own household.[53]

Besides being shown scenes that arouse his pity and besides being introduced to historical figures who stimulate his critical faculties, Emile's education in human compassion will include experiences of active social service. "By what bizarre turn of mind are we taught so many useless things while the art of action is counted for nothing?" Rousseau asks, implicitly criticizing the overemphasis on "speculative studies" of most educational systems. "They claim they form us for society, and they instruct us as if each of us were going to spend his life in thinking alone in his cell or treating airy questions with disinterested men."[54] In contrast, Emile has been taught "to live," for he has been taught how to accept his own limitations and how to earn his bread. But Emile must also learn how to interact with people in a way that will not corrupt him and that will further attach him to his species. The best way for him to develop his sense of connectedness with others is to engage him in activities that benefit the poor and unfortunate. "The exercise of the social virtues brings the love of humanity to the depths of one's heart," Rousseau points out, "It is by doing good that one becomes good. Let the interest of indigents always be his. Let him assist them not only with his purse but with his care. . . . Let him be their representative; he will never again in his life fulfil so noble a function."[55] But again, Rousseau warns, such acts of humanitarian concern ought not to be overdone, for Emile's first duty is "toward himself," and any beneficence that causes the benefactor to become vain or prideful is to be avoided.

Most important, at the end of this phase of his education in compassion and social consciousness what distinguishes Emile from "your pupil" is a desire for peace. "Emile dislikes both turmoil and quarrels, not only among men but even among animals." Such sentiments have been a deliberate purpose of Emile's educational experience from his earliest years. "This spirit of peace is an effect of his education which, not having fomented *amour propre* and a high opinion of himself, has diverted him from seeking his pleasure in domination and in another's unhappiness." Emile's natural sentiment of compassion for others has not been quenched by vanity or pride; he "suffers when he sees suffering."

> Emile therefore loves peace. . . . If he sees discord reigning among his comrades, he seeks to reconcile them; if he sees men afflicted, he informs himself as to the subject of their suffering; if he sees two men who hate each other, he wants to know the cause of their enmity; if he sees an oppressed man groaning under the vexations of the powerful and the rich, he finds out what maneuvers are used to cover those vexations.

"And," Rousseau concludes, hinting that Emile would give open-minded attention to proposals such as the Abbé de Saint-Pierre's *Project for Perpetual Peace*, "with the interest he takes in all men who are miserable, the means of ending their ills are never indifferent to him." Later on, Rousseau adds, "The love of mankind is nothing other than the love of justice."[56]

The next three courses in the curriculum that Rousseau designs for Emile build upon his lessons in social consciousness and gradually bring him to the point where he is ready to understand the principles of political and public right outlined at the end of Book V. In the "Profession of Faith of a Savoyard Vicar" in the middle of Book IV, Rousseau presents an example of spiritual reasoning that indirectly offers Emile a way to discover a faith in free will, a benevolent God, the immortality of the human soul, and the power of his own conscience—aspects of faith threatened by the theories of skepticism, sensationalism, and materialism that Enlightenment *philosophes* had derived from Locke.[57] In his brief essay on "taste" or aesthetic judgment at the end of Book IV, Rousseau discusses ways to help Emile develop an appreciation for simplicity and truth in speech and writing, and, in the form of a fantasy about how he would live "if I were rich," celebrates the sensuality of pastoral life, making at the end a forceful critique of "exclusive" pleasures like hunting and of "the demon of property" that "infects everything it touches."[58] Finally, in guiding Emile's courtship of Sophie, which fills most of Book V, Rousseau shows how Emile's passion for Sophie's virtues (a passion artfully nurtured by his teacher in Emile's imagination even before he met Sophie in real life) can have the effect of enabling Emile himself to become more virtuous: for the first time in his education he learns that he needs to control his impulses for the sake of another's happiness and self-esteem.

There is a wealth of political and pedagogical wisdom to be discovered in the three long "courses" of Emile's education that span the two hundred pages from the middle of Book IV to the middle of Book V; there is also, especially in the section that focuses on Sophie's education, much to be questioned and criticized. But my concern here is not the totality of Rousseau's treatise on natural education but only those aspects of it that are clearly related to Rousseau's interest in limiting war and promoting peace—interests expressed in his writings on "The State of War" and on the Abbé de Saint Pierre's *Project for Perpetual Peace* during the period directly preceding the publication of *Emile*.

One brief but important episode in the story of Emile and Sophie's courtship, however, must not be overlooked. Rousseau tells how one evening Emile and his teacher fail to arrive at Sophie's house at the appointed hour and only appear late the next morning. Sophie's anxiousness of the night before turns to anger and disdain when she sees Emile; she is haughty and cold toward him for being late. Finally the teacher explains that on their way the day before, they had come upon a peasant who had fallen from his horse and broken his leg; they had carried him home only to discover his wife in the throes of labor pains, and so, having made one long detour, Emile now had to set out in search of a doctor. At the end of the account Emile tells Sophie firmly that while she is the "arbiter of my fate" and could by her lack of love cause him to "die of pain," still she cannot make him "forget the rights of humanity." These rights, Emile continues, "are more sacred

to me than yours. I will never give them up for you." At these words
Sophie's ill humor dissolves; she gives Emile a kiss on the cheek and
at that moment agrees to be his wife.⁵⁹ The passage signifies explicitly
that Emile's love for Sophie has not weakened his social consciousness;
indeed, as husband and wife they will devote themselves to improving
the lives of the people around them.

Emile's most difficult lesson in sublimating his youthful passions
comes when the teacher, as the last lesson he will provide for Emile,
makes him leave Sophie to travel for two years around Europe studying the political institutions of the times. Until now, Emile has been
naturally good; having been sheltered from the influences that might
stimulate the corrupting instincts of *amour propre*, he has been pro-
tected from vices instead of having to submit himself to duty. But being
good is not the same thing as being virtuous. The virtuous man, as the
teacher tells Emile, is "he who knows how to conquer his affections;
for then he follows his reason and his conscience." In effect, there is
no real virtue without some form of inner struggle. "Command your
heart, Emile, and you will be virtuous," he tells his pupil before an-
nouncing to him the necessity of leaving Sophie. "You must leave in
order to return worthy of her."⁶⁰ The young man who will artfully be
given a notion of what political legitimacy and international security
might look like should he happen to find them on his travels is thus a
man who has not only had his natural goodness preserved but who has
also learned the more difficult lesson of putting his duties before his
inclinations.

With the final "course" on political institutions, one is brought full
circle back to where the Introduction to this study began. Here at the
end of Book V of *Emile*, Rousseau provides the reader both with an
outline of the main questions dealt with in the *Social Contract* and with a
list of questions that refer to his writings on war and peace. This tactic
not only provides *Emile*'s readers with a kind of internal advertisement
for Rousseau's other work but, more seriously, it indicates how close
the connections are between his educational thought and his political
thought. In their proposed overview of the ideal social contract Emile
and his teacher will first examine "whether men are born enslaved or
free, associated with one another or independent," "whether they join
together voluntarily or by force," and whether force can establish any
legitimate right over another human being. From there the explorations
will lead first to the notion of a tacit social contract needed to establish
that a people is a people and then to the idea of a general will that
provides the basis for such a society. The notion of law based on the
general will is, says Rousseau at this point, a subject that is "entirely
new" and needs investigation, as does the question of representation.

Finally, the travelers will focus on forms of government and the relationship between the size of the state and the relative power of the sovereign and the subjects—a study that will conclude that "there is not a single and absolute constitution of government, but that there ought to be as many governments differing in nature as there are states differing in size."[61]

"Once we have thus considered each species of civil society in itself," Rousseau goes on to say as he makes the transition from questions concerning domestic politics to questions concerning international politics,

> we shall compare them in order to observe their diverse relations: some large, others small; some strong, others weak; attacking, resisting, and destroying one another and in this continual action and reaction, responsible for more misery and loss of life than if men had all kept their initial freedom.

Rousseau's wording here is close to that of a passage in "The State of War," and in the following sentence it is almost identical to a passage in his "Summary" of the *Project for Perpetual Peace*:

> We shall examine whether the establishment of society accomplished too much or too little; whether individuals—who are subject to laws and to men, while societies among themselves maintain the independence of nature—remain exposed to the ills of both conditions without having their advantages; and whether it would be better to have no civil society in the world than to have many.

Such a "mixed condition," Rousseau observes, resembles one described by the Stoic philosopher Seneca in which it is permitted neither to be fully prepared for war nor secure in peace, and this leads Rousseau to ask, "Is it not this partial and imperfect association which produces tyranny and war; and are not tyranny and war the greatest plagues of humanity?"[62]

At this point Rousseau refers explicitly to his writings on war and peace of the previous decade, mentioning first the possible "remedies for these disadvantages" provided by treaties and confederations, then the Abbé de Saint-Pierre's *Project for Perpetual Peace*, and finally "the true principles of the right of war" and "why Grotius and others presented only false ones." Significantly, it is at this moment that Rousseau has Emile interrupt his teacher with a question about the plausibility of all that he is describing, and once again one is reminded of Glaucon's interruption of Socrates as he was constructing *his* ideal of justice in Plato's *Republic*: "Someone might say that we are building our edifice with wood and not with men, so exactly do we align each piece with the ruler!" observes Emile, and his teacher gives an appropriately Socratic reply. "It is true, my friend, but keep in mind that right is not bent by men's passions and that our first concern was to establish the true principles of political right."[63] At the end of his course on political institutions, Rousseau is reaffirming the precept with which the course began: "It is necessary to know what ought to be in order to judge soundly what is."[64]

As the final pages of Book V indicate, Emile's education in political institutions does not turn him into either a patriot or a revolutionary. Emile may have learned to recognize a legitimate government when he sees one, but the final scenes show him returning from his travels convinced that, for the time being, there are no existing forms of political life worth committing himself to. His sole desire at this point is to find a little farm someplace where he and Sophie can peacefully and freely work together to improve the land and be helpful to their neighbors. Having experienced an education that has made him fit to be neither a warrior nor a victim (to use Freeman Dyson's words), Emile now wants simply "to live and let live."[65]

And yet Rousseau insists at the end of the book that Emile will not be able to avoid his civic responsibilities altogether. When the young graduate impetuously declares that "I shall not be free in this land or that land . . . I shall be free everywhere on earth. . . . What difference does it make where I am? Wherever there are men, I am at the home of my brothers," the tutor gently reprimands him: "This extravagant disinterestedness does not displease me at your age," he says, but "he who does not have a [homeland] at least has a country. . . . Where is the good man who owes nothing to his country? Whatever country it is, he owes what is most precious to man—the morality of his actions and the love of virtue." Reminding Emile that the citizens of Rome often had to go "from the plow to the consulate," the tutor says firmly that "if the prince or the state calls you to the service of the [homeland], leave everything to go to fulfill the honorable function of citizen in the post assigned to you." However, he continues, with an ironic smile, "If this function is onerous to you, there is a decent and sure means to free yourself from it—to fulfill it with enough integrity so that it will not be left to you for long."[66] Thus while the "fully formed" gentle and cosmopolitan Emile is undoubtedly very different from the fiercely patriotic citizen who is the object of the civic education proposed for Poland, Emile nevertheless emerges as a "humanitarian" citizen—one who is comfortable in the world at large and generally critical of his own government, but who nevertheless fulfills civic duties and social responsibilities with compassion and commitment.

In an age dominated by the Hobbesian view that happiness is the "restless desire of power after power," Emile's final attitude of stoic pacifism may look like a romantic form of political passivity. And yet, at a time when humankind possesses forms of technology capable of destroying the planet and all of its inhabitants, an education that produces a young man who respects the necessities of nature, whose integrity prevents him from harming others, and who has learned to feel compassion for humanity rightfully merits our attention. Rousseau recognizes that the program he has outlined in *Emile* may contain "difficulties" that are "unsurmountable." But he argues,

> it is still certain that in applying oneself to overcoming them, one does overcome them up to a certain point. I show the goal that must be set; I do not say that it can be reached. But I do say that he who comes nearest to it will have succeeded best.[67]

Rousseau's lifelong effort to prove Hobbes wrong—to show that human survival does *not* naturally require human aggression—needs closer study today than at any other time in history.

CONCLUSION

THIS BOOK has had a threefold purpose. First, I have tried to show how the writings that Rousseau drafted on war and peace in the years between 1754 and 1759 influenced the evolution of his political and educational thought. With the fragments on war restored to a more coherent ordɛ·, one can now see that the experience of grappling with the issues raised by Hobbes and Grotius concerning "The State of War"—both in the sense of the condition of war and in the sense of war as a function of the state—helped Rousseau to formulate crucial assumptions about human nature, slavery, and right that a few years later would provide the pushing-off points for the central principles of the *Social Contract*. Similarly, the experience during the same period of summarizing and evaluating a *Project for Perpetual Peace* that would enable sovereign states to unite in a confederation for international security undoubtedly helped to stimulate Rousseau's final exposition, three years later, of an ideal political society that would enable individuals to unite for the sake of personal security.

In addition to shaping the evolution of his political principles, Rousseau's writings on war and peace contributed significantly to his principles of education. Underlying both the plan for civic education sketched out in *Considerations on the Government of Poland* and the program of natural education elaborated in full in *Emile* is the explicit intention to prevent the development of human aggressiveness and to promote nonthreatening forms of human strength—an intention undoubtedly grounded in Rousseau's persistent concern to find ways to limit international war and promote international peace. From this perspective it is not an overstatement to assert that Rousseau's mature political and educational thought developed *by way of* his interest in international relations.

But the aim of *Reading Rousseau in the Nuclear Age* is not only to contribute to a deeper understanding of the evolution of Rousseau's political consciousness. In the course of showing the importance of international relations in the formation of Rousseau's political and educational principles, I have also demonstrated that several of Rousseau's most insightful theoretical distinctions gain a new and broader relevance when they are seen in the context of his interest in the relations among states. Woven into all of Rousseau's political writings and into the discussion of them presented in this book are three theoretical distinctions that have long been recognized as basic to his political and educational thought, but that now can be seen as fundamental to his thinking about international relations as well. The first is the distinction between *amour de soi*, the human instinct of self-preservation, and *amour propre*, the social instinct of competition. Originally set forth in the *Discourse on the Origin of Inequality* and widely recognized as the foundation of Rousseau's understanding of human motivation and behavior, this distinction, as I have shown in Chapter 1, implicitly underlies Rousseau's understanding of the motivation and behavior of nation-states as well. The argument that human aggression arises out of relationships of dependency and envy can now be seen to be as important for an analysis of international behavior as it is for an analysis of personal or political behavior and might usefully be brought into debates on contemporary issues ranging from the role of multinational corporations to our reliance on foreign oil supplies.

Another important concept is Rousseau's distinction between fact and right. Throughout his writings, Rousseau insisted on being clear about the difference between what is and what ought to be: Just because circumstances are a certain way does not mean that they should be that way or, by implication, that they will always be that way. The distinction between fact and right thus opens the way for the possibility of political change. Again, although long acknowledged as one of Rousseau's important teachings about the internal politics of the state, this distinction—as is evident in the important transition from actual war to legitimate war at the end of the unfinished manuscript on "The State of War"—can now be seen as a crucial feature of Rousseau's writings about the state's external relations, and it too might profitably be adapted to contemporary questions. While in *fact* the power to declare war has recently become less the responsibility of the people and more the prerogative of the president, for example, is it *right* that a single person should have such power? While it is a *fact* that modern states possess weapons that obliterate the distinction between combatants and noncombatants and threaten future life on earth, do states have the *right* to possess such weapons? Often the "realist" approach to international relations ignores such questions.

Closely related to Rousseau's distinction between fact and right is the distinction between nature and convention. A conceptual dichotomy that was familiar to classical political theorists but that Rousseau interpreted in new ways in his response to Hobbes, the distinction between what happens by itself and what can happen only as a result of human agency is perhaps the most important of all Rousseau's principles to keep alive in contemporary political discourse. A general will or feeling of identity with others is not natural, Rousseau insisted, both in his dialogue with Diderot and in his treatise on natural education, but it is creatable; likewise, a secure peacekeeping structure cannot be expected to come about naturally "without the help of art" but must instead be deliberately and artfully created. All three of these basic conceptual distinctions—the distinctions between *amour de soi* and *amour propre*, between fact and right, and between nature and convention—are as potentially important to today's vocabulary of international political theory as they are to the vocabulary of domestic political theory.

But one must not read Rousseau expecting to find easy answers to today's crucial questions about war, peace, and education. The third aim of this book has been to suggest that Rousseau's purpose was not to provide answers but only to sharpen judgment. His purpose in painting the portrait of natural man in the *Discourse on the Origin of Inequality* was to enable us "to judge our present state correctly," his purpose in presenting Emile with an outline of the *Social Contract* was to enable his pupil "to know what ought to be in order to judge soundly what is," and his purpose in making the Abbé de Saint-Pierre's *Project for Perpetual Peace* available to posterity was to enable readers "to judge by [it] whether the government is right or wrong." As a political educator for the present age, Rousseau's usefulness lies less in providing answers than in clarifying choices.

Indeed, as Rousseau's writings on war and peace demonstrate, the nation-state system itself brings with it the necessity of choice. Although war is not natural to individuals—that Rousseau made clear in his response to Hobbes—war is natural to states, particularly to states caught up in the interlocking "interests" of culture and commerce. But rather than lead to a political dead-end, as Stanley Hoffmann and others have argued, Rousseau's analysis of "The State of War" leads to a crucial political intersection. After pointing to the ironic contradiction between the civil order that has been established within the modern state and the horrifying destructiveness of modern wars between states, Rousseau encourages us to ask whether our political institutions have accomplished "either too much or too little"—whether, in other words, nation-states are not at the point where it is necessary either to limit themselves to more circumscribed and autonomous forms of political association in which they self-consciously choose to remain relatively small and self-reliant, defensive, and frugal, or to progress in their political development toward a confederation for peace in which they self-consciously choose to forgo national systems of defense in favor of more effective forms of collective security.

The alternatives are not easy ones. To choose more limited forms of political life would permit a young or small nation to turn inward and educate its citizens to become unified and proud, but such a choice would also mean resisting many of the attractions of international trade and cultural exchange. Alternatively, to choose a "project for perpetual peace" would secure the benefits of the international "system," but it would also mean relinquishing the claims of patriotic citizenship and settling instead for forms of socialization that encourage the more benign behaviors of humanitarian citizenship. For to want *both* military autonomy *and* economic interdependence at the same time, Rousseau implies, is to want contradictory things.[1]

Rousseau's heart was in the former choice, and throughout his political writings he expressed a deeply felt nostalgia for the forms of heroism and virtue that devotion to a tightly knit and self-contained community can inspire in its citizens. And yet, as his powerful responses to the Abbé de Saint-Pierre's *Project for Perpetual Peace* show, Rousseau also understood the need for modern nation-states that have been seduced by the material advantages of a global economy eventually to create political institutions that can provide an effective means of preventing the hostilities engendered by economic dependencies from breaking into war.

Today the history of relations among states may be moving toward an important turning point. On the one hand, the persistence of economic nationalism, military rivalries, and religious, ethnic, and ideological factionalism seems to point to an intensification of the anarchy characteristic of international relations in the past. On the other hand, recent signs of openness in relations between the United States and the Soviet Union, a growing awareness of the dangers of nuclear war, and widespread concern about how best to protect our fragile ecosphere all suggest that we may not be far from a new movement toward interdependence and some form of world order. At this crucial juncture Rousseau's analysis of the competing claims of freedom and security, his eloquent reminders of what is gained and what is lost by entering a social contract, and his compelling portraits of both the humanitarian and the patriot provide a fruitful starting point for the political and educational choices that lie ahead.

Most important, perhaps, Rousseau's political and educational writings indicate that the divergent values of patriotism and humanitarianism are not mutually exclusive in the long run. Emile's story shows that the carefully educated humanitarian can also become a responsible member of a small community, and Rousseau's account of the origin of the general will shows that the habits of identifying with "a small republic" can gradually be developed into a sense of identification with "the large one." Although we must "choose between making a man and making a citizen, for one cannot do both at the same time," we can do both at *different* times. Nations that were insular and self-protective in the early stages of their development can eventually mature into political bodies willing to join with others to promote a more general will through international law.

In the middle of Book I of the *Social Contract* where Rousseau finally completes his discussion of what a legitimate social contract is *not* (it is not based on the use of force or on any natural inequalities) and finally embarks on his exposition of what a legitimate social contract *is* (it is a product of deliberate human will, and is based on freedom), one reads the following statement.

> I assume that men have reached that point in the state of nature where the circumstances which threaten their self-preservation are stronger than the forces each individual can use to maintain himself in that condition. Then that primitive state can no longer continue and the human race would perish if it did not change its way of life.[2]

By recognizing the importance of international relations in the shaping of the essential lessons of the *Social Contract*, one gains a new appreciation for the relevance of Rousseau's thinking for the crucial choices of contemporary life. For as Rousseau made clear in the *Discourse on the Origin of Inequality*, in his unfinished manuscript on "The State of War," in his "Summary" of the Abbé de Saint-Pierre's *Project for Perpetual Peace*, and in *Emile*, it is states, not individuals, that currently remain in the state of nature, and in the late twentieth century, even more than in Rousseau's time, it is states, rather than individuals, which "have reached that point where the circumstances that threaten their self-preservation are stronger than the forces that each [state] can use to maintain [itself] in that condition." The time has surely come to heed Rousseau's warning that the human race will perish if it does not change its way of life.

APPENDICES

A

ROUSSEAU'S UNFINISHED MANUSCRIPT ON "THE STATE OF WAR"

I open my books about rights and morals, I listen to scholars and legal experts, and inspired by their suggestive discourses, I deplore the miseries of nature, admire the peace and justice established by the civil order, bless the wisdom of public institutions, and find consolation for being a man by seeing myself as a citizen. Well instructed as to my duties and my happiness, I close the books, leave the lecture room, and look around me. There I see a miserable people groaning under an iron yoke, the whole human race crushed by a handful of oppressors, and an enraged mob overwhelmed by pain and hunger whose blood and tears the rich drink in peace. And everywhere the strong are armed against the weak with the formidable power of the law.

All of this happens peacefully and without resistance. With a tranquility like that of Odysseus's imprisoned companions waiting to be devoured by the Cyclops, we can only groan and be quiet. But I must draw a veil over these horrors. I lift my eyes and look into the distance. There I see fires and flames, deserted countrysides, pillaged villages. Monstrous men, where are you dragging these poor creatures? I hear a terrible noise, an uproar, screams! I draw near. Before me is a panorama of murder—ten thousand slaughtered men, the dead piled up in heaps, the dying trampled by horses—and everywhere the sight of death and agony. And yet all of this is the fruit of peaceful institutions. Pity and indignation rise up from the depths of my heart. Barbarous philosopher, come read us your book on a battlefield!

What human soul would not be sickened by such painful scenes? But one is no longer a man if one pleads the cause of humanity. Justice and truth must be twisted in the interest of the strongest. That is now the rule. The poor cannot provide pensions or employment, they do not grant academic honors or endow university chairs, so why should we protect them? Magnanimous princes, I speak in the name of the literary class: oppress the people in sound conscience. It is from you alone that we expect everything; the people can give us nothing.

How then will a feeble voice make itself heard above so many selfish clamors? Must I simply keep quiet? Cannot a voice from the heart break through these oppressive silences? No. Without entering into horrifying details that would be considered satirical if only because they are true, I will limit myself, as I have always done, to examining human institutions by means of their principles; to correcting, if it is possible, the false ideas given about them by self-interested authors; and, at the very least, to ensuring that injustice and violence do not shamelessly take on the names of right and equity.

WHEN I reflect upon the condition of the human race, the first thing that I notice is a manifest contradiction in its constitution. As individuals we live in a civil state and are subject to laws, but as nations each enjoys the liberty of nature.[1] The resulting continual vacillation makes our situation worse than if these distinctions were unknown. For living simultaneously in the social order and in the state of nature, we are subjected to the evils of both without gaining the security of either. The perfection of the social order consists, it is true, in the conjunction of force and law. But for this it is necessary that law direct force. According to the notion that princes must be absolutely independent, however, force alone, which appears as law to its own citizens and "raison d'état" to foreigners, deprives the latter of the power and the former of the will to resist, so that in the end the vain name of justice serves only to safeguard violence.

As for what is called the law of nations, it is clear that without any real sanction these laws are only illusions that are more tenuous even than the notion of natural law. The latter at least addresses itself to the heart of individuals, whereas decisions based on the law of nations, having no other guarantee than the utility of the one who submits to them, are respected only as long as those decisions confirm one's own self-interest. In the double condition in which we find ourselves, by doing too much or too little for whichever of the two systems we happen to prefer, we in fact have done nothing at all, and thereby have put ourselves in the worst possible position. This, it seems to me, is the true origin of public calamities.

For a moment let us put these ideas in opposition to the horrible system of Hobbes. We will find, contrary to his absurd doctrine, that far from the state of war being natural to man, war is born out of peace, or at least out of the precautions men have taken to assure themselves of peace. But before entering into this discussion, let us try to explain that which it . . .[2]

[Who could imagine without shuddering the insane system of a natural war of every man against every man? What a strange animal this man must be who believes that his own well-being depends upon the destruction of his species! And how could anyone think that this species, so monstrous and detestable, could last even two generations? But it is to extremes such as these that the desire, or rather the fury, to establish despotism and passive obedience has led one of the greatest geniuses that ever lived. Such an insidious theory was surely worthy of its underlying purpose.

The social state that governs all our natural inclinations cannot, however, eliminate them. In spite of our prejudices and in spite of ourselves, our natural inclinations speak to us from the depths of our hearts and often lead us back to the truth that we have abandoned as fantasy. If a destructive and mutual enmity were essential to our constitution, it would make itself felt even more and would burst forth, unopposed, from within every social bond. The fierce hatred of humanity would eat away at the heart of man. He would mourn at the birth of his children, rejoice at the death of his brothers, and kill every sleeping man he happened to come across.

The benevolence that enables us to share in the happiness of our fellow men, the compassion that identifies us with those who suffer and that touches us with their pain, would be unknown sentiments and contrary to nature. A sensitive and sympathetic man would be considered a monster, and we would be naturally that which we have taken great pains to become in the midst of the corruption that surrounds us.

In vain could our sophist argue that this mutual enmity might not be innate and immediate but that it is founded on an inevitable competition resulting from the right of each for all things. For the sentiment of this alleged right is no more natural to man than the war that it gives birth to.][3]

I have said before and cannot repeat too often that the error of Hobbes and the *philosophes* is to confuse natural man with the man that they have before their eyes, and to transport into one system a being which could only exist in another.[4] Man wishes for his own well-being and for all that can contribute to it—this is incontestable. But by nature the well-being of man is limited to physical necessity. For when he has a healthy soul and his body is not in pain, what does his natural constitution lack to make him happy? He who has nothing desires few things; he who commands no one has few ambitions. But surplus awakens greed: The more one accumulates, the more one desires. Those who

have much want to have all, and the mad passion for universal monarchy has only tormented the hearts of great kings. This is in the nature
of things—this is how the passions expand. A superficial philosopher
observes souls that are endlessly kneaded and allowed to ferment in the
yeast of society and believes he has observed man. But in order to know
man well, he must know how to separate out the natural growth of the
sentiments. And it is not among city dwellers that he must search to
find nature's first imprint on the human heart.

Thus, this analytic method offers only mystery and abyss where
those who are most wise understand the least. Let someone ask the *philosophes* why morals are corrupted in proportion to the enlightenment
of minds. Being unable to find the cause, they will have the audacity
to deny the fact. Let someone ask them why primitive people brought
among us share neither our passions nor our pleasures and do not worry
about the things that we desire with so much fervor. Either the *philosophes* will never explain this or they will explain it with the principles put
forth by me. They know only what they see, and they have never seen
nature. They may very well know a bourgeois from Paris or London,
but they will never know man.

But even if it were true that this unlimited and uncontrollable greed
had developed in every man to the extent that Hobbes presumes, still
it would not bring on that state of universal war of each against all
that he has described in such odious terms. For the frenzied desire
to appropriate everything for oneself is incompatible with the desire
to destroy one's fellow men. The victor in such a war would face the
world alone, and having gained everything he would enjoy nothing.
What good are riches if they cannot be exchanged? What good would
it be to possess the whole universe if one were its only survivor? Can
one man's belly devour all the earth's fruit? Who would harvest for
him all the world's crops? Who would carry the word of his empire
to the vast wastelands where he himself could never live? What would
he do with his treasures, who would consume his commodities, before
whose eyes would he display his power? I know: Instead of massacring
everyone, he would put them all in chains and then he at least would
own some slaves. And this of course would immediately change things,
for as soon as destruction itself is no longer the issue, the state of war
as such disappears. May the reader here suspend his judgment; I will
return to this point.[5]

Man is naturally peaceful and shy; at the slightest danger his first
movement is to flee. He only becomes emboldened by force of habit
and experience. Honor, self-interest, prejudice, vengeance—all the
passions that can make him brave the perils of death—are far from him
in the state of nature. It is only after having associated with one man

that he determines to kill another. He only becomes soldier after having been citizen. It is not in natural man that one finds the great propensities for war. But I need not dwell on a system that is as revolting as it is absurd, and that has been refuted a thousand times.

In the state of nature there is thus no general war of every man against every man; the human race was not created simply to destroy itself. But it still remains for us to consider those accidental and specific wars that might arise between two or several individuals.[6]

If natural law were inscribed only on human reason, it would hardly be capable of directing most of our actions. But it is also indelibly engraved in the human heart. It is from the heart that natural law speaks to man more powerfully than all the precepts of philosophers. It is from there that it cries out to him that he may not sacrifice the life of his fellow man except to save his own, and that even when he sees himself obliged to do so, he cannot but feel a sense of horror at the idea of killing in cold blood.

I can imagine that in the unmediated quarrels that sometimes arise in the state of nature an irritated man might happen to kill another, either openly or by surprise. But think what a strange position this same man would be in were he to find himself in a real war where he could not save his own life except at the expense of another's—and by virtue of an agreement established between them that one must die so that the other might live. War is a continual state, but the constant relationships that the state of war presupposes can rarely be found between man and man. Everything among individuals is in a continual flux which incessantly alters their interests and ties. The subject of a dispute thus appears and disappears in almost an instant, a quarrel begins and ends in a day, and while there may be conflicts and killings there is never, or at least very rarely, long-standing enmity or general war.

Nor does the state of war exist between individuals in the civil state. For there the life of all the citizens is within the power of the sovereign, and each one has no more right to dispose of another's life than he has to dispose of his own. As for duels, threats, rivalries, or individual challenges, except for those times when a military constitution is illegitimately and barbarously abused, what has ensued is not an actual state of war but rather a single conflict which was settled at a specific time and place—so that a second battle required a new call to arms. (One exception to this was the private wars suspended by daily truces —called the "Peace of God"—which received official sanction during the reign of Louis IX. But this example is unique in history.)

One might still ask whether kings who are in fact independent of human power could initiate private wars between themselves—independently of those of the state. But this is obviously an idle question since, as everyone knows, princes do not make a practice of sparing others for the sake of exposing themselves. Furthermore this question depends on another that is not up to me to decide—which is whether or not the prince himself is subject to the laws of the state. For if he is subject to them, his person and his life belong to the state just like every other citizen's does. But if the prince is above the laws, then he lives in the pure state of nature and need not account for his actions—either to his subjects or to anyone else.

CONCERNING CIVIL SOCIETY

We now enter into a new order of things where we see men united by an artificial accord coming together to cut one another's throats, and where all the horrors of war arise from the efforts that were taken to prevent it. But first of all it is important to formulate more exact notions than we have up until now about the essence of this body politic. Here the reader must realize that it will be less a matter of history and facts than of right and justice, and that I examine things by their nature rather than by our prejudices.

From the first formed society the formation of all the others necessarily follows. These must either become part of the first or unite to resist it; they must imitate it or be swallowed up by it.

Thus the whole face of the earth is changed. Everywhere nature has disappeared and human art has taken its place, independence and natural liberty have given way to laws and to slavery, and there no longer exists a free being. The philosopher searches for man and does not find him.[7]

But it would be vain to think that we had crushed nature completely, for nature has broken loose and can be found where least expected. The independence that was wrenched from man has sought refuge in civil societies; and these great bodies, left to their own impulses, produce shocks whose terror is proportional to their mass.

But, one may ask, if each one of these political bodies has a stable base, why must they come into conflict? Should their own constitutions not keep them in peace? Must states, like men, search outside themselves to provide for their needs? Can political bodies not be self-sufficient? Are competition and trade an inevitable source of discord? And is not the fact that in all the countries of the world inhabitants existed before commerce the invincible proof that they could subsist without it?[8]

To the above question I could answer simply with facts and then I would have no rebuttals to fear. But I have not forgotten that I am reasoning about the nature of things and not about events, which could have a thousand particular causes that have nothing to do with the basic principles. Let us examine closely the way political bodies are constituted. For although it may be true theoretically that each one could be self-sufficient, we will find that in fact their relations with each other cannot help but be more intimate than the relations among individuals are.

Natural man, after all, has no necessary ties to his fellow men; he can survive in good health without their assistance. Indeed, he needs the attentions of men less than he needs the fruit of the earth, and the earth produces more than enough to feed all of its inhabitants. Add to this that the extent of man's strength and size has been fixed by nature: No matter how he imagines himself, his faculties are limited. His life is short, his years are numbered, fortune cannot stretch his stomach, his passions multiply in vain, his pleasures have their measure, his heart too its natural confines, his capacity for enjoyment is always the same. His ideas may convince him of his grandeur, but in his life he is always small.

The state, in contrast, since it is an artificial body, has no fixed measure and is never sure of its proper size. It can always expand, and yet it always feels weak as long as there are other states that are stronger than itself. Its security, its defense, demand that it try to appear more powerful than its neighbors; and it can only grow, feed itself, and test its strength at their expense. Even if it does not actually need to seek its subsistance beyond its own borders, it is ceaselessly on the lookout for new members who might give it a more stable base. For the inequality of men has limits put in place by the hands of nature, but the inequalities of states can grow incessantly, until one alone absorbes all the others.

Its power thus being purely relative, the political body is forced ceaselessly to compare itself in order to know itself.[9] It depends on its surroundings, and must take an interest in all that happens there. For in vain might it wish simply to keep to itself without risking gain or loss; whether a state becomes small or great, weak or strong, depends on whether its neighbor expands or pulls back, adds to its forces or reduces them. Finally even political stability, insofar as it results in a more systematic foreign policy, can give an added forcefulness to a state's actions and thus make its conflicts more severe.

It seems that we have made it our task to reverse all the true ideas about things. Natural man is above all inclined to rest. To eat and to sleep are the only needs he knows, and hunger alone pulls him from his idleness. And yet we have turned him into a furious being who is always ready to torment his fellows because of passions that he knows nothing of. Conversely, we consider the passions that are aroused by all the stimulations of society not to exist. A thousand writers have dared to say that the state is without passion and that there is no "raison d'état" other than reason itself. And yet anyone can see that the essence of society consists in the activity of its members and that a state without motion would be dead. As if all the histories of the world do not show that the societies that are the best constituted are also the most active, and that both internally and externally the continued action and reaction of all their members provide proof of the vigor of the body as a whole.

The difference between human art and the work of nature is felt in its effects. Citizens may call themselves members of a state, but in fact they cannot unite themselves to it like the members of a physical body are united. It is impossible for each of them not to have an individual and separate existence that suffices for his own preservation. The nerves are less sensitive, the muscles are less strong, all the ligaments are more lax, and the slightest accident can tear everything apart.

When one considers how inferior the public force in the body politic is to the sum of private forces, how much there is, so to speak, of friction in the play of the whole machine, one will find that, all due allowance being made, the frailest man has more strength for his own preservation than the most robust state.

For the state to survive it is thus necessary that the intensity of its passions supplement the intensity of its actions, and that its will become animated to the extent that its strength becomes slack. This is the law of self-preservation that nature herself established among the species and which sustains them all in spite of their inequality. It is also, I must say in passing, the reason why smaller states have in proportion more vigor than larger ones. For public vitality does not increase with territory. The further a society extends itself, the weaker grows its will, and the great body that is overburdened with its own weight soon sinks down, falls into decline, and perishes.

AFTER having seen the earth become covered with new states, after having discovered among them a general relationship which tends toward their mutual destruction, it remains for us to see what exactly it is that constitutes their existence, their well-being, and their life, in order then to identify the kinds of hostilities by which they are able to attack and harm one another.

It is from the social pact that the body politic receives its unity and its *"moi commun."* The government and the laws determine the robustness of its constitution, the hearts of its citizens give it its life, their courage and their customs determine its durability, and the only actions that it undertakes freely and that it can be accountable for are those dictated by the general will. It is by these actions that we can judge whether the being that produced them is well or poorly constituted.

Thus as long as there exists a common will to observe the social pact and its laws, the social pact will continue to survive; and as long as this will manifests itself as external acts, the state is not destroyed. But without ceasing to exist, the state can find itself at a point of vigor or decline from which—weak, healthy, or ill, and tending either to destroy itself or to assert itself—its power can grow or alter in an infinite number of ways, almost all of which are contingent upon its wellbeing. This immense detail is not within my subject matter, but here is a summation of that which relates to it.

THE GENERAL IDEA OF WAR BETWEEN STATE AND STATE

The life principle of the body politic, and, if I may say so, the heart of the state, is the social pact, which, if harmed in any way, immediately dies, falls apart, and dissolves. But this pact is not a charter made out of parchment that can simply be torn apart into shreds. It is written into the general will, where it is not at all easy to get rid of.

Unable at first to be broken up all at once, the social pact can be attacked part by part. If the body is invulnerable, its separate members can be struck at one by one. If its life cannot be taken, at least its health can be altered. If the source of its life cannot be reached, that which maintains it—the government, laws, customs, holdings, possessions, men—can still be destroyed. When everything that preserves it is annihilated, the state will finally die.

All these means are used or can be used in a war of one power against another, and they are also often the conditions imposed by the conquerors as a way further to harm a disarmed and defeated state. For the objective of all the harm inflicted on one's enemy at war is to force him to accept those things that he will have to suffer even more from when at peace. History gives us plenty of examples of every form of these hostilities. I need not go so far as to mention pecuniary contributions of merchandise or commodities, nor of captured territory or transported inhabitants. Annual tributes in the form of human beings are even not such a rare thing. Without having to go back to King Minos and the Athenians, we know that the emperors of Mexico attacked their neighbors only for the purpose of obtaining captives to sacrifice, and in our own day the wars between the kings of Guinea and their treaties with the peoples of Europe have no object other than the trading and selling of slaves.

That the purpose and the effect of war may only be to alter the constitution of the enemy state is also not difficult to justify. The Greek republics attacked one another less in order to take away one another's liberty than to change the form of their governments, and they changed the government of those who were defeated only to hold them in a more servile dependence. The Macedonians and all the conquerors of Sparta always gave great importance to abolishing the laws of Lycurgus, and the Romans believed that there was no greater sign of their clemency toward a subjected people than to leave them their own laws. We know, moreover, that one of their maxims of politics was to foment in their enemies and to keep away from themselves the effeminate and sedentary arts that enervate and soften men. Leave to the Tarentins their angry Gods, said Fabius, when he was asked to bring to Rome the statues and paintings that embellished the town of Tarentum; and to Marcellus is rightly imputed the first decadence of Roman customs for not having followed the same policy toward Syracuse. So true is this that a clever conqueror can cause more harm to the defeated by what he leaves to them than by what he takes away, and conversely that an avid usurper often harms himself more than his enemy by the evils he causes indirectly. This moral influence has always been seen as very important by truly enlightened princes. The only punishment that Cyrus had to impose on the rebellious Lydians was a soft and effeminate life, and the manner in which the tyrant Aristodemus went about maintaining the inhabitants of Cumae in their dependence is too curious not to be mentioned.

WHAT THE STATE OF WAR IS

[Although these two words *war* and *peace* appear to be exactly correlative, the second contains a broader significance, since peace can be troubled or interrupted in many different ways without leading to war. Repose, unity, concord, and all the notions of benevolence and mutual affection seem contained in the sweet name of peace. It brings to one's soul a fullness of sentiment that makes us love simultaneously our own existence and that of others; it represents the tie among beings that unites them into a universal system. Its full meaning is to be found in the spirit of God, whom nothing can harm and who desires the preservation of all the beings that he has created.

The constitution of this universe does not permit all the sensible beings that compose it to concur at the same time in their mutual happiness. Instead, the happiness of one is the misfortune of another, and thus according to the law of nature each gives himself preference, both when he works to his own advantage and when he works to the disadvantage of others. As soon as peace is upset on the side of the one who suffers, then not only is it natural to rebuff the hurt that is directed at us, but, in cases when an intelligent being sees that this hurt comes from the ill will of someone else, it is natural to get angry and seek to counter it. From this arises discord, quarrels, sometimes conflicts, but still not war.

Finally, when things have arrived at the point where a rational being is convinced that the care for its own preservation is incompatible not only with the well-being of another but with that other's existence, then this being takes up arms and seeks to destroy the other with the same ardor with which it seeks to preserve itself, and for the same reason. The one that is attacked, sensing that the security of its existence is incompatible with the existence of the aggressor, attacks in turn with all its strength the life of the one who is after him. This manifest will to destroy each other and all the actions that it gives rise to produce between the two enemies a relation that is called war.

From the above it follows that war does not consist of one or a few unpremeditated conflicts, or even of homicide or murder as long as they are committed in a brief fit of anger. Instead, war consists in the constant, reflected, and manifest will to destroy one's enemy. For in order to judge that the existence of this enemy is incompatible with our well-being, one needs coolness and reason—both of which produce a lasting resolve; and in order for the relationship to be mutual, the enemy in turn, knowing that its life is in jeopardy, must have the intention to defend its own life at the risk of ours. All these ideas are contained in the word war.

The public effects of this will reduced into acts are called hostilities. But whether or not there are hostilities, the relation of war, once established, can only cease by means of a formal peace. Otherwise, each of the two enemies, having no proof that the other has ceased resenting its existence, cannot or should not cease defending its own life at the cost of the other's.

These differences lead to a certain distinction in terminology. When both sides continue to engage in acts of hostility, there is what is properly called the *waging of war*. On the other hand, when two self-declared enemies remain stationary and take no offensive actions against each other, the relationship has not in any way changed, but so long as there are no actual effects there is what is called only *a state of war*. Long wars that people get tired of but that they cannot end ordinarily produce this state. Sometimes, far from being lulled into inaction, the animosity needs only to wait for a favorable moment to surprise the enemy, and then often the state of war that produces this release is more dangerous than war itself.

It has been argued whether a truce, a suspension of arms, a "Peace of God" are a state of war or peace. It is clear from the preceding notions that they all constitute a modified state of war in which the two enemies tie their own hands without losing or disguising the will to harm each other. They make preparations, pile up weapons and materials for a siege, and all the nonspecified military operations continue apace. This is enough to show that intentions have not changed. It is also the same when two enemies meet in neutral territory without attacking each other.][10]

These examples are sufficient to give an idea of the diverse ways in which a state can become weakened, and of those whose use as a means to harm one's enemies seems authorized by war. In regard to treaties—which actually provide the conditions for some of the above situations—what are such forms of peace in the end but a continual war that is all the more cruel because the enemy can no longer defend itself? But I will speak of this again in another place.[11]

One must add to the above examples all of those overt signs of hostility that announce an aggressive intent—such as refusing to give a sovereign power its proper titles, ignoring its rights, rejecting its claims, depriving its subjects of the freedom to trade, arousing its enemies, or, in short, infringing upon the law of nations under any pretext whatsoever.

These diverse means of offending a body politic are not all equally practical or equally useful to the one who employs them, and those resulting both in our own advantage and in the enemy's disadvantage are naturally preferred. Land, money, men—all the spoils that can be appropriated—thus become the principal objectives of reciprocal hostilities. As vile greed imperceptibly changes people's thinking about things, war finally degenerates into brigandage, and men who were once enemies and warriors gradually turn into tyrants and thieves.

To avoid adopting these new ideas unthinkingly, let us clarify them with a definition that will be so simple that no one will be able to abuse it.

I thus define *war* between one power and another the effect of a mutual, constant, and manifest intention to destroy the enemy state, or at least to weaken it by all possible means. This intention carried into action is *war* properly so called; but as long as it does not come into effect it is only the *state of war*.[12]

I foresee an objection: Since, according to me, the state of war is natural between sovereign powers, why does the intention of which it is the result need to be made manifest? To that I answer that until now

I have been speaking of the natural state, that now I am speaking of the legitimate state, and that hereafter I will make it clear why, to make it legitimate, war requires a formal declaration.

FUNDAMENTAL DISTINCTIONS

I beg my readers not to forget that I am looking not for that which makes war advantageous to the one who wages it, but for that which makes it legitimate. To be just almost always costs something; is one for that reason excused from being so?

If there has never been, and never could be, an actual war between private individuals, whom therefore does it take place between? Who can really be called enemies? To this I answer that war takes place between public persons. And what is a public person? To this I answer that it is an artificial being that one calls sovereign, which is brought into existence by the social pact, and whose collective will carries the name of law. Applying the preceding distinctions here, we thus can say that in the effects of war it is the sovereign that inflicts the harm but the state that receives it.

If war only takes place between artificial beings, then there need be no enmity between men, and one might therefore wage war without taking a single person's life. But this requires an explanation.

If we look at things strictly from the standpoint of the social pact, land, money, men, and all that is included within the definition of the state belong to it without reservation. But since the rights of society are unable to suppress the rights of nature that they themselves are founded on, all these objects ought to be considered under a double relationship—that is, the land both as public territory and as the patrimony of private individuals, material goods as belonging in one sense to the sovereign and in another sense to the owners of property, and people both as citizens and as men.

As an artificial being, the body politic is essentially only a creature of reason. Remove public convention, and at that instant the state is destroyed without the slightest alteration in all that comprises it; and never will all the conventions of men be able to change this physical nature of things.[13]

What is it then to make war on a sovereign? It is to attack public convention and everything that results from it, for the essence of the state consists only in that. If the social pact could be broken apart in one blow, at that instant there would no longer be war; and by this one blow the state would be killed without a single man having died. Aristotle says that to authorize the cruelties that they inflicted on the helots, the Spartan Ephors, before taking them over, made a solemn declaration of war against them. This declaration was as superfluous as it was brutal. The state of war existed between them if only because some were masters and the others were slaves. There is no doubting that because the Spartans killed the helots, the helots had every right to kill the Spartans.

B

ROUSSEAU'S "SUMMARY" OF THE ABBÉ DE SAINT-PIERRE'S *PROJECT FOR PERPETUAL PEACE*

Tunc genus humanum positis sibi consulat armis,
Inque vicem gens omnis amet.
—Lucan, lib. I, 60[1]

Just as there is no greater nor more beautiful and useful project for the human spirit to reflect upon than one which aims at a perpetual and universal peace among all the peoples of Europe, so there is no author who better deserves the attention of the public than one who proposes the means for putting this project into effect. It is even difficult for a sane and virtuous person not to become enthusiastic about such a project, for in this case I am not sure whether the dreams of a truly human heart whose own zeal makes everything seem easy are not to be preferred to that cold and calculating reason which always finds in its indifference to the public good the first obstacle to everything that might benefit it.

I do not doubt that many readers are armed in advance skeptically to resist persuasion in these matters, and I pity them for so stubbornly mistaking hard-headedness as realism. But I hope that at least a few good souls will share the gratifying feelings with which I take up my pen on a subject so vital to humanity. I am about to see, at least in my mind, men coming together and loving each other; I am about to imagine a sweet and peaceful society of brothers, living in an eternal concord, all led by the same beliefs, all content with common pleasures; and, realizing in myself such a touching scene, the image of a happiness which does not exist will allow me to enjoy a few moments of one that does.

I could not withhold my sentiments from these first lines, but now let us reason realistically. Determined to put forth nothing that I cannot prove, I believe I can ask the reader in turn to deny nothing that he cannot refute. For it is not the true polemicists whom I fear so much as those who, while refusing to accept any proofs, yet have no objections to bring to them.

It is not necessary to have thought long about the means of perfecting any government to perceive the difficulties and obstacles that arise less from its constitution than from its foreign policy—to the extent that we are forced to give over to our defense most of the attention that should be devoted to enforcing the law and to think more about being in a state of readiness to resist others than about perfecting the government itself. Indeed, if our social order were, as it is claimed to be, the work of reason rather than of the passions, would we have taken so long to see that as far as our well-being is concerned we have accomplished either too much or too little; that each one of us being both in the civil state with his fellow citizens and in the state of nature with the whole rest of the world, we have prevented private wars only so as to set off public wars, which are a thousand times worse; and that by uniting with a few men we have really become the enemies of mankind?

If there is any means of removing these dangerous contradictions it can only be by a form of confederative government, which, by uniting nations with ties similar to those which unite individuals, submits each of them equally to the authority of laws. This form of government, moreover, appears preferable to any other in that it combines at the same time the advantages of both large and small states. it is externally secure because of its power, internally sound because of its laws, and it is the only form which is able to include subjects, leaders, and foreigners on an equal basis.

Although this form of government seems new in certain respects and has only been well understood in modern times, the ancients were not ignorant of the concept. The Greeks had their Amphictyons, the Etruscans their Iucumonies, the Romans their *feriae*, the Gauls their *cités*, and Greece's last moments were made even more illustrious by the Achaean League.[2] But none of these confederations approach the wisdom of the union of German states, or the Helvetian League, or the Estates-General.[3] If these political bodies are still small in number and far from realizing their full potential, it is because what is best does not always work the way we think it should, and because in politics as in morals the reach of our knowledge rarely proves anything except the extent of our wrongs.

Besides these public confederations, others less apparent and yet no less real may form tacitly through common interests, ideological ties, similar customs, or other circumstances that permit mutual relations to survive among divided peoples. It is thus that all the powers of Europe constitute among themselves a sort of system in which they are united by a common religion, by a common sense of the customary laws governing the relations among states [*droit des gens*], by manners, literature, and commerce, and by a sort of equilibrium which is the necessary effect of all that, and which, without anyone consciously maintaining it, would nevertheless not be as easy to disturb as many people might think.

This society of European peoples has not always existed, but the particular causes that gave birth to it serve to maintain it still. Indeed, before the conquests of the Romans all the peoples of this part of the world, barbarous and unknown to one another, had nothing in common except their quality as human beings—a quality which, greatly suppressed at that time by slavery, hardly differentiated them spiritually from beasts. The Greeks, with their rationalism and vanity, thus came to distinguish two kinds of humanity—one (their own), which was made to command, and the other (which comprised the rest of the world), simply to serve. The result of this principle was that to the Greeks a Gaul or an Iberian meant no more than a Kaffir or an American, nor did the barbarians have any more affinity among themselves than the Greeks had for any of them.

But when this naturally sovereign people had been subjected to the Romans who had been its slaves, and when one whole part of the known world had suffered under the same yoke, a political and civil union gradually developed among all the members of the common Empire. This union was held together by the either quite wise or quite foolish practice of bestowing on the conquered peoples all the rights of the conquerors, and above all by the famous decree of Claudius, which incorporated all the subjects of Rome into the ranks of her citizens.

The political network that thus united all the members into one body was reinforced by civil institutions and laws that determined in an equitable, clear, and precise manner (at least as much as was possible in such a vast empire) the duties and reciprocal rights of the prince and of his subjects and of the citizens among themselves. The Theodosian Code and later the Codex of Justinian constituted an additional network of justice and reason, which was substituted at an opportune moment for that of the sovereign, who was then visibly becoming quite weak. This substitution greatly slowed down the decline of the Empire and preserved for it a sort of authority even over the barbarians who eventually became the cause of its ruin.

A third tie, stronger than the preceding ones, was that of religion, and no one can deny that it is, above all, to Christianity that Europe even today owes the kind of society that has been perpetuated among its members—to the extent that one who has not adopted the sentiment of the others on this point remains a stranger among them. Christianity, so maligned at its birth, served finally as a refuge for its detractors. After having persecuted Christianity so cruelly and so vainly, the Roman Empire found in it the resources that it could no longer find among its own forces. The Empire came to value conversion more than victory, it sent bishops to repair the mistakes of generals, and it triumphed with priests when its soldiers were defeated. It is thus that the Franks, the Goths, the Bourguignons, the Lombards, the Avares, and thousands of others finally recognized the authority of the Empire after having subjugated it, and in appearance at least, received with the law of the Gospel the law of the prince who had had it preached to them.

So great was the respect still held for this great expiring body that until the last moment its destroyers honored themselves with its titles. We find the same conquerors who had brought down the Empire becoming its officials, the greatest kings accepting—soliciting even—patrician honors or the prefecture or the consulat, and, like a lion who flatters the man whom he might devour, we find these fierce conquerors paying homage to an imperial throne that they themselves had the power to overthrow.

That is how the priesthood and the Empire formed the social bond among diverse people who, without having any real community of interests, of rights, or of dependence, did have one of common values and opinions, and whose influence still remains even when its principle has been destroyed. The ancient pretense of the Roman Empire has continued to form a sort of liaison among the members that composed it; and once Rome had become dominant in a new way after the fall of the Empire, there remained from this double tie[4] a more tightly knit society among the nations of Europe where the center of these two powers was located than in other parts of the world where different peoples, too spread out to have intercourse with each other, have never had any common meeting ground.

Add to this the particular situation of Europe, which is more evenly peopled, more consistently fertile, better united in all its parts than other continents; the continual blending of interests, which ties of blood and the business of commerce, of the arts, and of the colonies have stimulated among sovereigns; the multitude of rivers and the variety of their currents, which make easy all kinds of communication; the restless temperament of the inhabitants, which leads them to travel ceaselessly and to visit each other frequently; the invention of printing and the general love of literature, which have brought people together into a community of science and of knowledge; finally, the number and small size of the states, which, joined with the need for luxury and the diversity of the climates, makes each one necessary to the others. All these factors together make Europe not just an idealized collection of peoples who have only a name in common, like Asia or Africa, but a real society with its own religion, manners, customs, and even laws, from which no single nation composing it could withdraw without immediately causing problems for the others.

When we see, on the other hand, the endless conflicts, violence, usurpations, revolts, wars, and murders that daily lay waste to this respectable abode of the wise, this brilliant haven for the sciences and the arts; when we compare our elegant speeches with our horrifying procedures, the humanity of our maxims with the cruelty of our actions, the gentleness of our religion with the brutality of our prejudices, the wisdom of our politics in theory with its harshness in practice, our benevolent leaders with our miserable people, our moderate governments with our cruel wars—then we hardly know how to reconcile such strange contradictions, and the so-called fraternity of the peoples of Europe seems nothing more than a name of derision to express with irony their mutual hate.

In all this, however, things are only following their natural course. Any society without leaders or without laws, its union formed or maintained by chance, must necessarily degenerate into quarrels or dissention at the first change in circumstance. The ancient union of the peoples of Europe has complicated their interests and their rights in a thousand ways; they overlap at so many points that the slightest movement of some cannot help but trouble the others; their divisions are all the more deadly as their ties are more intimate; and their frequent quarrels have almost the same cruelty as civil wars.

Let us agree then that the relative state of the powers of Europe is properly speaking a state of war, and that all the partial treaties among certain of these powers are but temporary truces rather than true states of peace—either because such treaties commonly have no other guarantee than the contracting parties themselves or because the rights of each of them are never determined in any fundamental way—and thus that these half-stifled rights (or the claims substituted for them between powers that recognize no superior) will infallibly become the source of new wars as soon as different circumstances have given new strengths to the claimants.

International public law, moreover, having never been established or authorized in concert, having no general principles, and varying incessantly according to time and place, is full of contradictory rules that can only be tested by the right of the strongest. With reason having no definite guide and in questionable matters always leaning toward personal self-interest, war thus becomes inevitable even when each side would like to be just. With all good intentions, all that can be done is to settle these kinds of problems by means of arms, or to assuage them by temporary treaties. Soon, however, to the occasions that rekindle the same quarrels are added others that modify them. Then everything gets more confused, everything gets more complicated, no one sees clearly, usurpation passes for right and weakness for injustice, and in the midst of this continual disorder each party gradually becomes so unsettled that if it were possible to return to basic original rights there would be few sovereigns in Europe who would not be obliged to give up everything they now possess.

Another seed of war, more hidden and no less real, is that things do not change form in changing their nature. States that are hereditary in effect may remain elective in appearance, parliaments or representative bodies can be found in monarchies and hereditary chiefs in republics, a dependent power may still keep up an appearance of liberty, the various peoples subjected under a same power may not be governed by the same laws, and the order of succession may be different in the different states of the same sovereign. Finally, each government has a tendency to change without its being possible to hinder this progress. These are the general and particular causes that unite us in order to destroy us, and that make us write such beautiful social doctrines with hands forever tainted with human blood.

But once the causes of an evil are known, they are sufficient to indicate a remedy, if one exists. Everyone can see that society is formed by common interests; that discord arises out of opposing ones; that since a thousand fortuitous events can change and modify these interests, then once there is a society it is necessary to have a coercive force to organize and coordinate the movements of its members so that the common interests and reciprocal ties are given the solidity they would not be able to have by themselves.

It would be a great error, however, to hope that the violent state of things could ever change simply by the force of circumstances and without the help of art. The European system has precisely the degree of solidity that can maintain it in a perpetual agitation without overthrowing it completely; and if our troubles cannot increase, still less can they end, for any great revolution is henceforth impossible.[5]

In order to give some necessary evidence to the above statements, let us begin by taking a general glance at the present state of Europe. The location of the mountains, the seas, and the rivers, which serve as borders to the nations that inhabit Europe, seems to have determined their number and size; and one could say that the political order of this part of the world is, in certain respects, the work of nature.

Therefore let us not think that such a highly praised equilibrium was established by anyone or that anyone has purposely done anything to preserve it. It is found to exist, and those who do not feel in themselves enough strength to break it apart hide their particular views under the pretext of sustaining it. But whether one thinks about it or not, this equilibrium subsists, and needs nothing but itself to survive, without interference from anyone; and when it disintegrates for a moment on one side, it soon reestablishes itself on the other—to the extent that if the princes whom we accuse of aspiring to universal monarchy really did aspire to it, they would thereby demonstrate more ambition than talent. For how could one envisage such a plan for one moment without immediately perceiving its folly? How can anyone avoid seeing that there is no power in Europe superior enough ever to become its master? Conquerors who have succeeded in overthrowing states have always appeared with unexpected military forces or with strangely armed foreign troups before peoples who were either disarmed or divided or completely lacking in discipline. But where could a European prince, aiming to overthrow all the others, find such an unprecedented force, since the most powerful state is still such a small part of the whole and since the others would be on their guard against such an attack? Could he have more soldiers than all of them? He could not—or would all the sooner be ruined, or his soldiers would be less effective by virtue of their greater number. Could he have troops that were better trained? He would have proportionately fewer of them. Besides, discipline is everywhere pretty much the same, or quickly becomes so. Would he have more money? The sources of funds are common to all, and in any case, money alone has never been the cause of great victories. Could he make a sudden invasion? Famine or fortresses would slow his pace. Would he gain power step by step? He would then give his enemies the means to unite to resist him; his time, his money, and his men would soon disappear. Would he divide the other powers in order to conquer them one by one? The European ethos would make this policy useless, and even the most narrow-minded prince would not give in to this ploy. In sum, because no single one of them could gain exclusive command over resources, the resistance would, in the long run, equal the effort, and time would soon repair the sudden accidents of fortune, if not for each prince in particular, at least for the general constitution.

Shall we now whimsically suppose that two or three powers could agree to subject all the rest? These three powers, whichever they were, could not together make up half of Europe. Moreover, the other half would certainly unite against them, and the aggressors would have to overcome something stronger than themselves. I will add that the views of each one would be too opposed to those of the others and that there would reign too great a jealousy among them for them to be able to form such a plan. I also will add that if they were able to form the plan, to execute it, and to have any kind of success, this success in itself would seed discord among them: It would not be possible for the spoils to be so fairly divided that each one would be equally satisfied with his own share; and the least happy would soon oppose the progress of the others, who, for a similar reason, would quickly become divided among themselves. Indeed, I doubt whether, since the world has existed, there have ever been three or even two great powers well enough united to subjugate others without fighting among themselves over the responsibilities or the profits of war, and without soon providing, by their misunderstandings, additional resources for the weaker powers. Thus, however one looks at it, it is not likely that any prince or league could henceforth change in any considerable or permanent way the present status of things among us.

This is not to say that the Alps, the Rhine, the sea, the Pyrenees, are insurmountable obstacles to ambition, but that these obstacles are fortified by others that reinforce them or that restore states back to the same limits when temporary attempts have been made to transgress them. What provides the real basis of the European system is certainly in part the interplay of negotiations, which almost always ends up in a mutual balance. But the system has another, even more solid support. This is the body of Germanic states placed in the center of Europe, which demands respect from all the others and serves perhaps much more for the maintenance of its neighbors than for that of its own members. A body that is formidable to outsiders on account of its size and its population, it is also useful to everyone else on account of its constitution, which by denying the means and the will to conquer creates an obstruction for conquerors. Despite the defects of this constitution, it is certain that as long as it lasts the equilibrium of Europe will never be broken, that no prince will have to fear being dethroned by another, and that the Treaty of Westphalia will perhaps forever be the basis of the political system among us.[6] Thus the public law that the Germans study with so much care is yet more important than they think and is not only the Germanic public law but in certain respects the public law of all of Europe.

But if the present system is unshakable, it is by the same token all the more violent, for there is among the European powers an action and reaction which, while not dislodging them completely, hold them in a continual agitation. Such efforts are always futile and always recurring, like the currents of the sea that ceaselessly agitate the surface without ever changing its level, and the people are incessantly devastated, without any visible rewards for the sovereigns.

It would be easy for me to deduce the same truth from the individual interests of all the courts of Europe, for I could easily show that these interests coincide in a way that could hold all their forces in mutual respect, except that the ideas of commerce and money have produced a kind of political fanaticism that makes the apparent interests of princes change every day. Since everything now depends on the rather bizarre economic theories that happen to pass through the heads of ministers, it has become impossible to form any firm convictions about princes' true interests. Nevertheless, commerce does tend on a daily basis to move toward an equilibrium: By depriving certain powers of the exclusive advantage that they might gain from it, commerce deprives them at the same time of one of the great means that they have to make others obey them.[7]

If I have insisted on the equal distribution of power that results in Europe from its present situation, it was to point to a consequence that is important for the establishment of any more general association. For, in order to form a solid and durable confederation, it would be necessary to put all the members in such a mutual dependence not only that no one singly would be in a condition to resist all the others, but also that particular associations that might be harmful to the whole would meet in it obstacles sufficient to prevent their execution. Without such mutual dependence the confederation would be useless, and each one while appearing to be subjected, would really remain independent. Now, if these obstacles are such as I have described them above, when at present all the powers are in complete liberty to form leagues and offensive treaties with each other, just imagine what they might be if there were a great armed league, always ready to intervene against those who would like to start to destroy it or resist it. This suffices to show that such an association would not consist simply of futile deliberations that each participant could ignore at will; instead, it would give rise to an effective power capable of forcing ambitious men to keep within the limits of the general treaty.

Three incontestable truths result from this exposition. First, that except for Turkey there reigns among all the peoples of Europe a social bond that is imperfect but tighter than the general and loose ties of humanity; second, that the imperfection of this society makes the condition of those who compose it worse than it would be were there no social structures at all; third, that the original bonds that make this society harmful simultaneously make it easy to perfect: All of its members could draw their happiness from that which at present causes their misery and could change into an eternal peace the state of war that now reigns among them.

Now let us see how this great work, begun by chance, could be achieved by reason, and how, by taking on the force and the solidity of a true body politic, the free and voluntary society that unites all the European states could change into a real Confederation. By giving to this association the perfection it now lacks, it is clear that such an institution would destroy its present abuses, extend its advantages, and force all its members to cooperate for the common good. But for that it is necessary that this Confederation be so general that no considerable power could refuse it; that it have a judiciary tribunal to establish laws and regulations that would be binding on its members; that it have a compulsory and coercive force to constrain each state to submit to the common deliberations, whether by taking action or abstaining from action; finally, that it be firm and durable, to prevent members from seceding from it at will the moment they believe their particular interests to be contrary to the general interest. These are the sure signs that will show whether or not the institution is wise, useful, and sound. Now we must extend this supposition to an analysis of what effects might result from it, what means are proper for establishing it, and what reasonable hopes one could have for putting it into effect.

From time to time there occurs among us various general assemblies called Congresses to which envoys are solemnly sent from all parts of Europe only to return just as they went, where they gather together but have nothing to say, where all public issues are dealt with in private ways, where they deliberate about whether the table should be round or square, whether the room will have more or fewer exits, whether such and such a dignitary will have his back or his front facing the window, whether another will have to travel two inches more or less to make the trip, and about a thousand other questions of equal importance that have been uselessly stirred up for the past three centuries and that are assuredly worthy of preoccupying our own statesmen today.

It could happen, however, that the members of one of these assemblies might at some point be gifted with common sense, nor is it impossible that they might sincerely wish for the well-being of the public; nor, for reasons which will be given below, is it inconceivable that after having smoothed out many of the difficulties, the delegates to one of these Congresses could receive orders from their respective sovereigns to sign the general Confederation, which I assume to be summarily contained in the following five Articles.

By the first Article the contracting sovereigns would establish among themselves a perpetual and irrevocable alliance and would name delegates to hold, in a designated place, an assembly or a permanent congress, in which all the differences between the contracting parties would be regulated and settled by means of arbitration or judgment.

The second Article would specify the number of sovereigns whose voices the delegates would represent in the assembly, those who would be invited to comply with the treaty, the order, the time, and the manner in which the presidency would pass from one to another by equal intervals, and finally the relative quota of contributions and the manner of levying them to provide for common expenses.

The third Article of the Confederation would guarantee to each of its members the possession and the government of all the states that it at present possesses; likewise its elective or hereditary succession according to how it is established by the fundamental laws of each country; and, in order to suppress all at once the source of contentions that incessantly arise, it would be agreed to take the current possession and the most recent treaties as the basis for all mutual rights of the contracting powers, renouncing forever and reciprocally any prior pretensions. Any future contentious successions and other devolving rights would all be regulated by the arbitration of the assembly, without its being permitted to exact reparation by violent means, or to take up arms against each other under any pretext whatsoever.

The fourth Article would specify the cases in which any ally who infringes on the treaty would be put under a ban by the rest of Europe and proscribed as a public enemy, that is to say, if it refused to execute the judgments of the great alliance—whether by making preparations for war, negotiating treaties contrary to the confederation, or taking up arms either to resist it or to attack any one of the allies.

It would also be agreed by the same Article that the Confederation would be armed and would act offensively and at common expense against any banned state until the latter had put down its arms, executed the judgments and the rules of the assembly, repaired its wrongs, paid back its costs, and made reparation for the preparations for a war that was contrary to the treaty.

Finally, the fifth Article would give the delegates of the European body the power to form in the assembly—with a plurality of votes needed for adoption and a three-quarters majority needed for ratification five years after, according to instructions from their sovereigns— rules that they might judge important to procure all possible advantages for the European Republic and for each of its members. But no part of these five fundamental Articles could be changed without the unanimous consent of the confederees.

These five Articles, thus abridged and couched in general rules, are,

I admit, subject to a thousand minor difficulties, some of which would require long clarification. But minor difficulties can be removed if need be, and it is not they that are the main issue in an enterprise of the importance of this one. When the question of the routine duties of the assembly's police force comes up, there will be a thousand obstacles but ten thousand means of overcoming them. Right now it is a question whether, according to the nature of things, the enterprise is possible or not. We would get lost in a volume of trivia if it were necessary to foresee and answer everything. In holding to incontestable principles we cannot hope to satisfy everyone or to resolve every objection or say how everything will turn out; it is sufficient to show that it can be done.

What then must we look at in order to judge this system well? Two questions only, for I have no wish to insult my reader by having to prove to him that in general the state of peace is preferable to the state of war.

The first question is whether the proposed Confederation would be sure to attain its purpose and would be sufficient to give Europe a solid and perpetual peace.

The second is whether it is in the interest of the sovereigns to establish this confederation and to purchase a continual peace at this price.

When both the general and the particular usefulness of the plan has been demonstrated, it will be hard to see what rational motive could prevent an institution that depends only on the will of the interested parties from going into effect.

To discuss the first Article, let us apply here what I have said above about the general system of Europe and about the common effort which keeps each power for the most part within its own borders and prevents it from completely crushing the others. To make my reasoning on this point more clear, I will add here the list of nineteen powers which may be assumed to constitute the European Republic; with each one having an equal voice there would thus be nineteen voices in the assembly, i.e.,

The Roman Emperor
The Emperor of Russia
The King of France
The King of Spain
The King of England
The Estates-General
The King of Denmark
Sweden
Poland
The King of Portugal
The Sovereign of Rome

The King of Prussia
The Bavarian Elector and his Associates
The Palatine Elector and his Associates
The Swiss and their Associates
The Ecclesiastical Electors and their Associates
The Republic of Venice and its Associates
The King of Naples
The King of Sardinia

Several less considerable sovereigns, such as the Republic of Genoa, the Ducs of Modena and Parma, and others, having been omitted from this list, will be added to the less powerful members in the form of associates and will have along with them a right to vote similar to the *votum curiatum* of the counts of the Empire. It is useless to make this enumeration more precise here because until the execution of the project, minor alterations might occur that would require its reforming but would change nothing about the foundation of the system.

One need only to glance at this list to see that it is obviously not possible either for any of the powers that constitute it to be in a position to resist all the others united into one body, or for a partial league to form that would be capable of taking over the whole Confederation.

For how would such a league be formed? Would it be formed out of the most powerful states? We have shown how it could not last long, and we can now easily see that it would be incompatible both with the particular system of each great power and with the inseparable interests of the Confederation's constitution. Could a league be formed out of one large state and several small ones? But the other large states, united in the Confederation, could soon overpower the league, and one must sense that with the great alliance always united and armed it would be easy for it, by virtue of the fourth Article, to prevent and to suppress from the start any partial and seditious alliance that might try to trouble the peace and public order. Just look at what happens in the Germanic body, despite the abuses of its police and the extreme inequality of its members. Is there a single one, even among the most powerful, that would dare to expose itself to a ban by the Empire by overtly offending its constitution unless it believed that it had good reason not to fear that the Empire would be willing to act against it?

Thus I take it as demonstrated that the European Assembly once established would never have a rebellion to fear, and that even though some abuses might appear, they would never go so far as to elude the objective of the institution. It remains to see how well this main objective would be fulfilled by the institution itself.

For that, let us consider the motives that cause princes to take up arms. These motives are either to make conquests, or to defend oneself from an invasion, or to weaken a too-powerful neighbor, or to uphold one's rights when those rights have been infringed upon, or to settle a difference that cannot be settled amicably, or, finally, to fulfill the responsibilities of a treaty. There has never been a cause or pretext for war that does not fall under one of these six headings. Now, it is evident that not one of these six motives could exist in the proposed new state of things.

First, any form of invasion would have to be renounced because of the impossibility of its success. Any invader would be sure to be stopped in his tracks by forces much greater than those he could muster alone, and by risking all, he would be powerless to gain anything. An ambitious prince who wishes to gain power in Europe usually does two things. He begins by fortifying himself with good alliances, and then he tries to take his enemy by surprise. But individual alliances will serve no purpose against a more powerful and permanent alliance; and without any real reason for being armed, no prince would be able to do so without being noticed, warned, and punished by the Confederation, which would always be in a state of preparedness.

The same reason that deprives each prince of all hope of invasion relieves him at the same time of all fear of being attacked. And not only would his states be guaranteed by the whole of Europe and made as secure to him as the personal possessions of citizens in a well-regulated nation are, but as much more so than if he were their sole and only protector as Europe as a whole is stronger than he alone.

There is no reason to want to weaken a neighbor from whom one no longer has anything to fear, and there is not even a temptation to do so when one has no hope of succeeding.

Regarding the protection of one's rights, it is first of all necessary to say that an infinite number of quibbles and obscure pretensions and quarrels would be eliminated by the third Article of the Confederation, which regulates definitively all the reciprocal rights of the allied sovereigns on the basis of their present possessions. Thus all the demands and possible pretensions would become clear in the future and would be judged in the assembly as they might arise. In addition, if anyone infringes on my rights, I must uphold them by the same means. But, within the terms of the Confederation, no one could infringe on my rights by force without incurring the ban of the assembly. Thus it would no longer be by force that I now should defend those rights. The same can be said of insults, damages, reparations, and all the different unforeseen events that can arise between two sovereigns. The same power that must defend their rights must also settle their grievances.

As for the last motive for going to war, the solution offered by the Confederation is right before our eyes. First we can see that, no longer having any aggressor to fear, there would be no longer any need for defensive treaties, and that since one could not devise a treaty that was more solid and more secure than the great Confederation, any others would be useless, illegitimate, and consequently nil.

It would thus be impossible that the Confederation, once established, could let fall a single seed of war between the Confederees, and that the objective of perpetual peace could not be perfectly fulfilled by carrying out the proposed system.

It now remains for us to examine the other question, which has to do with the advantages for the contracting parties, for it is obvious that it would be futile to speak of the public self-interest to the detriment of private self-interest. Proving that peace is in general preferable to war says nothing to someone who believes that he has reasons to prefer war over peace; indeed, showing him the means of establishing a durable peace is only going to arouse his opposition.

Such a person will argue, in effect, that with this plan you are taking away the sovereigns' right to determine justice for themselves—that is to say, their precious right to be unjust when they please. You are taking away their power to grow at the expense of their neighbors; you are making them give up the apparatus of power and of terror with which they love to frighten the world—that glory of conquest from which they derive their honor; finally you are forcing them to become equitable and peaceful. How will they be compensated for such cruel deprivations?

Here I would not dare to reply, as the Abbé de Saint-Pierre does, that the true glory of princes consists in procuring the happiness of their subjects and the well-being of the public; that the whole of their self-interest is subordinate to their reputation and that their reputation among sensible men is measured by how much good they have done for the people; that the institution of a perpetual peace, being the greatest initiative that had ever been undertaken, would be the most capable of covering its author with an everlasting glory; that this same initiative, while being the most advantageous for the people, still would be the most honorable for the sovereigns—the only one, moreover, that is not tainted with blood, rape, tears, and curses; and finally that the most certain means of standing out from the crowd of kings would be to work for the welfare of the public. In the offices of ministers such lofty words may have brought ridicule to the Abbé and his projects, but let us not be mistaken like them about his underlying reasoning. Whatever may be true about the virtues of princes, let us speak only in terms of their own self-interest.

All the powers of Europe have rights or claims relative to one another. However, these rights are inherently unable to be elucidated in any absolute way, both because there is no common or constant rule with which to judge them and because they are often founded on ambivalent or uncertain facts. Nor can the conflicts that they cause ever be completely settled in any permanent way—as much because of the lack of any competent arbiter as because each prince will heedlessly take any chance he can get to revoke the concessions that were forced upon him, either by treaties made by the more powerful or by his defeat in a bitter war.

It is therefore an error to think only about one's own claims upon others and to forget the claims that others have upon us, for there is no means on either side to make these reciprocal claims valid. Once it becomes clear that these things all depend on chance, then simple common sense forbids us to risk our present possessions for a future gain, even when the odds for success are even. Certainly everyone blames a well-to-do man who, in the hope of doubling his holdings, dares risk them all with a throw of the dice. But we have made it clear that, in plans for expansion, each one, even in the present system, would find a resistance superior to his effort. It follows from this that, since the more powerful have no reason to play the game and the weak have no hope of profiting from it, it would be a benefit for all to renounce what they desire in the interests of guaranteeing what they have.

Let us consider the expenditure of men, of money, of force of all kinds, the impoverishment into which even the most propitious war throws any state, and let us compare this damage to the advantages that might be drawn from it. We will find that the victor often has lost when he thinks he has won, and that, being always weaker after the war than he was before, his only consolation is to see the defeated suffering even more than himself. But even this advantage is more apparent than real, because whatever superiority one might have gained over one's adversary is at the same time lost in respect to the neutral states, which, without changing their status, fortify themselves in direct relation to what the combatants have lost.

If every king has not yet renounced the lust for conquest, it seems that the wiser of them are at least beginning to see that wars cost more than they are worth. In this regard, without entering into a thousand distinctions that would lead us too far afield, we can say in general that a prince who, to extend his frontiers, loses as many former subjects as he acquires new ones, thus becomes weaker through his desire to grow. With a greater territory to defend, he no longer has any defenders. Moreover, we cannot ignore that, in the manner in which war is waged today, it is not in the armies that the greatest fatalities occur. It is there that we may find the most apparent and obvious losses, but at the same time throughout the state the increase in the number of those who will never be born, the rise in taxes, the interruption of commerce, the desertion of the countryside, and the abandonment of agriculture all cause a more serious and irreparable harm than the loss of men who die. Such evils, while perhaps not immediately evident, make themselves known painfully later on, and it is then that people are surprised at being so weak after supposedly making themselves so strong.

What also makes conquest less tempting is that it is now known how to double or triple one's power not only without extending one's territory but sometimes by contracting it, as was done very wisely by the emperor Hadrian. It is clear that men alone constitute the force of kings, and a proposition that follows from what I have just said is that of two states that nourish the same number of inhabitants, the one occupying the least territory is really the more powerful. It is by means of good laws, wise policies, and economic foresight that a judicious sovereign, without leaving anything to chance, can thus add to his strength. The real victories that he will gain over his neighbors will be whatever beneficial institutions he develops in his own states. The number of new subjects born under him are worth as much as the number of enemies that he might have killed.

It would be useless to object here that I am proving too much and that if things were really the way I represent them and each sovereign had a true common interest in maintaining peace, then peace would be established by itself and would last forever without any confederation. This would be to engage in very poor reasoning in the present situation. For although it would be much better for everyone always to be at peace, the common lack of security in this respect makes it so that each one, lacking any assurance of being able to avoid war, tries at least to begin it with an advantage in case the occasion presents itself, and to anticipate his neighbor—who in turn does not miss any favorable occasion to anticipate him. Hence many wars, even offensive wars, result less from the desire to usurp the interests of others than from the unjust precautions that each side takes to make its own interests secure. However worthy a commitment to the public good might be in general, given the objectives that are followed in politics and even in morality, it is certain that these commitments become dangerous to anyone who persists in practicing them with others when no one else practices them with him.

I have nothing to say about military parades or displays of weaponry, for without either fear or hope providing a solid justification for them, these displays become nothing but a kind of infantile game, and kings are not supposed to play with toys. Nor will I say anything about military prowess, for if there remain a few monsters who would be distressed at having no one to massacre, then the solution would not be to try to reason with them but rather to deprive them of the means of exercising their murderous rage.

Since the third Article anticipates all plausible reasons for war, there would be no motive to start a war against others that others could not just as well use to start a war against us; at the same time it would be a great advantage to be freed from the risk of being alone against all.

As for the mutual dependence on the common tribunal, it is clear that this would in no way diminish the rights of sovereignty, but on the contrary would strengthen them. Again because of the stipulations of the third Article, the tribunal would make the rights of sovereignty even more assured than they are now by guaranteeing to each not only his security against any foreign invasion but also his authority in respect to any internal rebellion. Consequently princes would not be less absolute, and their crown would be even more secure. By submitting themselves to the judgment of the assembly in their quarrels among their peers and by depriving themselves of the dangerous power of seizing the property of others, they would only assure themselves of their real rights and renounce those that they do not have. Moreover, there is a big difference between depending on others and simply depending on a body of which one is a member and where each is a leader in turn. For, in this latter case, each one is responsible for the guarantees that would assure his own liberty. This liberty might be alienated in the hands of a master, but it is strengthened in the hands of one's peers.

The example of the Germanic body confirms the above truth, for even though the sovereignty of its members has been altered in many respects by its constitution, and although they may consequently be in a less favorable situation than the members of a European body would be, there is nevertheless not a single member, however jealous it might be of its own authority, which would wish, even if it could, to assume an absolute independence by detaching itself from the Empire. Notice, moreover, that since the Germanic body has a permanent leader, the authority of this leader must have a tendency constantly to be usurped —something which could not happen in the European assembly where the presidency will alternate without regard to the differences in power.

To all these considerations is added another, which is much more important for people who are as avid for money as princes always are. That is, the great facility of gaining additional wealth—both from all the advantages that would accrue to their people and to themselves from the continual peace and from the excessive expense that would be spared by the reforming of the military state and by the elimination of the multitude of fortresses and troops that use up revenue and become every day a heavier burden on the people and on the princes themselves. I know that it would not be agreeable to all sovereigns to disband their troops and be completely without armed forces on hand to stifle unexpected uprisings or to push back a sudden invasion;[8] I know also that they would have to furnish a contingent to the Confederation, both to guard the frontiers of Europe and to maintain the Confederative army intended to defend, if need be, the decrees of the assembly. But once these expenses had been paid and the contingencies of war forever done away with, there would remain still more than half the usual military expenses to be divided between the needs of the people and the treasury of the prince. In this way the people would pay much less; the prince, being much richer, would be able to stimulate commerce, agriculture, the arts, and to develop useful institutions that would further increase the people's wealth and his own; and the state would thus have a much more perfect security than that which it could gain from armies and from the whole apparatus of war, which never ceases to weaken it even in times of peace.

One might argue that the countries on the frontiers of Europe would thereby be in a more disadvantageous position and might correspondingly have wars to sustain either with Turkey or with Africa or with the Tartars.

To this I answer (1) that those countries are in the same position today and that consequently it would not be citing a positive disadvantage but simply one less advantage and an inevitable inconvenience that their situation exposes them to; (2) that freed from all uneasiness from the European side, they would be in a much better position to resist an external threat; (3) that getting rid of all the defenses in the interior of Europe and the costs necessary to maintain them would put the Confederation in a position to establish a large number of defenses on the frontiers with no extra burden on the confederees; (4) that these defenses—constructed, maintained, and commissioned at common expense—would similarly provide defenses and savings for the powers at the borders whose states were being guarded; (5) that the armies of the Confederation, distributed within the confines of Europe, would always be ready to repel an aggressor; (6) and, finally, that a body as formidable as the European Republic would discourage foreigners from the desire to attack any of its members—just as the Germanic body, though infinitely less powerful, still is powerful enough to make itself respected by its neighbors and to protect effectively all the princes that compose it.

One might also argue that if Europeans were to have no more wars among themselves, the art of military strategy might fall gradually into oblivion, that troops would lose their courage and their discipline, and that there would be no more generals or soldiers, and Europe would remain at the mercy of the first foreign invader.

To this I answer that one of two things would happen: either Europe's neighbors would attack and make war, or they would fear the Confederation and leave Europe in peace.

In the first case, here would be the chances for cultivating military genius and talents, to arm and assemble troops. The armies of the Confederation would become in this case the school for Europe: They would go to the frontier to learn war; but in the heart of Europe the people would enjoy peace, and thus the advantages of both would be joined. Why do we think that to become a warrior we must always fight at home? And are the French less brave because the provinces of Touraine and Anjou are not at war with one another?

In the second case, we would no longer be armed, it is true, but there would be no need to be, for what good would it to be to practice for war with no one to wage it against? Which is better, to cultivate a deadly art or to make it useless? If we could discover a secret for enjoying constant good health, would it make sense to reject it so as not to deprive doctors of the occasions for gaining their expertise? It remains to be seen in this parallel which of the two arts is the more beneficial in itself and thus merits being preserved.

One need not feel threatened by the possibility of sudden invasion. It is well known that Europe has nothing to fear and that this "first invader" will never come. We no longer live in those times when barbarian onslaughts seemed to come upon us from out of the blue. Ever since our curious eyes learned how to search into the far corners of the earth, there is nothing that can approach us without being perceived from a great distance. There is no power in the world that is now in a position to threaten the whole of Europe; and if there ever were to be one, either we would have the time to prepare for it, or if we were united in one body, we would at least be in a better position to resist it than if we had to end some long conflict quickly and reunify our forces all at once.

We have just seen that once they are carefully examined, all the so-called inconveniences of the status of confederation can be reduced to nothing. We now ask whether anyone on earth would dare to say as much for the inconveniences that result from the present manner of settling differences between princes by the right of the strongest—that is, from the state of anarchy and war that is necessarily brought on by each sovereign's absolute and mutual independence within the imperfect social context that holds sway among us in Europe. In order to give us a better perspective with which to weigh these latter inconveniences, I will summarize them in a few words which I will leave the reader to examine on his own.

1. No assured right except that of the strongest.
2. Continual and inevitable changes in the relationships among peoples that prevent any one of them from being able to hold on to the power that it currently enjoys.
3. No perfect security as long as one's neighbors are not either subjected or annihilated.
4. General impossibility of annihilating them, seeing that subjugating the first one simply brings on others.
5. Precautions and immense expenses for keeping oneself on guard.
6. Lack of forces and of defense against minorities and against revolts. For when the state is divided, who can defend one part against the other?
7. Lack of security in mutual engagements.
8. Never any justice to hope for from others without immense costs and losses, which do not always procure it, and which the disputed object rarely makes up for.
9. Inevitable risk of one's state and even of one's life in the pursuit of these rights.
10. The necessity of taking part in spite of oneself in the quarrels of one's neighbors and of waging war when one least wants it.
11. The interruption of commerce and of public resources at the moment when they are most necessary.
12. A continual danger from a powerful neighbor, if one is weak, and from a league, if one is strong.
13. Finally, the futility of wisdom where events are governed by chance, the continual desolation of the people, the weakening of the state both during successes and during reversals, and the total impossibility of ever establishing a good government, of relying on one's own possessions, or of bringing happiness either to oneself or to others.[9]

Let us recapitulate in the same way the advantages to be gained by the confederated princes from European arbitration.

1. Complete assurance that their present and future conflicts would always be terminated without any war—an assurance incomparably more useful for sovereigns than a similar assurance of never having to engage in lawsuits would be for individuals.
2. The removal or at least the reduction to a minor role of the causes of conflict by the erasure of all prior claims—an act which will compensate for what they give up and secure what they possess.
3. Complete and perpetual security both for the person of the prince

and for that of his family, and for his states, and for the order of succession fixed by the laws of each country—as much against the ambition of unjust and power-hungry pretenders as against the revolts of rebel subjects.

4. Perfect security for the administration of all reciprocal agreements between one prince and another to be guaranteed by the European Republic.
5. Liberty and perfect and perpetual security in regard to commerce, both between state and state and for each state in distant regions.
6. Total and perpetual cutting back of prodigious military expenditures on land and at sea in times of war and a considerable lowering of ordinary expenditures in times of peace.
7. Evident progress in agriculture and in population growth, in the wealth of the state, and in the revenues of the prince.
8. Greater ease in establishing projects that could add to the glory and authority of the sovereign, the resources of the public, and the happiness of the people.

As I have said before, I will leave to the judgment of my readers both the examination of all these articles and the comparison of the state of peace that would result from the Confederation with the state of war that results from European anarchy.

If we have reasoned well in the exposition of this project, it is demonstrated, first, that the establishment of perpetual peace depends solely on the consent of sovereigns and presents no difficulty other than their resistance; second, that this establishment would be useful to them in every way and that there is no comparison even for them between its inconveniences and its advantages; third, that it is reasonable to suppose that their will accords with their self-interest; finally, that this establishment, once it is developed according to the proposed plan, would be solid and durable and would fulfill its objective perfectly. Doubtless this is not to say that sovereigns will adopt this project (who can speak for the reasoning of others?) but only that if they were to adopt it, they would be acting with respect to their own true interests. For it must be observed that we have not been considering men such as they ought to be—good, generous, disinterested, and loving the public well-being from a humanitarian standpoint—but such as they are—unjust, greedy, and looking to their own self-interest above all else. The only thing that we have assumed about them is that they are both rational enough to perceive what is useful to them and courageous enough to work toward their own happiness. If, despite all this, the project remains unfulfilled, it is not therefore because it is too idealistic; rather, it is because men are insane and because it is a sort of folly to remain wise in the midst of those who are mad.

C

ROUSSEAU'S "CRITIQUE" OF THE ABBÉ DE SAINT-PIERRE'S *PROJECT FOR PERPETUAL PEACE*

As the most worthy cause to which a good man might devote himself, the *Project for Perpetual Peace* must also have been, among all the projects of the Abbé de Saint-Pierre, the one that he thought about the most and the one that he pursued with the greatest obstinancy. For how else could one explain the missionary zeal with which he clung to this project—despite the obvious impossibility of its success, the ridicule that it brought upon him every day, and the hostility that he was made continually to suffer. It seems that this humane soul was so single-mindedly focused on the public good that he measured the efforts that he gave things solely on the basis of their usefulness, without ever letting himself be discouraged by obstacles and without ever thinking about his own personal self-interest.

If ever a moral truth has been demonstrated, it seems to me that it is the general and the specific usefulness of this project. The advantages that would result from its formation both for each prince and for each nation, as well as for Europe as a whole, are immense, clear, and uncontestable. One cannot imagine anything more solid and more precise than the arguments with which the author supports his case. Indeed, so much would the experience allow each individual to gain from the common good, that to realize the European Republic for one day would be enough to make it last forever. However, these same princes who would defend the European Republic with all their might once it existed would now be opposed even to its being set up, and they would invariably prevent it from being established with just as much energy as they would prevent it from being destroyed. The work of the Abbé de Saint-Pierre thus would seem both ineffectual for producing peace and superfluous for maintaining it. Some impatient reader will say that it is therefore nothing but vain speculation. No, it is a solid and sensible book, and it is very important that it exists.

Let us begin by examining the difficulties of those who do not judge arguments with reason but only with events and who have nothing to object to in this project other than that it has not been tried. In effect, they doubtlessly will say, if the advantages are so real, why have the sovereigns of Europe not adopted them already? Why do they neglect their own self-interest, if this self-interest has now been made so clear? Do we see them rejecting all the other ways of increasing their revenues and their power? If this project were as good for that purpose as is claimed, is it plausible that they would be less impressed with it than with those which have failed them so many times before, or that they would prefer a thousand risky chances to one sure gain?

Clearly, all this is plausible unless we pretend that the wisdom of all these sovereigns is equal to their ambition and that the more strongly they desire their own advantages the better they can see them. Instead, the great penalty for excessive *amour propre* is forever to resort to the means that abuse it, and the very heat of the passions is what almost always prevents them from reaching their goal. We must distinguish, then, in politics as well as in morality, real interest from apparent interest. The first is to be found in perpetual peace—that has been demonstrated in the *Project*. The second can be found in the condition of absolute independence that draws sovereigns away from the rule of law in order to submit them to the rule of chance—like a mad sailor who, to show off his knowledge and intimidate his crew, would prefer to drift dangerously among the reefs during a storm than to secure his ship with an anchor.

The whole preoccupation of kings, or of those to whom they delegate their duties, centers on two sole objectives—to extend their domination outside their borders and to make it more absolute within. Any other purpose either relates to one of these two or else only serves as a pretext for them. Examples of such pretexts are the notions of "public well-being," the "happiness of the people," and the "glory of the nation"—words that are never mentioned in official circles and are so ineptly used in political statements that they usually signify some unpleasant announcement and make the people groan in anticipation of their masters' paternal solicitude.

Judge, on the basis of these two fundamental principles, how princes might receive a proposal that strikes directly at the first and is hardly favorable to the second. For it is clear that with the European Assembly the government of each state would be just as clearly defined as its borders, that princes could not be guaranteed their security from the revolts of their subjects without at the same time guaranteeing their subjects security from the tyranny of princes, and that otherwise the institution could not survive. Now, I ask if there is in the whole world even one sovereign who, limited thus forever in his most cherished projects, would support without indignation the idea of seeing himself forced to be just, not only toward foreigners but even toward his own subjects.

Conversely, it is quite easy to understand how on the one hand, war and invasions, and on the other hand, the progress of despotism, mutually reinforce each other; how, in a nation of slaves, money and men are taken discretely for the purpose of subduing others; how, reciprocally, war furnishes one pretext for monetary extortions and another pretext, no less specious, for continually having large armies to keep the people in check. Finally, anyone can see that aggressive princes make at least as much war against their own people as against their enemies and that the condition of the winners is in reality no better than that of the losers. "I have beaten the Romans," wrote Hannibal to the Carthaginians. "Send me some troops. I have laid Italy under contribution; send me some money." This is the significance of the *Te Deums*, the victory fires, and the celebrations of the people at the triumphs of their masters.

As for the conflicts between one prince and another, can anyone hope to submit to a superior tribunal men who dare boast that their power comes only from their swords and who would not pay their respects even to God except that he is in heaven? Would sovereigns submit their disputes to judicial methods that the whole structure of laws has not yet been able to force individuals to apply to theirs? It is rare for a typical gentleman who has been offended to condescend to bring his complaint before the tribunal of the Marechaux de France;[1] and yet you expect that a king would bring his complaint to a European Assembly? Moreover, there is this difference, that the one sins against the laws and exposes his life from two sides, whereas the other exposes only his subjects, exercises a right in taking up arms that is endorsed by the whole human race, and claims to be accountable only to God.

A prince who places his survival on the chances of war is not unaware that he runs certain risks, but he pays less attention to the risks than to the advantages that he anticipates. For he fears fortune far less than he hopes to profit from his own skill. If he is powerful, he counts on his own forces; if he is weak, he counts on his allies. Furthermore, war can be useful to him internally as a way of getting rid of domestic complaints, of weakening subjects who are unruly, even of suffering reversals—for the clever politician knows how to take advantage of his own defeats. I hope my readers recognize that it is not I who reason in this way, but the sophist of the court who prefers a large territory and a few poor and submissive subjects to the secure realm that a happy and flourishing people ruled by justice and the law could provide him.

By the same principle he also refutes for himself the argument based

on the suspension of commerce, the drop in population, the disruption
of finances, and the real losses that a futile war can cause. Always to
evaluate a sovereign's gains and losses in monetary terms makes for a
very faulty form of calculation, for the extent of one's actual power
cannot be measured by how many millions one possesses. The schemes
of a prince form a never-ending upward spiral. He wants to have more
power in order to increase his wealth and to increase his wealth in order
to have more power. He will sacrifice each in turn to acquire that which
is lacking. But it is, in the end, only to be able to possess both together
that he pursues each one separately, for in order to be the master of
both men and things one must have at the same time both glory and
gold.

We must add, in considering the great commercial advantages that
would result from a general and perpetual peace, that while they are
obviously in themselves certain and incontestable, being common to
all they would not be relative advantages to anyone. Since advantage
is usually only sensed by virtue of difference, to add to one's relative
power one must seek out only exclusive gains.

Ceaselessly deceived by the appearance of things, princes will therefore reject this peace when judging it by their own self-interest. Just
think, then, what will happen when they leave such judgments to their
ministers, whose interests are always opposed to those of the people
and almost always opposed to those of the prince. Ministers need war
to make themselves necessary, to precipitate the prince into crises that
he cannot get out of without them, and to cause the loss of the state,
if it is necessary, rather than the loss of their jobs. They need war to
harass the people in the guise of public safety, to find work for their
protégés, to make money on the markets, and to form a thousand corrupt monopolies in secret. They need it to satisfy their passions and
to push each other out of office. They need it to preoccupy the prince
and remove him from the court while dangerous intrigues arise among
them. Such resources would all be lost to them if there were a perpetual peace. And the public keeps on demanding why, if the project is
possible, it has not been adopted! They fail to see that there is nothing
impossible about the project except its adoption. And what will the
ministers do to oppose it? What they have always done—they will turn
it to ridicule.

Nor is it possible to believe along with the Abbé de Saint-Pierre
that, even with the good will which neither princes nor ministers will
ever have, it would be easy to find a favorable moment to set this system
in motion. For that it would be necessary that the sum of individual
interests would not outweigh the common interest, and that each one
would believe that he had found in the good of all the greatest good that

he could hope for for himself. Now this would require a convergence of wisdom among so many different minds and a convergence of aims among so many different interests that one could hardly hope to get the happy agreement of all these necessary circumstances simply by chance. The only way to make up for the failure of this agreement to come about by chance would be to make it come about by force. Then it would no longer be a question of persuading but of compelling, and then what would be needed is not to write books but to levy troops.

Thus, although the project was very wise, the means of putting it into effect reflect the naiveté of the author. He innocently imagined that all you would need to do is to assemble a committee, propose his articles, have everyone sign them, and that would be it. We must conclude that, as with all the projects of this good man, he could envision quite well the effect of things after they had been established, but he judged with too little sophistication the methods for getting them established in the first place.

To prove that the project for a Christian Republic is not mere fantasy, I would simply like to name its first author, for assuredly Henri IV was no fool, nor was Sully a visionary. The Abbé de Saint-Pierre looked back to these great authorities with the purpose of bringing their system up to date. But what a difference there is in the times, in the circumstances, in the actual propositions of the system, in its method, and in its author!

In order to evaluate the earlier project, let us look at the general situation of things at the moment chosen by Henri IV for the execution of his plan.

Charles V had such immense power that he had begun to aspire to use his great resources (and his great talents for making the most out of those resources) to create a kind of universal monarchy. His son, even richer than he but not quite so powerful and stubbornly pursuing a policy that he was not capable of carrying out completely, began to make all of Europe increasingly uneasy. At the same time Austria had gained such ascendancy over the other powers that no prince was secure unless he was on good terms with her.[2]

Philippe III, less clever even than his father, inherited all of the latter's pretensions. The fear of Spanish hegemony still held Europe in respect, but Spain continued to dominate more through the habit of commanding than through the power of making herself obeyed, for the revolt of the Netherlands, the mobilizing of troops against England, and the civil wars in France had depleted the armies of Spain and the treasures of the Americas. The House of Hapsburg, now divided into two branches, was no longer acting in concert, and although in Germany the Emperor tried to maintain or to recover the authority of

Charles V, he succeeded only in alienating the princes and fomenting leagues, which almost managed to dethrone him.

Thus the way was paved well in advance for the decline of the Hapsburgs and the reestablishment of common liberty. However, no one dared to be the first to shake off the yoke and to expose himself to war all alone. Even the example of Henri IV had had a discouraging effect, since it had turned out so badly. Moreover, except for the Duke of Savoy, who was too weak and too overwhelmed to initiate anything, there was not, among so many sovereigns, one capable man in a position to formulate and sustain such an enterprise. They all seemed only to be waiting for time and circumstances to provide them with the right moment to break out of their chains.

That was the general state of things when Henri IV formulated his plan for the Christian Republic and prepared to put it into effect. A project quite grand, quite admirable in itself, and whose honor I do not wish to tarnish, but which, having as its underlying rationale the hope of bringing down a formidable enemy, gained from this motive an impetus that it would have had difficulty drawing from its collective utility alone.

Let us now look at the means by which this great man was prepared for such a lofty undertaking.

I would easily rank first in importance his broad understanding of the difficulties of the project. For having formed this plan since his childhood, he meditated on it throughout his life, and left its actual fulfillment for his old age—a pattern of behavior that is evidence both of the passionate and sustained commitment necessary for overcoming great obstacles in times of difficulty and of the patient and reflective wisdom that enables one to smooth the way with long-term foresight and preparation. For there is a great difference between those necessary undertakings that common sense leaves to chance and those that success alone can justify; having been able to get along without the latter, one has no desire to attempt them unless guaranteed of success. With such a great undertaking—which required the coordination of so many men but which so many men also had an interest in thwarting —it was as essential as it was difficult to keep everything a deep secret until the moment of its execution. It seems that although he had gotten the greater part of Europe on his side, and although he was aligned with the most powerful sovereigns of the time, he never had but one confidant who knew the full extent of his plan. By a kind of luck that heaven would bestow only on the best of kings, this confidant was a minister of great integrity.[3]

But even though no one knew about these grand designs, they all were silently moving toward their fulfillment. Twice Sully went to

London to strengthen ties with James I, and Charles IX of Sweden was brought in from the side. The league was concluded with the Protestants of Germany, and even the Italian princes could be depended upon. Everyone concurred with the great aim without really being able to say what that aim was—like workers who labor separately at parts of a new machine without knowing either its form or its function.

What helped this general movement along? Was it a perpetual peace, which no one foresaw and few even cared about? Was it public concern, which is never any private person's concern? The Abbé de Saint-Pierre might have thought so! But in fact each one worked only with regard to his own individual self-interest, which Henri had the ingenuity to show them all in a very attractive guise. The King of England needed to do something about the frequent conspiracies among the Catholics in his realm, all of which were fomented by Spain; he found an additional advantage in the independence of the Low Countries, which were costing him much to maintain and which put him every day closer to the outbreak of a war that he feared—or that he would prefer to participate in along with everyone else so as to get it over with once and for all. The King of Sweden wanted to be assured of Pomerania and to be able to get a toehold in Germany. The Palatine Elector, at that time a Protestant and chief of the Augsburg Confession, had his sights set on Bohemia, and was ready to go along with anything that was planned by the King of England. The German princes wanted to repress the attempted usurpations of the Hapsburgs. The Duke of Savoy gained Milan and the crown of Lombardy, which he passionately desired. Even the Pope, tired of Spanish tyranny, took part in the plan by being promised the Realm of Naples. The Dutch, who got paid better than anyone else, were given the assurance of their liberty. In sum, beyond the common interest in weakening a proud power that had wanted to become preeminent, each ruler had a particular, vital, and deeply felt interest of his own. And because it was agreed that the conquests would be shared by all the allies except France and England, who were not to keep anything for themselves, each prince's interests were not compromised by any counterbalancing fear of merely substituting one tyrant for the other, and those who were the most nervous about the ambition of Henri IV were sufficiently calmed by France and England's restraint.

But this wise prince was not unaware that in reserving nothing for himself by the treaty, he nevertheless would gain more from it than anyone else. For, without adding anything to his own patrimony, simply to divide the patrimony of the one ruler who was more powerful than he would suffice to make Henri the most powerful; and it is clear that by taking all the precautions necessary to assure the success of the enterprise he did not neglect those that would give him the key position in the body that he aimed to set up.

Furthermore, these preparations were not at all limited to forming strong international leagues and contracting alliances with his own neighbors and those of the enemy. By interesting so many people in the demise of the foremost power of Europe, he did not neglect to put himself in a position to take his turn at the same role. He used fifteen years of peace to make preparations worthy of the enterprise which he was planning. He filled his treasuries with money and his arsenals with artillery, arms, and munitions; he managed distant resources for unforeseen needs. But more important, he governed his people wisely, imperceptibly rooting out all seeds of discord, and putting his finances in such good order that they could pay for everything without oppressing his subjects. Thus tranquil within and respected without, he was finally in a position to maintain sixty thousand men and twenty warships, to be able to go outside his realm without leaving behind any source of disorder, and to make war for six years without tapping into his ordinary revenues or adding a single cent of new taxes.

To so many preparations must be added the same zeal and the same prudence for the direction of the enterprise that had originally motivated its formulation, as much on the part of his minister as on his own part. Finally, add a leader such as he to head the expeditions, whereas his adversary had no one comparable to oppose him, and you can judge whether his hopes for success lacked anything that would herald a happy outcome.

Without knowing his views, Europe watched his extensive preparations attentively, and, with a certain amount of trepidation, waited to see what would happen. A minor pretext was to set off this great upheaval—a war that would end all wars was to make way for immortal peace—when an event, which was made even more shocking by the mystery surrounding it, came to banish forever this last hope of the world. The same blow that ended the days of this good king plunged Europe back into eternal wars that she can scarcely hope to see come to an end. Nevertheless, those were the elements that Henri IV brought together to form the same enterprise that the Abbé de Saint-Pierre claimed to create with a book.

We may not say, therefore, that if his system has not been adopted, it is because it was not good; on the contrary, we must say that it was too good to be adopted. For evil and abuse, which so many men profit from, happen by themselves, but whatever is useful to the public must be brought by force—seeing as special interests are almost always opposed to it. Doubtless perpetual peace is at present a project that seems absurd; but were we to be given a Henri IV and a Sully, perpetual peace might become a project that once again would seem reasonable. Instead, let us admire such a fine plan, but be consoled that we will never see it come about, for that can only happen by means that humanity might find violent and fearful.

We will not see federative leagues establishing themselves except by revolution, and, on this principle, who would dare to say whether this European league is to be desired or to be feared? It would perhaps cause more harm in one moment than it could prevent for centuries to come.

NOTES
BIBLIOGRAPHY
INDEX

Notes

INTRODUCTION

1. For bibliographic summaries of some of these earlier uses of Rousseau, see Alfred Cobban, *Rousseau and the Modern State* (London: Archon Books, 1964), 13–31; Lester Crocker, *Rousseau's "Social Contract": An Interpretive Essay* (Cleveland: Case Western Reserve University Press, 1968), 115–133; and Ernst Cassirer, *The Question of Jean-Jacques Rousseau*, ed. and trans. Peter Gay (Bloomington: Indiana University Press, 1967), 3–30.

2. *Daedalus*, Summer 1978, vii.

3. See, for example, Jean-Jacques Rousseau, *On the Social Contract, with "Geneva Manuscript" and "Political Economy,"* ed. Roger D. Masters, trans. Judith R. Masters (New York: St. Martin's Press, 1978), 1–40; Roger Masters, *The Political Philosophy of Rousseau* (Princeton: Princeton University Press, 1968); Jean-Jacques Rousseau, *Emile: or On Education*, ed. and trans. Allan Bloom (New York: Basic Books, 1979), 3–28; and Jean-Jacques Rousseau, *Politics and the Arts: Letter to M. d'Alembert on the Theater*, ed. and trans. Allan Bloom (Ithaca: Cornell University Press, 1960).

4. See, for example, Maurice Cranston, *Jean-Jacques: The Early Life and Work of Jean-Jacques Rousseau, 1712–1754* (New York: Norton, 1982); and Robert Derathé, *Jean-Jacques Rousseau et la science politique de son temps* (Paris: Librairie Philosophique J. Vrin, 1970). For an earlier example, see Ernst Cassirer, *Rousseau, Kant, Goethe: Two Essays*, trans. James Gutmann, Paul Oskar Kristeller, and John Herman Randall, Jr. (Princeton: Princeton University Press, 1963).

5. Stephen Ellenburg, *Rousseau's Political Philosophy: An Interpretation from Within* (Ithaca: Cornell University Press, 1976); Michel Launay, *Jean-Jacques Rousseau, Écrivain politique 1712–1762* (Grenoble: Association pour une Coopérative d'Édition et de Recherche, 1971); and James Miller, *Rousseau, Dreamer of Democracy* (New Haven: Yale University Press, 1984).

6. Rousseau, *Emile*, 466; Jean-Jacques Rousseau, *Oeuvres complètes*, ed. Ber-

nard Gagnebin and Marcel Raymond, Bibliothèque de la Pléiade, 4 vols. (Paris: Gallimard, 1959–1969), IV:848. In this and subsequent notes where I cite other scholars' English translations of Rousseau's work, I include the corresponding page references to the Pléiade edition of Rousseau's *Oeuvres complètes,* hereafter to be abbreviated as *OC.*

7. Ibid., 466–467; *OC,* IV:848. To show its link to Grotius's *Rights of War and Peace,* I have translated *droit de la guerre* as "rights of war" throughout.

8. Georges Lassudrie-Duchène, *Jean-Jacques Rousseau et le droit des gens* (Paris: Imprimerie Henri Jouve, 1906); J. L. Windenberger, *Essai sur le système de politique étrangère de J.-J. Rousseau: La République Confédérative des petits États* (Paris: Alphonse Picard et Fils, 1900). See also Cuno Hofer, *L'Influence de J.-J. Rousseau sur le droit de la guerre* (Genève: Georg & Cie., 1916).

9. Jean-Jacques Rousseau, *A Lasting Peace through the Federation of Europe and The State of War,* trans. C. E. Vaughan (London: Constable, 1917). Reprinted in *The Theory of International Relations: Selected Texts from Gentili to Treitsche,* ed. M. G. Forsyth, H. M. A. Keens-Soper, and P. Savigear (London: Allen and Unwin, 1970), 127–180.

10. Jean-Jacques Rousseau, *L'État de Guerre and Projet de Paix Perpétuelle,* ed. Shirley Patterson (New York: G. P. Putnam's, 1920). See also Jean-Jacques Rousseau, "A Project of Perpetual Peace: Rousseau's Essay," trans. Edith M. Nutall (London: Richard Dobden-Sanderson, 1922), reprinted in *Peace Projects of the Eighteenth Century,* ed. Blanche Wiesen Cook, Sandi E. Cooper, and Charles Chatfield (New York: Garland, 1974).

11. Kenneth N. Waltz, *Man, the State, and War: A Theoretical Analysis* (New York: Columbia University Press, 1954), 165–186.

12. F. H. Hinsley, *Power and the Pursuit of Peace: Theory and Practice in the History of Relations between States* (Cambridge: Cambridge University Press, 1963), 46–61.

13. Stanley Hoffmann, "Rousseau on War and Peace," *American Political Science Review* 17 (June 1963): 317–353. Reprinted also in Stanley Hoffmann, *The State of War* (New York: Praeger, 1965), 54–87.

A recent British dissertation builds on the interpretations put forth by Hinsley and Hoffmann. Stressing the tension between Rousseau's "moralism" and his "pessimism," the author argues that "Rousseau can be said to have a realist view of international relations in that he assumes that there can be no essential harmony of interest among nations, and that war or the threat of war will inevitably remain indispensable to rulers who dictate public policy, indeed, even to well governed states which still have their own particular interest." Christine Jane Carter, *Rousseau and the Problem of War* (New York: Garland, 1987), 210.

14. The debate over these issues goes to the heart of questions about whether Rousseau had a "unified" or a "dualistic" world view, and whether his work is essentially cohesive or essentially contradictory. The bibliography on this question is vast; for salient examples of those authors who stress the dualism or the contradictions in Rousseau's work see C. E. Vaughan's "Introduction" to Jean-Jacques Rousseau, *The Political Writings of Jean Jacques Rousseau,* ed. C. E. Vaughan, 2 vols. (New York: Wiley, 1962), I:1–117; Roger D. Masters, *The*

Political Philosophy of Rousseau (Princeton: Princeton University Press, 1968); and Judith N. Shklar, *Men and Citizens: A Study of Rousseau's Social Theory* (Cambridge: Cambridge University Press, 1969). For those who stress the unity in Rousseau's work see Cassirer, *The Question of Jean-Jacques Rousseau*; Ellenburg, *Rousseau's Political Philosophy*; and Miller, *Rousseau, Dreamer of Democracy*.

15. See Grace G. Roosevelt, "A Reconstruction of Rousseau's Fragments on the State of War," *History of Political Thought* 8 (Summer 1987): 225–244; and Grace G. Roosevelt, "Rousseau and the Strange Fabrications of the Count d'Antraigues," in process.

16. Le Comte d'Antraigues, *Quelle est la situation de l'Assemblée nationale?* Cited in Windenberger, *Essai sur le système de politique étrangère de J.-J. Rousseau*, 55–56; and by Vaughan in Rousseau, *Political Writings*, II:135.

17. Rousseau, *OC*, I:404–405.

18. Rousseau, *Emile*, 467; *OC*, IV:849.

19. Rousseau, *Social Contract*, 46, 104, 132; *OC*, III:349, 431, 470.

20. Rousseau, *Political Writings*, ed. Vaughan, II:136. In his biography of d'Antraigues, Pingaud speculated that d'Antraigues met Rousseau "either in the Lyonnais region, at the home of the Marquis de Tourette, their friend in common, or at the home of Angianier de Saint Germain, the pious Catholic who had the privilege of never offending the Genevan philosopher." The biography goes on to say that d'Antraigues was occasionally received by Rousseau in his garret on the rue Platrière and gave d'Antraigues, on 14 March 1774, as a sign of their friendship, "a drawing by Leseur representing the death of Socrates, some translations of Salluste and Tacitus, and a sequel to the *Social Contract*." Pingaud supports these claims by pointing out that a drawing by Leseur of the death of Socrates was sold at an auction in London in 1878 and had on its frame, in d'Antraigues hand, a note saying that it had been given to him by J.-J. Rousseau, who in turn had received it from the Prince of Conti in 1770. Windenberger, in his *Essai sur le système de politique étrangère de J.-J. Rousseau*, quotes from Pingaud's work and uses further evidence about the translations to support his view that d'Antraigues actually did receive a sequel to the *Social Contract* from Rousseau by pointing out that the French Ministry of Foreign Affairs has in its possession a letter from d'Antraigues that refers to his efforts to publish a translation of Sallust by Jean-Jacques Rousseau. The implication here is that since the existence of both the print and the translation was corroborated by other sources, the existence of a sequel to the *Social Contract* is also quite plausible. Windenberger fails to emphasize, however, that in both of the above cases the corroboration is based on the words of d'Antraigues himself. See Windenberger, *Essai sur le système de politique étrangère de J.-J. Rousseau*, 57.

21. Cobban's exploration, in *Rousseau and the Modern State*, of the potentially conservative nationalistic strains in Rousseau's writing made him naturally interested in an aristocrat whose writings reveal both a nostalgia for feudal forms of loyalty and a passionate appropriation of Rousseauean ideals of popular sovereignty. Cobban's researches on d'Antraigues led him to examine the contents of a box of letters that had been found in a house in London where the son

of the count had once lived. Among the contents were about twenty letters purportedly written by Rousseau, though not in Rousseau's handwriting, and exhibiting characteristics of composition and handwriting that made them resemble Rousseau's rough drafts. Such idiosyncrasies, plus the fact that one of the letters had been accepted as a "genuine" copy by an authority on the Rousseau correspondence, led Cobban and Elmes to guess that a number of the letters, while not actually written by Rousseau, might have been *based on* actual letters that d'Antraigues had received from Rousseau. The article also points out that while there is no hard evidence about their being friends, d'Antraigues "enjoyed the reputation of having been an intimate friend and disciple of Rousseau." They also mention references to Rousseau scattered among the private papers of d'Antraigues, including early manuscripts that bear margin notes such as "corrigé par J.-J. R le 2 août 1775." Alfred Cobban and R. S. Elmes, "A Disciple of Jean-Jacques Rousseau: The Comte d'Antraigues," *Revue d'histoire littéraire de la France* 43 (1936):183–184.

22. Jean-Jacques Rousseau, *Correspondance complète*, ed. R. A. Leigh, 43 vols. (Geneva: Institut et Musée Voltaire, 1984), vol. XXXVII, Appendices 589–590, p. 370.

23. Rousseau, *OC*, III:608–610. In this and subsequent references to "The State of War," I have used my own translation of the French text. See Appendix A for the full translation.

24. For an account of the discovery of this fragment, see Bernard Gagnebin, "Un inédit de Rousseau sur l'état de guerre," in *De Rousard à Breton: Recueil d'essais. Hommages à Marcel Raymond* (Paris: Librairie José Corti, 1967), 103–105. The fragment appears in *OC*, III: 1899–1904.

25. Rousseau, *Correspondance complète*, V:50–51. In his introduction to Rousseau's works on the Abbé de Saint-Pierre, Sven Stelling-Michaud also speculates that "The State of War" is a draft for Rousseau's "Principles of the Rights of War." See *OC*, III:cxxv.

26. It is difficult to know exactly when in the 1750s "The State of War" was drafted. Some commentators have guessed that it was drafted in 1756 or later, at around the time Rousseau was working on his responses to the Abbé de Saint-Pierre's *Project for Perpetual Peace*. This view would be supported by Rousseau's reference to the manuscript in the 8 March 1758 letter to Rey. It seems to me, however, that the similarities in phrasing between "The State of War" and the second *Discourse* would suggest that the manuscript was drafted quite a bit earlier—perhaps during Rousseau's 1754 trip to Geneva. That the manuscript could not have been drafted *prior* to the second *Discourse* is clear from Rousseau's statement in "The State of War" that "I have said before and cannot repeat too often that the error of Hobbes and the *philosophes* is to confuse natural man with the man that they have before their eyes," a statement that obviously refers to the opening theme of the second *Discourse*. For an earlier discussion of Rousseau's drafting of the manuscript, see Vaughan's introduction in Rousseau, *Political Writings*, I:284.

CHAPTER I
WAR AND HUMAN NATURE

1. For this and subsequent citations from "The State of War," see Appendix A; *OC*, III:601–612, 1899–1904.

2. For a recent collection of essays on the theme of Rousseau's relation to Hobbes, see Howard R. Cell and James I. MacAdam, *Rousseau's Response to Hobbes* (New York: Peter Lang, 1988).

3. Cranston, *Jean-Jacques*, 79, 206.

4. Derathé, *Rousseau et la science politique*, 104.

5. Thomas Hobbes, *Leviathan* (New York: Liberal Arts Press, 1958), 24.

6. Ibid., 86–87.

7. Ibid., 87.

8. Ibid., 106–107.

9. Ibid., 108.

10. Ibid.

11. Ibid., 109–114.

12. Ibid., 106, 118, 142.

13. Ibid., 165.

14. Ibid., 169.

15. Derathé, *Rousseau et la science politique*, 101–102.

16. *Encyclopédie ou Dictionnaire raisonné des sciences, des arts, et des métiers*, par une société de gens de lettres, 36 vols. (Lausanne and Berne, 1782), XVII:589. Cited by Derathé, *Rousseau et la science politique*, 104.

17. "Th'ill Times, and Ills born with me, I bemoan: / For Fame had rumour'd, that a Fleet at Sea, / Wou'd cause our Nations Catastrophe: / And hereupon it was my Mother Dear / Did bring forth Twins at once, both Me, and Fear." From Thomas Hobbes, *The Life of Mr. Thomas Hobbes of Malmesbury* (London, 1689), 2.

18. Jean-Jacques Rousseau, *Confessions*, trans. J. M. Cohen (Harmondsworth, England: Penguin, 1953), 19; *OC*, I:7.

19. Ibid., 30; *OC*, I:20.

20. A note about gender. In most of Rousseau's political and educational writings he was referring exclusively to the male members of the human species. In my translation of and references to these writings I have thus often found it necessary to revert to the unmodern practice of using the word "man" and the pronoun "he" to refer to the human beings whom Rousseau is writing about.

21. Jean-Jacques Rousseau, *The First and Second Discourses*, ed. Roger D. Masters, trans. Roger D. Masters and Judith R. Masters (New York: St. Martin's Press, 1964), 62; *OC*, III:28.

22. Ibid., 91; *OC*, III:122.

23. Ibid., *OC*, III:122. Translation mine. Rousseau's critique of Hobbesian natural man is similar to that of Montesquieu, who had earlier stated that Hobbes "attributes to mankind before the establishment of society what can happen but in consequence of this establishment." Montesquieu, *The Spirit of the Laws*, trans. Thomas Nugent (New York: Hafner, 1949), 3–5.

24. Rousseau, *Discourses*, 93; *OC*, III:123.

25. Ibid., 105; *OC*, III:134–135. Some critics have used recent anthropological findings to argue that since hominids probably always lived in groups, Rousseau's hypothesis concerning "solitary" natural man is unfounded and therefore useless. Others have emphasized that the questions about human history that Rousseau raises in the second *Discourse* remain the central questions of evolutionary biology, ethology, and human anthropology. (See Roger Masters, "Jean-Jacques Is Alive and Well: Rousseau and Contemporary Sociobiology," and Robert Wokler, "Perfectible Apes in Decadent Cultures: Rousseau's Anthropology Revisited," *Daedalus* [Summer 1978]: 93–134.) I would argue that Rousseau's account of the state of nature is less important for its scientific veracity than as a normative standard with which to evaluate human change.

26. Rousseau, *Emile*, 80; *OC*, IV:304.

27. Rousseau, *Discourses*, 116; *OC*, III:143.

28. Ibid., 129; *OC*, III:153.

29. Ibid., 222, 175; *OC*, III:219, 189.

30. Ibid., 130; *OC*, III:154.

31. Ibid., 133; *OC*, III:156–157. A similar point is made by Richard E. Leakey and Roger Lewin in their critique of Konrad Lorenz's assumptions about human aggression. "An animal that develops a proclivity for killing its fellows thrusts itself into an evolutionarily disadvantageous position. . . . As the evolutionary success is the production of as many descendants as possible, an innate drive for killing individuals of one's own species would soon have wiped that species out." Richard E. Leakey and Roger Lewin, *Origins* (New York: Dutton, 1977), 197–198.

32. In this section of the second *Discourse*, Rousseau mentions in passing the example of a stag hunt that Kenneth Waltz and others put at the center of their analysis of Rousseau's theory of international relations. At this stage of development, if a group of hunters agreed to cooperate to catch a stag, Rousseau says, and a hare happened to pass by within reach of one of them, it is certain that the hunter would abandon the group to pursue the hare "without scruple," even if it meant jeopardizing the long-term interests of the group. Waltz argues that this fable effectively represents the way that units in any system lacking a central law-enforcing authority will act and that it illustrates what he terms the "third image" of international relations theory in which the cause of war is seen to lie in the system of independent states rather than in human nature or in particular forms of government (see Waltz, *Man, the State, and War*, 170). Although the stag hunt analogy can accurately be applied to Rousseau's understanding of international relations, it should be stressed that the example constitutes a relatively minor section of the second *Discourse* and was never used by Rousseau himself to describe relations among states. The implication in a recent textbook on international relations theory that Rousseau's stag hunt anticipates the use of game theory by foreign policy strategists thus gives a somewhat distorted view of Rousseau's intentions. See Paul R. Viotti and Mark V. Kauppi, *International Relations Theory: Realism, Pluralism, Globalism* (New York: Macmillan, 1987), 49–50.

33. Rousseau, *Discourses*, 147; *OC*, III:168.

34. Ibid., 150–151; *OC*, III:171.

35. Ibid., 151–152; *OC*, III:171.

36. Ibid., 155–157; *OC*, III:174–176.

37. Ibid., 160; *OC*, III:177.

38. Ibid., 160–161; *OC*, III:178–179.

39. Indeed, Rousseau has often been claimed as a precursor of anarchism. For a critique of this claim, which focuses on the *Discourse on the Origin of Inequality*, see Aubrey Rosenberg, "*The Discourse on Inequality*: A Primer for Anarchists?" in *Études sur les "Discours" de Rousseau/Studies on Rousseau's "Discourses,"* ed. Jean Terrasse, Pensé libre, No. 1 (Ottawa: Association nord-américaine des études Jean-Jacques Rousseau, 1988), 141–151.

40. Rousseau, *Social Contract*, 50; *OC*, III:357. Although Locke's name is not mentioned as the object of Rousseau's description of the state of nature either in the second *Discourse* or in "The State of War," Locke's ambiguous comments about the possibility of war in the state of nature make it possible that Rousseau's critique is directed as much against him as against Hobbes and Grotius. See John Locke, *Locke's Two Treatises of Government*, ed. and with an introduction by Peter Laslett (Cambridge: Cambridge University Press, 1967), 296–300.

41. Hinsley, *Power and the Pursuit of Peace*, Chap. 3; Hoffmann, "Rousseau on War and Peace," 317–333.

42. Randolph S. Bourne, *War and the Intellectuals: Collected Essays, 1915–1919*, ed. Carl Resek (New York: Harper Torchbooks, 1964), 69.

43. Hobbes, *Leviathan*, 61.

44. For a discussion of the distinction between "nature" and "convention" (*physis* and *nomos*) in classical political theory, see Ernest Barker's "Introduction" to Aristotle, *The Politics of Aristotle*, ed. and trans. Ernest Barker (New York: Oxford University Press, 1970), xlviii. For fruitful discussions of Hobbes's relationship to classical "liberal" thought, see, for example, C. B. Macpherson, *The Political Theory of Possessive Individualism: Hobbes to Locke* (Oxford: Oxford University Press, 1962), 1–106; George H. Sabine, *A History of Political Theory* (New York: Holt, Rinehart and Winston, 1961), 455–475; and Sheldon S. Wolin, *Politics and Vision: Continuity and Innovation in Western Political Thought* (Boston: Little, Brown, 1960), 239–285.

45. Thomas Hobbes, *Man and Citizen*, ed. and with an introduction by Bernard Gert (Garden City, N.Y.: Doubleday Anchor Books, 1972), 205.

46. Rousseau, *Social Contract*, 46; *OC*, III:351.

47. Ibid., 46–47; *OC*, III:351–352.

48. Ibid., 48; *OC*, III:354.

49. Ibid., 52; *OC*, III:359.

CHAPTER 2

WAR AND THE STATE

1. Hugo Grotius, *The Rights of War and Peace: Selections from De Jure Belli ac Pacis*, trans. W. S. M. Knight. Reprinted in *Peace Projects of the Seventeenth Century* (New York: Garland, 1972), 29. Italics mine.

2. Derathé, *Jean-Jacques Rousseau et la science politique*, 66–78.

3. See my "Introduction."

4. Jean Jacques Rousseau, *The Minor Educational Writings of Jean Jacques Rousseau*, ed. and trans. William Boyd (New York: Teachers College Press, 1962), 37; *OC*, IV:50–51.

5. Rousseau, *Discourses*, 86–87; *OC*, III:118.

6. Rousseau, *Emile*, 458; *OC*, IV:836.

7. Rousseau, *Social Contract*, 47; *OC*, III:352–353. Later in the *Social Contract*, Rousseau implies that Grotius's false principles derive from his fear of offending the monarchs upon whom his livelihood depended: "Grotius—taking refuge in France . . . and wanting to pay court to Louis XIII to whom his book is dedicated—spares nothing to divest the people of all their rights and to endow kings with them as artfully as possible." Ibid., 60; *OC*, III:370.

8. Grotius, *The Rights of War and Peace*, 35.

9. Ibid., 35–36.

10. Rousseau, *Emile*, 458; *OC*, IV:836. Making the same point, Voltaire quipped that if a prince should disband his troops, neglect his fortifications, and spend his time reading Grotius's work on international law, he would certainly not keep his kingdom for long. Cited by Merle Perkins, *Voltaire's Concept of International Order*, Studies on Voltaire and the Eighteenth Century, vol. 36 (Geneva: Institut et Musée Voltaire, 1965), 82.

11. Hugo Grotius, *De Jure Belli ac Pacis*, trans. Francis W. Kelsey, The Classics of International Law, No. 3 (Oxford: Clarendon Press, 1925), 103–106. For this and subsequent citations I have chosen to use a different edition of *De Jure Belli* because the Garland edition (cited in note 1), though a more modern translation, includes only selections and does not contain the full passage cited here.

12. Ibid., 516.

13. Rousseau, *Social Contract*, 47; *OC*, III:353.

14. Grotius, *De Jure Belli*, 635, 639.

15. Ibid., 648–649.

16. Ibid., 690–691.

17. James Turner Johnson, in *Ideology, Reason, and the Limitation of War: Religious and Secular Concepts, 1200–1740* (Princeton: Princeton University Press, 1975), shows that the medieval just-war theory was far from being a uniform doctrine and that, from early on, it was a product of both secular and religious influences.

18. James Turner Johnson, *Just War Tradition and the Restraint of War: A Moral and Historical Inquiry* (Princeton: Princeton University Press, 1981), 85.

19. Grotius, *De Jure Belli*, 15.

20. Rousseau, *Discourses*, 94; *OC*, III:124.

21. Ibid., 95; *OC*, III:125.

22. Ibid., 133; *OC*, III:150–157.

23. For a close look at what Rousseau does borrow from the "natural law" school of jurisprudence, see Derathé, *Rousseau et la science politique*, esp. 151–168. For a history of natural law terminology, see 386–397.

24. Rousseau, *OC*, II:816–817. Translation mine. Ironically, Rousseau has a footnote to this line indicating that the "barbarian peoples" he refers to here are the Corsicans, a reference that contradicts Rousseau's later advice to the Corsicans to "depend on yourselves only." Jean-Jacques Rousseau, "Constitutional Project for Corsica," in *Rousseau: Political Writings*, trans. and ed. F. M. Watkins (Edinburgh: Thomas Nelson and Sons, 1953), 280; *OC*, III:903.

25. Rousseau, *Discourses*, 46; *OC*, III:15.

26. For some relatively recent works that stress this interpretation, see, for example, Crocker, *Rousseau's "Social Contract,"* 6; Jean Bethke Elshtain, *Women and War* (New York: Basic Books, 1987), 59–63; and Hannah Arendt, *On Revolution* (New York: Penguin, 1977), 97.

27. Rousseau, *OC*, III:54–55, 91. I am indebted to Launay's *Rousseau, écrivain politique* for most of these insights on the development of Rousseau's political consciousness.

28. Quoted in Perkins, *Voltaire's Concept of International Order*, 81.

29. The digressive nature of this part of Rousseau's manuscript on "The State of War" may account for its getting separated from the longer fragment. See my Introduction.

30. Gagnebin, "Un inédit de Rousseau," in *De Ronsard à Breton*, 105.

31. W. B. Gallie, ed., *Philosophers of Peace and War: Kant, Clausewitz, Marx, Engels and Tolstoy* (Cambridge: Cambridge University Press, 1978), 50. While stressing the political aspect of war, Rousseau never implies that politics *is* war. For an interesting discussion of a dangerous convergence of these concepts in the thought of Clausewitz, Lenin, and Mao, see Elshtain, *Women and War*, 76–86.

32. For an illuminating discussion of this issue, see Carter, *Rousseau and the Problem of War*, 108–111.

33. Cobban, *Rousseau and the Modern State*, 182–184.

34. Robert Derathé stresses this aspect of Rousseau's thought in his fine article "Jean-Jacques Rousseau et le progrès des idées humanitaires du XVIe au XVIIIe siècle," *Revue internationale de la Croix Rouge*, October 1958, 527.

35. For a thorough analysis of the just-war tradition, see Johnson, *Just War Tradition and the Restraint of War*.

36. Grotius, *De Jure Belli*, 639; and Rousseau, *Social Contract*, 51; *OC*, III: 357.

37. Rousseau, *OC*, III:615.

38. Rousseau, *Social Contract*, 50–51; *OC*, III:357. In making these distinctions, Rousseau may well have been influenced by the views of Montesquieu, who, in *The Spirit of the Laws*, argued that "from the destruction of the state it does not at all follow that the people who compose it ought also to be destroyed. The state is the association of men, not the men themselves; the citizen may perish, and the man remain" (Montesquieu, *Spirit of the Laws*, 135); and by Locke, who argued, in the *Second Treatise of Government*, that a lawful conqueror "has an Absolute Power over the Lives or Fortunes of those who by an Unjust War have forfeited them; but not over the Lives or Fortunes of those, who engaged not in the War, nor over the Possessions even of those, who were

actually engaged in it" (Locke, *Locke's Two Treatises of Government*, 406–409). Recently, Michael Walzer has argued that Montesquieu's and Rousseau's attempt to restrict the rights of war to actual combatants "is still too permissive a view," for "if the citizen is killed or the state destroyed, something of the man dies too" (Michael Walzer, *Just and Unjust Wars: A Moral Argument with Historical Illustrations* [New York: Basic Books, 1977], 113). Walzer's qualification is valid in a context that assumes the political rights of individuals, but, as Robert Derathé points out in an early article analyzing Rousseau's place in the just-war tradition, it is also important to see Rousseau's views in the context of the political thought of his time. Looked at from a historical perspective, it is clear that Rousseau's definition of who constitutes the enemy was much more limited than that of Grotius or even of the Catholic just-war theorists Suarez and Victoria. Derathé, "Jean-Jacques Rousseau et le progrès des idées humanitaires," 526–527. For a more detailed evaluation of Rousseau's contribution to the principle of noncombatant immunity, see Lassudrie-Duchène, *Rousseau et le droit des gens*, 379.

39. Rousseau, *Social Contract*, 51; *OC*, III:158. By not distinguishing whether the defeated had unjustly perpetrated the war or not, Rousseau's principles here go well beyond those of Locke, who argued that defeat of those who undertake an unjust war is the sole basis for despotic rule: "Despotical Power . . . is the effect . . . of Forfeiture, which the aggressor makes of his own Life, when he puts himself into a state of war with another" (Locke, *Two Treatises of Government*, 400–401). This point is made by Derathé in "Rousseau et des idées humanitaires," 527.

40. Rousseau, *OC*, III:615.

41. Rousseau, *Social Contract*, 51; *OC*, III:358.

42. See, for example, Hofer, *L'influence de J.-J. Rousseau sur le droit de la guerre*, and Lassudrie-Duchène, *Rousseau et le droit des gens*, esp. 330–392.

43. Rousseau, *Social Contract*, 51; *OC*, III:358.

44. Rousseau, *OC*, III:614–615.

45. Ibid.

46. See, especially, Rousseau, *Discourses*, 167; *OC*, III:183. Locke had also argued that no one has the right to enslave himself to another man. See Locke, *Two Treatises of Government*, 302.

47. Rousseau, *Social Contract*, 50–51; *OC*, III:358.

48. Ibid., 51–52; *OC*, III:358.

49. Rousseau, *Rousseau: Political Writings*, ed. Watkins, 237; *OC*, III:1013.

50. See, in particular, Launay, *Rousseau, écrivain politique*; and Miller, *Rousseau, Dreamer of Democracy*.

CHAPTER 3
A GENERAL WILL OF THE HUMAN RACE?

1. As Patrick Riley has pointed out, the term *volonté générale* had been used by a number of seventeenth-century religious writers to describe God's will, but it gradually became more secularized as a concept in the course of the eighteenth century (Patrick Riley, "The General Will Before Rousseau," *Politi-*

cal Theory, November 1978, 485–516). Hannah Arendt and others implicate these religious origins of the concept when they blame Rousseau for the excesses of the French Revolution and claim that "the general will of Rousseau and Robespierre is still this divine will which needs only to will in order to produce a law" (Arendt, *On Revolution*, 183). Other interpreters, such as Roger Masters and James Miller, stress the extent to which Rousseau's notion of the general will offers a potentially useful solution to the classical secular problem of rationally reconciling what is good for one's group and what is good for oneself. See Roger Masters and Christopher Kelly, "Rousseau's *Social Contract*, the Common Good, and Guilt," paper delivered at the biannual colloquium of the North American Association for the Study of Jean-Jacques Rousseau, at Columbia University, 30 May 1987 (publication forthcoming); and Miller, *Rousseau, Dreamer of Democracy*, 62–63. James MacAdam likewise implies that the general will is what brings together *any* association of men united in a common interest and that the general will of the social contract is simply the most general will of a particular civil society. See James I. MacAdam, "Hobbes v. Rousseau: Man v. Law," in Cell and MacAdam, *Rousseau's Response to Hobbes*, 26, 44; see also Terrence Edward Cook, "Rousseau: Education and Politics," Ph.D. dissertation, Princeton University, 1971, 195–198.

2. For a beautifully written and well-balanced account of Diderot and Rousseau's relationship, see Arthur M. Wilson, *Diderot* (New York: Oxford University Press, 1972), esp. Chaps. 5, 6, 19, 22. For specifics about Rousseau's and Diderot's interests in music, see René Hubert, *Rousseau et l'Encyclopédie: Essai sur la formation des idées politiques de Rousseau (1752–1756)* (Paris: J. Gamber, 1928), 21.

3. Rousseau, *Confessions*, 324; *OC*, I:347.

4. It is not a question here of trying to fathom Diderot's actual convictions about the general will. While the article on "Natural Right" appeared over Diderot's name, there is little evidence that he believed what he wrote about the concept. As Lelend Thielemann in "Diderot and Hobbes" points out, the article does not accurately reflect Diderot's skepticism, and its main ideas may have been borrowed (or even copied) from Buffier's *De l'origine & de la nature du droit & de l'équité* (1732). See Otis E. Fellows and Norman L. Torrey, eds., *Diderot Studies* (Syracuse: Syracuse University Press, 1952), 2:247–250.

5. Diderot's article on "Droit Naturel" appears in Rousseau, *Political Writings*, ed. Vaughan, I:429–433. Translation mine.

6. Twentieth-century scholars have generally asserted that Diderot's violent reasoner referred not to Hobbes but to *Rousseau*, and this erroneous assertion, I believe, has colored their interpretation of the differences between Diderot's and Rousseau's conception of the general will. Both C. E. Vaughan and Roger Masters argue that Diderot's intention to attribute the role of the violent reasoner to Rousseau can be shown by the fact that later in the "Geneva Manuscript" Rousseau "takes on" the role of the violent reasoner, and because in two of his letters Rousseau makes it clear that he felt implicated in Diderot's use of the epithet. (See *Political Writings*, I:424, 427; and Masters, *Political Philosophy of Rousseau*, 262.) But Rousseau's later defensiveness toward Diderot does not necessarily support the claim that Diderot had Rousseau in mind when he cre-

ated the dialogue of the violent reasoner. For, in 1755, not only were Rousseau and Diderot still close friends, but Rousseau had recently, in his *Discourse on the Origin of Inequality*, publicly refuted the Hobbesian view of original natural man as a "violent reasoner."

In the paragraph of the article on "Natural Right" that follows the dialogue of the violent reasoner, however, there may be a teasing reference to Rousseau, for there Diderot asserts that both a just man and an evil man would have to admit that the search for a solution to the violent reasoner's dilemma must be rational and that anyone who refuses to believe in human reason "ought to be treated by the rest of his species as a fearful beast." Here Diderot may indeed be making a jab at Rousseau—particularly given Rousseau's portrayal, in the second *Discourse*, of man as an instinctive rather than a rational being (and his claim in its preface that, analogous to the disfigurement wrought by time upon the statue of Glaucus, the effect of social progress had been to make man resemble a "ferocious beast"). While Rousseau may have been the model for Diderot's "fearful beast," still it is unlikely that he could have been cast by Diderot as a "violent reasoner." This is an important distinction that Rousseau scholars, and even Rousseau himself in his periods of feeling persecuted by his former friends, often failed to make.

7. Rousseau, *Political Writings*, ed. Vaughan, I:432.

8. Ibid., 433.

9. For Rousseau's affinity for Plato and the close relationship between the *Social Contract* and the *Republic*, see Vaughan's "Introduction" to Rousseau, *Political Writings*, ed. Vaughan, I:1–3; and Masters's "Introduction" to *Social Contract*, 18–20. For an imaginative discussion of the parallels between Rousseau's work and a number of Socratic and biblical sources, see Madeleine B. Ellis, *Rousseau's Socratic Aemilian Myths: A Literary Collation of "Emile" and the "Social Contract"* (Columbus: Ohio State University Press, 1977).

10. Rousseau, "Geneva Manuscript," 157; *OC*, III:281.

11. Ibid., 158; *OC*, III:282.

12. Ibid.

13. Ibid., 158–159; *OC*, III:283.

14. Ibid., 159–160; *OC*, III:284.

15. Ibid., 160; *OC*, III:285.

16. Gerardo Zampaglione, *The Idea of Peace in Antiquity*, trans. Richard Dunn (Notre Dame: University of Notre Dame Press, 1973), 92.

17. Rousseau, "Geneva Manuscript," 160; *OC*, III:285.

18. Ibid., 161; *OC*, III:286.

19. Diderot was often referred to as "the philosopher" by his friends. See Wilson, *Diderot*, 70–71, 174.

20. Rousseau, "Geneva Manuscript," 161; *OC*, III:286.

21. Ibid.; *OC*, III:286.

22. Plato, *The Republic of Plato*, trans. Allan Bloom (New York: Basic Books, 1968), 35.

23. Rousseau, "Geneva Manuscript," 162–163; *OC*, III:288–289. I have added spacing for emphasis.

24. For an interpretation that stresses the pessimistic implications of Rousseau's writings, see Frederick Watkins's introduction to Rousseau, *Political Writings*, xxx–xxxiv.

25. For a summary of the criticism of this aspect of Rousseau's thought, see Cobban, *Rousseau and the Modern State*, 13–31.

26. Rousseau, "Geneva Manuscript," 161–162; *OC*, III:287.

27. For a contemporary description of how involvement in local community concerns can develop into a broader consciousness of global issues, see Robert N. Bellah et al., *Habits of the Heart: Individualism and Commitment in American Life* (Berkeley: University of California Press, 1985), 158–163, 192–195.

28. Rousseau, *Social Contract*, 47; *OC*, III:351.

29. Ibid., 53; *OC*, III:360.

30. Ibid., 52; *OC*, III:359.

31. Ibid., 53; *OC*, III:360.

32. Ibid., 64; *OC*, III:375.

33. Ibid., 53; *OC*, III:360–361.

34. Ibid., 55–56; *OC*, III:364.

35. Miller, *Rousseau, Dreamer of Democracy*, 62.

36. Rousseau, *Social Contract*, 66; *OC*, III:378–379.

37. Ibid., 61; *OC*, III:371.

38. Ibid., 55; *OC*, III:363.

39. Ibid., 61; *OC*, III:371.

40. Ibid., 67; *OC*, III:380.

41. For a discussion of the role of Rousseau's legislator that stresses its scope and importance more than I do here, see Hilail Gildin, *Rousseau's "Social Contract": The Design of the Argument* (Chicago: University of Chicago Press, 1983), 67–91.

42. Rousseau, "Political Economy," 212; *OC*, III:245. In making a similar point, Terrence Cook argues that one can find in Rousseau's *Essay on the Origin of Languages* an analogy for the gradual development within a people of more universal concepts of justice. As Cook reads it, the essay suggests that while sentiments of compassion and pity were originally confined to the intimate circle of the family because of limited cognitive learning experiences, gradually such notions came to be extended to include a collectivity of many families; eventually, "when the social relations of this people formed by widened compassionate identification are ordered by humanly contrived laws, a civil society is formed." In the analysis that follows, Cook argues that "the pattern becomes clear: in Rousseau's theory, love of oneself is a precondition for love of one's family; and love of one's family is a precondition for love of one's people or compatriots" (Cook, "Rousseau: Education and Politics," 167–169). Although I generally agree with Cook's interpretation, it seems to me that he may be reading a bit too much into the *Essay on the Origin of Languages* about the political role of the family. For interpretations that stress the complexity of the relationship between family life and political life in the thought of Rousseau, see Jean Elshtain, *Mediations on Modern Political Thought* (New York: Praeger, 1986), 37–

54; Philip Abbott, *The Family on Trial: Special Relationships in Modern Political Thought* (University Park: Pennsylvania State University Press, 1981), 39–58; and Nicole Fermon, "The Politics of Sentiment: Rousseau's Teaching on the Family and the State," Ph.D. dissertation, Columbia University, 1988.

43. Ibid., 213; *OC*, III:246. This passage relates closely to Rousseau's assertion, in "The State of War," that the actions dictated by the general will enable one to "judge whether the being which produced them is well or poorly constituted." See Chap. 2.

44. Rousseau, "Geneva Manuscript," 191; *OC*, III:329.

45. For an account of realist international relations, see Hans J. Morgenthau, *Politics Among Nations: The Struggle for Power and Peace* (New York: Knopf, 1960).

CHAPTER 4
POLITICAL MAN AND PERPETUAL PEACE

1. Rousseau, "Geneva Manuscript," 161–62; *OC*, III:187.
2. Rousseau, *Confessions*, 394; *OC*, I:423.
3. Rousseau, *OC*, III:657.
4. Ibid., 664–665.
5. Rousseau, *Confessions*, 380; *OC*, I:407–408.
6. Ibid.; *OC*, I:408.
7. Rousseau, *OC*, III:672–682.
8. Rousseau, *Confessions*, 393; *OC*, I:422.
9. Ibid., 394; *OC*, I:423.
10. Among the several surveys of this history are Elizabeth V. Souleyman, *The Vision of World Peace in Seventeenth and Eighteenth-Century France* (New York: G. P. Putnam's, 1941); G. Putnam's introduction to Rousseau, *L'État de Guerre and Projet de Paix Perpétuelle*; Michael Howard, *War and the Liberal Conscience* (New Brunswick, N.J.: Rutgers University Press, 1986), 13–30; and James Turner Johnson, *The Quest for Peace: Three Moral Traditions in Western Cultural History* (Princeton: Princeton University Press, 1987). Johnson makes the point that the focus on peace plans in the seventeenth and eighteenth centuries is somewhat ironic, for in comparison to the religious wars of the preceding era and the revolutionary wars of the later period, the "sovereigns' wars" of 1648–1789 were relatively limited in aim, scope, and impact on the civilian population. See Johnson, *Quest for Peace*, 199–200.

11. Abbé de Saint-Pierre, *Projet pour rendre la paix perpétuelle en Europe*, présenté par Simone Goyard-Fabre (Paris: Editions Garnier Frères, 1981).

12. Rousseau, *OC*, III:658–659.

13. Ibid., 655–656. Italics mine. This passage includes a shrewd comment by Rousseau concerning state secrets: "We must not let ourselves be intimidated by what are called political secrets, which, if they were concerned with something positive, would not have been hidden from us. Such secrets are either dangerous or nonexistent so long as one's aim is to make the people happy —which is or at least should be the goal of all government. Achieving that goal has nothing mysterious about it, but such sinister shadiness hides motives

which are dangerous rather than incomprehensible; we are told that things are obscure only out of the fear that we might try to find out for ourselves." My translation.

14. Unless otherwise indicated, all quotations in this section are from my translation of Rousseau's "Extrait" of the Abbé de Saint-Pierre's *Projet de paix perpétuelle*, Appendix B; *OC*, III:563–589.

15. Although Rousseau uses the word *confédération* throughout the "Extrait," it is clear from his examples of confederations (which range from the Greek Amphictyonic League to the Estates-General) that the term refers to a broad spectrum of political structures, including what we today would call federations. In his article on "Political Economy," moreover, it is interesting to note that he apparently uses the words "compact" and "confederation" interchangeably. See Rousseau, "Political Economy," 23, 220, 230; *OC*, III: 246, 256, 270.

16. Rousseau, *OC*, III:658.

17. For a summary of the "internationalist" tradition, see Hedley Bull, *The Anarchical Society: A Study of Order in World Politics* (New York: Columbia University Press, 1977), esp. 21–46, 238–240; for a summary of the "liberal pacifist" tradition, see Howard, *War and the Liberal Conscience*, esp. 13–30.

18. Rousseau, *Social Contract*, 58; *OC*, III:367.

19. Ibid., 54; *OC*, III:363.

20. Ibid., 55, 59; *OC*, III:363, 368.

21. For a convincing statement of this argument, see Cobban, *Rousseau and the Modern State*, 186.

22. Rousseau, *Social Contract*, 104; *OC*, III:431.

23. The censor wanted to replace "I would not dare to reply, as the Abbé de Saint-Pierre does, that the true glory of princes consists in procuring the happiness of their subjects" with "I would dare reply." Rousseau objected to this change, but offered the following clever compromise: "I can absolutely not say 'I would dare' because it is not true that I would dare. But I propose an accommodation to this phrase: have 'I would not dare' left in the text and have 'I would dare' inserted as errata. The text would be my own thought; the errata that of the censor." See Rousseau, *OC*, III:1550.

24. It is clear from these passages that Michael Howard, in *War and the Liberal Conscience*, is misreading Rousseau when he argues (on p. 133) that Rousseau "sardonically" put forth "the dissolution of the sovereign state" as a solution to the problem of war. Howard's interpretation seems to result from a faulty intermingling of passages from "The State of War" and the *Project for Perpetual Peace*.

25. Rousseau, *Correspondance complète*, VI:90. The letter is dated 4 May 1759. Cited by Sven Stelling-Michaud in Rousseau, *OC*, III:cxxxii–cxxxiii.

26. Rousseau, *OC*, III:cxxxiii.

27. For an example of a peace plan that was not widely read, see the fascinating account of a project for peace written by a galley slave who successfully gained the attention and assistance of Benjamin Franklin while he was American ambassador to France. George Simpson Eddy, ed., *A Project of Universal and Perpetual Peace. Written by Pierre-André Gargaz, a former Galley-Slave,*

and Printed by Benjamin Franklin at Passy in the Year 1782 (New York: George Simpson Eddy, 1922).

28. Rousseau, *OC*, III:cxxxvi–cxxxvii.

29. Ibid., cxliv; Eric Foner, *Tom Paine and Revolutionary America* (New York: Oxford University Press, 1976), 77.

30. There are other differences as well. Like Hobbes, Kant stresses the similarity between the state of war and the state of nature, whereas Rousseau argued, as we saw in Chapter 1, that man in the state of nature is solitary and at peace. Kant also believed, unlike Rousseau but similar to Bentham and others, that world trade would help promote world peace, whereas Rousseau always tended to criticize commerce as a source of inequality and conflict. Finally, whereas Kant implied that the establishment of "law-governed external relations with other states" must occur *prior* to the establishment of "perfect civil constitutions," Rousseau, as is evident in his dialogue with Diderot over the general will, sees "willing generally" in the small republic necessarily prior to "willing generally" in the large one. Despite these differences, it is probable that Kant's original inspiration for considering the possibilities of perpetual peace came from Rousseau; as Kant points out in the *Idea for a Universal History*, "Rousseau's preference for the state of savagery does not appear so very mistaken if only we leave out of consideration this last stage which our species still has to surmount. We are cultivated to a high degree by art and science. We are civilised to the point of excess in all kinds of social courtesies and proprieties. But we are still a long way from the point where we could consider ourselves morally mature. . . . But as long as states apply all their resources to their vain and violent schemes of expansion, . . . no progress in this direction can be expected." Immanuel Kant, *Kant's Political Writings*, ed. Hans Reiss (Cambridge: Cambridge University Press, 1970), 49. For recent discussions of Kant's *Perpetual Peace*, see Howard, *War and the Liberal Conscience*, 25–27; Gallie, *Philosophers of Peace and War*, 8–36; Stanley Hoffmann, "Kant, Liberalism, and War," *American Political Science Review* 55 (June 1962): 331–340; and Hinsley, *Power and the Pursuit of Peace*, 62–80.

31. See Lassudrie-Duchène, *Jean-Jacques Rousseau et le droit des gens*; G. Lowes Dickinson's introduction to "A Project of Perpetual Peace: Rousseau's Essay," in *Peace Projects of the Eighteenth Century*, xvi–xxii; Vaughan, *Political Writings of Rousseau*, I:363; and Souleyman, *Vision of World Peace*, 91–92, 201.

32. Unless otherwise indicated, this quote and subsequent quotes in this section are from my translation of Rousseau's "Jugement" of the Abbé de Saint Pierre's *Projet de paix perpétuelle*, Appendix C; *OC*, III:590–600.

33. For a discussion of the various roles "the legislator" can have in Rousseau's political theory, see Gildin, *Rousseau's "Social Contract,"* 72.

34. Italics mine.

35. As Roger Masters indicates, Rousseau's use of a line from Virgil's *Aeneid* as the epigraph to the *Social Contract* implies that in the real world even a social contract may need to be instituted by force. The Latin epigraph, *"Foederis eaguas, dicamus leges,"* means "In an equitable federation, we will make laws." However, the line comes from a speech by the King of Latium, whose army

is defeated by Aeneas, paving the way for the founding of Rome on "the right of the strongest." Rousseau, *Social Contract*, 132 n. 3.

36. Rousseau, *Confessions*, 394; *OC*, I:423.

37. Rousseau, *OC*, III:600.

38. Ibid., 635.

39. Ibid., 637.

40. Ibid., 637–638.

41. See, for example, Rousseau, *Discourses*, 80 (*OC*, III:113), and *Rousseau, Juge de Jean-Jacques* (*OC*, I:935).

42. Rousseau, *Emile*, 42, 194; *OC*, IV:252, 468.

43. Rousseau, *Discourses*, 162; *OC*, III:180.

44. Ibid., 172; *OC*, III:187.

45. For a recent discussion of the use of Rousseau's works by the *sans culottes* of the French Revolution and for a review of the literature on the revolutionary import of Rousseau's writing, see Miller, *Rousseau, Dreamer of Democracy*, esp. 1–13; see also papers on the theme "Rousseau and the Revolution" delivered at the biannual colloquium of the North American Association for the study of Jean-Jacques Rousseau, held in Montreal in May 1989. Publication of the association's *Proceedings* is forthcoming.

46. Rousseau, *OC*, III:cxxxix.

CHAPTER 5

CIVIC EDUCATION AND NATIONAL DEFENSE

1. For background information on Poland in the eighteenth century, I have relied on C. E. Vaughan's "Introduction" to *Considérations sur le Gouvernement de Pologne*, in *The Political Writings of Jean-Jacques Rousseau*, II:360–390; F. M. Watkins's "Editorial Note," in Rousseau, *Rousseau's Political Writings*, ed. and trans. Watkins, xxxv; Norman Davies, *God's Playground: A History of Poland*, 2 vols. (New York: Columbia University Press, 1982); J. G. Pounds, *Poland between East and West* (Princeton, N.J.: Van Nostrand, 1964); and Michael Dobbs, K. S. Karol, and Dessa Trevisan, *Poland, Solidarity, Walesa* (New York: McGraw-Hill, 1981).

2. There is an excellent chronology of Rousseau's entire life in the Pléiade edition of the *Oeuvres complètes*, I:ci–cxvii. See also Jean Guéhenno, *Jean-Jacques Rousseau*, trans. John and Doreen Weightman, 2 vols. (London: Routledge and Kegan Paul, 1966), vol. II.

3. Rousseau, *OC*, III:ccxxxv, 1740.

4. Rousseau, *Political Writings*, ed. Vaughan, II:410.

5. Rousseau, *Political Writings*, ed. and trans. Watkins, 159; *OC*, III:953.

6. Ibid., 167; *OC*, III:959.

7. Rousseau had expressed similar hopes for Corsica before its popular rebellion against Genoa was effectively quenched by France. See ibid., xxxvii, 277–330; *OC*, III:901–950. There are many similarities between Rousseau's *Constitutional Project for Corsica* and his *Considerations on the Government of Poland*, but because the latter is the more substantial work, it is the one that I have chosen to focus on here.

8. Ibid., 160; *OC*, III:953–954.

9. Ibid., 160–161; *OC*, III:954.

10. Ibid., 161; *OC*, III:954. Here and elsewhere, I have substituted the word "homeland" for Watkins's word "fatherland" as the translation of *patrie*. Although "fatherland" may be the more accurate translation (since the root of *patrie* is *pater*, or "father"), the word is so loaded with modern imperialistic and paternalistic connotations that I believe it distorts Rousseau's meaning. "Homeland," however, has the advantage of stressing a nonexpansionist aspect of civic loyalty—an element that Rousseau believed essential for Poland's survival.

11. J. G. A. Pocock, *The Machiavellian Moment: Florentine Political Thought and the Atlantic Republican Tradition* (Princeton: Princeton University Press, 1975), 157.

12. Ibid., 194–200.

13. Niccolò Machiavelli, *The Prince* and *The Discourses* (New York: Modern Library, 1950), 119.

14. Rousseau, *Political Writings*, ed. and trans. Watkins, 193; *OC*, III:979.

15. Ibid., 198; *OC*, III:983. Although Rousseau takes care to spell out how Poland's representative system might be reformed, one must remember that in the *Social Contract* Rousseau argues against representation on principle. See Rousseau, *Social Contract*, 102; *OC*, III:429.

16. Ibid., 208; *OC*, III:991.

17. Ibid., 209; *OC*, III:991.

18. Machiavelli, *Discourses*, 397.

19. Rousseau, *Political Writings*, ed. and trans. Watkins, 186–187; *OC*, III:974.

20. James Harrington, *The Political Works of James Harrington*, ed. J. G. A. Pocock (Cambridge: Cambridge University Press, 1977), 181.

21. Rousseau, *Political Writings*, ed. and trans. Watkins, 253; *OC*, III:1026.

22. Rousseau, *Social Contract*, 121–122; *OC*, III:456.

23. Rousseau, *Political Writings*, ed. and trans. Watkins, 267; *OC*, III:1036–1037.

24. Ibid., 268; *OC*, III:1037.

25. See Appendix A; *OC*, III:605.

26. Ibid.; *OC*, III:606.

27. Rousseau, *Political Writings*, ed. and trans. Watkins, 167; *OC*, III:959.

28. Ibid., 167–168; *OC*, III:959.

29. Ibid., 162; *OC*, III:955.

30. Ibid., 168 (*OC*, III:960); and Rousseau, *Emile*, 40 (*OC*, I:250).

31. Rousseau, *Political Writings*, ed. and trans. Watkins, 169; *OC*, III:960–961.

32. Ibid., 171; *OC*, III:962.

33. Rousseau, *Emile*, 39; *OC*, IV:249.

34. Rousseau, *Political Writings*, ed. and trans. Watkins, 170; *OC*, III:961.

35. Rousseau, "Political Economy," 222; *OC*, III:259.

36. Rousseau, *Political Writings*, ed. and trans. Watkins, 176; *OC*, III:966.

37. Rousseau, *Emile*, 39–40; *OC*, IV:249.

38. Rousseau, *Political Writings*, ed. and trans. Watkins, 176; *OC*, III:966.
39. Ibid., 176–177; *OC*, III:966.
40. Ibid., 177; *OC*, III:966–967.
41. Ibid., 178; *OC*, III:968.
42. Ibid., 179; *OC*, III:968.
43. Cook, "Rousseau: Education and Politics," 102.
44. Rousseau, "Political Economy," 222; *OC*, III:259.
45. Ibid., 219; *OC*, III:255.
46. See also Rousseau, *Social Contract*, 129; *OC*, III:458–459.
47. Rousseau, *Political Writings*, ed. and trans. Watkins, 179; *OC*, III:968.
48. Ibid., 179; *OC*, III:968–969.
49. Ibid., 223–224; *OC*, III:1003.
50. A similar point was made in a series of lectures given at Teachers College, Columbia University, in the fall of 1985 by Michael Manley, the prime minister of Jamaica who was then out of office. He is an eloquent spokesman for Third World countries seeking to create independent paths of economic development that will help them overcome the debilitating dependencies left by a colonial past. Manley's talk stressed that the economic structures developed to serve wealthy capitalist nations are not necessarily suited to the political needs of younger or poorer nations. As Manley pointed out in criticizing some of the policies of the International Monetary Fund, "First World medicine doesn't always work on the Third World patient."
51. Rousseau, *Political Writings*, ed. and trans. Watkins, 224; *OC*, III:1003. In a footnote to the *Social Contract*, Rousseau makes a similar point: "Any type of foreign commerce, says the Marquis d'Argenson, creates almost nothing but a deceptive utility for a kingdom in general. It can enrich some private individuals, even some towns; but the whole nation gains nothing from it and the people is not better off because of it." Rousseau, *Social Contract*, 76; *OC*, III:392.
52. Ibid., 224–225; *OC*, III:1003–1004.
53. Ibid., 226–227; *OC*, III:1004–1005.
54. Ibid., 229; *OC*, III:1007.
55. Ibid., 230–231; *OC*, III:1008–1009. For further commentary on Rousseau's relationship with the Physiocrats, see Lucio Colletti, "Rousseau as Critic of 'Civil Society,'" *From Rousseau to Lenin: Studies in Ideology and Society* (New York: Monthly Review Press, 1972), 157–163.
56. Rousseau, *Political Writings*, ed. and trans. Watkins, 231; *OC*, III:1008.
57. Manley, lecture at Teachers College, 1985.
58. Rousseau, *Political Writings*, ed. and trans. Watkins, 235; *OC*, III:1011.
59. Ibid., 236; *OC*, III:1013.
60. Dietrich Fischer, *Preventing War in the Nuclear Age* (Totowa, N.J.: Rowman & Allanheld, 1984), 29. Although the capacity to inflict harm and the capacity to resist harm are always closely linked, the distinction is an important one to keep alive in any discussion of the meaning of security. For a thought-provoking discussion of defensive vs. offensive weapons systems, see also Freeman Dyson, *Weapons and Hope* (New York: Harper & Row, 1980), esp. 272–295.

61. Rousseau, *Political Writings*, ed. and trans. Watkins, 237, 242; *OC*, III: 1013, 1017. (See note on p. 1793.)

62. Pocock, *The Machiavellian Moment*, 198–199. In the *Social Contract*, Rousseau makes the comment that "there have been States so constituted that the necessity for conquests entered into their constitution itself, and that were forced to grow endlessly to maintain themselves. Perhaps they took great pride in this happy necessity, though it showed them, along with the limit of their size, the inevitable moment of their downfall." Rousseau, *Social Contract*, 73; *OC*, III:388.

63. Rousseau, *Political Writings*, ed. and trans. Watkins, 237; *OC*, III:1015–1016.

64. Ibid., 239–240; *OC*, III:1015. For a lively and thought-provoking contemporary account of the Swiss army (which in some ways remarkably resembles Rousseau's description of it in the eighteenth century), see John McPhee, *La Place de la Concorde Suisse* (New York: Farrar, Straus and Giroux, 1983). For a more serious proposal for civilian-based defense in Europe, see Gene Sharp, *Making Europe Unconquerable: The Potential of Civilian-based Deterrence and Defence* (Cambridge, Mass.: Ballinger, 1985).

65. Rousseau, *Political Writings*, ed. and trans. Watkins, 239–240; *OC*, III: 1015.

66. Ibid., 242–243; *OC*, III:1017–1018. I have substituted the word "terrain" for Watkins word "country" as the translation of *pays* here, for the notion of invading a "country" might give the mistaken impression that Rousseau was recommending offensive military tactics for the Polish cavalry.

67. Ibid., 243; *OC*, III:1018.

68. Ibid., 271; *OC*, III:1039.

69. As Norman Davies has recently pointed out, Rousseau's words were heeded in Poland "long after the cumulative wisdom of all the other *philosophes* had been completely forgotten." Davies, *God's Playground*, 369. On the other hand, part of their ability to resist Russian imperialism is of course to be found in the Polish people's strong faith in Catholicism, a force that Rousseau had little respect for and that he completely left out of his *Considerations*. In Rousseau's defense, it must be admitted that Catholicism in the eighteenth century could not have been perceived as having the same influence on popular liberation movements as it does today.

CHAPTER 6
NATURAL EDUCATION AND GEOPOLITICAL VIRTUE

1. For an insightful discussion of Rousseau's perception of authority, see Robert McClintock, "Rousseau and the Dilemma of Authority," *History of Education Quarterly*, Fall 1974, 313–321.

2. Rousseau, *Emile*, 40; *OC*, IV:250. As has been the case with the study of Rousseau's political writings, the study of Rousseau's pedagogical writings has sometimes suffered from the tendency to apply ideological categories of "individualism" and "socialism" to his principles. In William Boyd's otherwise

excellent and comprehensive work, *The Educational Theory of Jean-Jacques Rousseau* (New York: Russell and Russell, 1911), this tendency obscures Rousseau's insistence that different political settings call for different methods of education. Boyd presents Rousseau as having contradictory educational aims when in actuality Rousseau had dual aims: Civic education is appropriate for one kind of setting, natural education for another.

3. Rousseau, *Emile*, 35; *OC*, IV:243.

4. Although differing in many ways in their understanding of education and human psychology, Rousseau's "divided" modern man is similar at many points to the narcissistic personality described by Christopher Lasch. The final product of bourgeois individualism, the narcissist is characterized by inner emptiness, false posturing, illusions of grandeur, and an inability to accept the limits of the human condition. See Christopher Lasch, *The Culture of Narcissism: American Life in an Age of Diminishing Expectations* (New York: Warner Books, 1979), 22–23, 51–61, 118–119. These are precisely the characteristics that Rousseau tries to avoid in the education of Emile.

5. Rousseau, *Emile*, 39, 40; *OC*, IV:248, 250.

6. My understanding of Rousseau's response to Locke's views on education has been broadened by Joseph Featherstone's article "Rousseau and Modernity," *Daedalus*, Summer 1978, 167–192. For other comparisons of Locke's and Rousseau's political assumptions, see Colletti, *From Rousseau to Lenin*, 171–175; Shklar, *Men and Citizens*, 36–57; and Ellenburg, *Rousseau's Political Philosophy*, 35–55. See also, John Dewey's acknowledgment of his debt to Rousseau, in *Democracy and Education* (New York: The Free Press, 1944), 91–94.

7. John Locke, *The Educational Writings of John Locke*, ed. James L. Axtell (Cambridge: Cambridge University Press, 1968), 123–133, 139, 180, 270, 206.

8. Ibid., 148, 177.

9. Ibid., 140, 146. For a more extensive list of the "contradictions" Rousseau found in Locke's *Thoughts Concerning Education*, see Ellenburg, *Rousseau's Political Philosophy*, 281.

10. Rousseau, *Minor Educational Writings*, esp. 24. For Rousseau's own acknowledgment of his shortcomings as a tutor, see *Confessions*, 253; *OC*, I:267.

11. Locke, *Educational Writings*, 155–156.

12. "Reputation" and "opinion" will, however, be the guiding standard for Sophie's education, which is the subject of most of Book V of *Emile*. As Rousseau says there, "the principle of woman's education ought to be contrary in this respect to the system of our education. Opinion is the grave of virtue among men and its throne among women" (Rousseau, *Emile*, 365; *OC*, IV: 702–703). This aspect of Rousseau's pedagogy has rightfully dismayed feminist readers of *Emile* from Mary Wollstonecraft to Susan Okin and Jean Elshtain (see Mary Wollstonecraft, *Vindication of the Rights of Woman* [Harmondsworth, England: Penguin, 1985], 107–108, 176–186; Susan Muller Okin, *Women in Western Political Thought* [Princeton: Princeton University Press, 1979], 133–139, 162–166; and Elshtain, *Meditations on Modern Political Thought*, 47–48). For a defense of Rousseau's views of women, see Joel Schwartz, *The Sexual Politics of Jean-Jacques Rousseau* (Chicago: University of Chicago Press, 1985).

Partly because it is only indirectly related to my theme, but mostly because the issue has been so thoroughly discussed by others, Sophie's education will be omitted from this study.

13. Rousseau, *Emile*, 41; *OC*, IV:251.

14. Ibid., 37, 38; *OC*, IV:245–246. In order to dramatize the difference between natural education and civic education, Rousseau describes the "denatured" behavior of a Spartan mother: "A Spartan woman had five sons in the army and was awaiting news of the battle. A Helot arrives; trembling, she asks him for news. 'Your five sons were killed.' 'Base slave, did I ask you that?' 'We won the victory.' The mother runs to the temple and gives thanks to the gods. This is the female citizen" (ibid., 40; *OC*, IV:249). Jean Elshtain has recently used this passage to criticize Rousseau's tendency to glorify "martial motherhood" (see Elshtain, *Women and War*, 62, 70–71). I would argue that the passage represents instead a hyperbolic example of the kind of mothering that Rousseau is *not* going to recommend for Emile.

15. Ibid., 38; *OC*, IV:247.

16. Ibid., 80; *OC*, IV:304.

17. Ibid., 64; *OC*, IV:285.

18. Ibid., 65, 48, 66; *OC*, IV:285, 261, 287.

19. Ibid., 68; *OC*, IV:290.

20. Ibid., 47; *OC*, IV:260. In regard to the "hardening" of the child's body mentioned here, it is interesting to compare the methods of childrearing that Rousseau proposes in *Emile* with the education that Dr. Jean-Marc Gaspard Itard devised for a feral child discovered in Aveyron in 1800. Instead of gradually habituating him to cold baths, as Rousseau proposes for Emile, Itard made a point of encouraging the wild boy of Aveyron to indulge in warm baths; instead of giving him simple and unrefined food, Itard tried to cultivate his pupil's taste for sweets and sauces. The difference in their methods can be seen as a direct consequence of the difference in their purposes. Rousseau's purpose was to enable Emile to resist manipulation by others, whereas Itard recognized that the only way he could socialize his pupil was to sensitize his appetites so that he would become manipulable. For the story of the wild boy of Aveyron's education, see Harlan Lane, *The Wild Boy of Aveyron* (Cambridge, Mass.: Harvard University Press, 1979); or see François Truffaut's wonderful film *The Wild Child*.

21. Rousseau, *Emile*, 78; *OC*, IV:301.

22. Ibid., 68; *OC*, IV:290.

23. Ibid.; *OC*, IV:290. For an interesting discussion of Rousseau in the context of contemporary ecological concerns, see Gilbert F. La Freniere, "Rousseau's First Discourse and the Idea of Progress," *Willamette Journal*, Fall 1983, 7–26.

24. Rousseau, *Emile*, 66, 85; *OC*, IV:287, 311.

25. Ibid., 85, 89; *OC*, IV:311, 316.

26. Ibid., 98, 100, 91, 89, 119; *OC*, IV:331, 333, 320, 317, 361.

27. Ibid., 93–94; *OC*, IV:323.

28. Ibid., 81, 117; *OC*, IV:305, 359.

29. Ibid., 160–161; *OC*, IV:422.

30. Ibid., 165; *OC*, IV:426.

31. Ibid., 165–166; *OC*, IV:427–428.

32. In Book I of the *Essay*, Locke had argued that there are no such things as innate ideas; in Book II, he had explained that complex ideas are derived from the simple ideas resulting from sensation and reflection; in Book III, he had discussed the problem of making words reflect accurately the ideas they represent; and in Book IV, he had broached the distinction between intuitive and empirical knowledge—but the connection between these topics is far from clear. John Locke, *An Essay Concerning Human Understanding* (Oxford: Clarendon Press, 1975).

33. Ibid., 229.

34. Rousseau, *Emile*, 168; *OC*, IV:430.

35. Although a number of recent works have addressed the curricular challenges of educating for global responsibility, there has not yet been, to my knowledge, any comprehensive attempt to integrate such concerns into a theory of moral development. For studies that seem to be pointing in this direction, see Jerome Frank, *Sanity and Survival* (New York: Vintage, 1968); Betty A. Reardon, *Comprehensive Peace Education: Educating for Global Responsibility* (New York: Teachers College Press, 1988); and Elise Boulding, *Building a Global Civic Culture: Education for an Interdependent World* (New York: Teachers College Press, 1988).

36. Rousseau, *Emile*, 167; *OC*, IV:429.

37. Ibid.; *OC*, IV:428. It is interesting to compare Rousseau's comments here with a discussion of the moral implications of recombinant DNA research by the noted biophysicist Robert Sinsheimer: "We begin to see that the truth is not enough, that the truth is necessary but not sufficient, that scientific inquiry, the revealer of truth, needs to be coupled with wisdom if our object is to advance the human condition. . . . Our thrusts in inquiry should not too far exceed our perception of their consequence. . . . We need to recognize that the great forces we now wield might—just might—drive us too swiftly toward some unseen chasm." Quoted by Nicholas Wade in *The Ultimate Experiment: Man-Made Evolution* (New York: Walker, 1977), 106–107. Excerpted in Philip Appleman, ed., *Darwin, A Norton Critical Edition* (New York: Norton, 1979), 291.

38. Rousseau, *Emile*, 168; *OC*, IV:430.

39. Ibid., 187; *OC*, IV:458–459.

40. Ibid., 184–185; *OC*, IV:455.

41. Rousseau, *Discourses*, 93; *OC*, III:123.

42. Rousseau, *Emile*, 185, 190; *OC*, IV:455, 462.

43. Ibid., 190; *OC*, IV:463.

44. Ibid., 194–195; *OC*, IV:468–469.

45. Ibid., 203; *OC*, IV:481.

46. Ibid., 211–214; *OC*, IV:489–494.

47. Ibid., 317; *OC*, IV:640.

48. Ibid., 213–214; *OC*, IV:493.

49. Ibid., 220; *OC*, IV:502.

50. Ibid., 221; *OC*, IV:503.

51. Ibid., 223–226; *OC*, IV:506–510.
52. Ibid., 231–233; *OC*, IV:517–520.
53. Ibid., 237, 240, 243; *OC*, IV:526, 530, 533–534.
54. Ibid., 249; *OC*, IV:543.
55. Ibid., 250; *OC*, IV:544.
56. Ibid., 251–252; *OC*, IV:544–545.
57. For a comprehensive examination of the epistemological issues of the Enlightenment, see Ernst Cassirer, *The Philosophy of the Enlightenment* (Princeton: Princeton University Press, 1951), esp. 93–133.
58. Rousseau, *Emile*, 354; *OC*, IV:690.
59. Ibid., 441; *OC*, IV:812–813.
60. Ibid., 444, 447, 448; *OC*, IV:818, 822, 823.
61. Ibid., 459–464; *OC*, IV:837–845.
62. Ibid., 466–467; *OC*, IV:848.
63. Ibid., 467; *OC*, IV:849.
64. Ibid., 458; *OC*, IV:836–837.
65. Dyson, *Weapons and Hope*, 4–5, 272–313.
66. Rousseau, *Emile*, 472–475; *OC*, IV:856–860.
67. Ibid, 94–95; *OC*, IV:325.

CONCLUSION

1. For a recent discussion of these conflicting aims, see Richard Falk's "intellectual biography" of the World Order Models Project (WOMP) in *The Promise of World Order: Essays in Normative International Relations* (Philadelphia: Temple University Press, 1987), 18–20.
2. Rousseau, *OC*, III:360.

APPENDIX A
"THE STATE OF WAR"

1. This point is made again by Rousseau in his *Extrait du Projet de paix perpétuelle*. See Rousseau, *OC*, III:564, or my translation of the *Projet de paix perpétuelle* in Appendix B. The point is also made in Rousseau, *Emile*, 466; *OC*, IV:848.
2. This sentence, which comes at the bottom of a page, is incomplete.
3. The bracketed paragraphs were crossed out in the original, but because they constitute an interesting part of Rousseau's attack on Hobbes, editors from Vaughan on have included them in their texts.
4. Rousseau has made this argument "before" in his *Discourse on the Origin of Inequality*. See Rousseau, *Discourses*, 91–95; *OC*, III:122–126.
5. Grotius argued that to enslave the defeated was one of the "rights" of conquest (see *De Jure Belli*, 690–691); and Hobbes argued that peace could legitimately be attained through conquest (see Hobbes, *Leviathan*, 165). Rousseau will "return to this point" at the end of the manuscript where he will argue that slavery is in fact a continuation of the state of war (a point that he develops even further in Chapter iv of Book I of the *Social Contract*).

6. Here Rousseau is moving from his critique of Hobbes's notion of a natural war of every man against every man to a critique of Grotius's identification, in Book I of *De Jure Belli*, of private war, public war, and mixed war.

7. See Rousseau, *Discourses*, 178; *OC*, III:192. "The reason Diogenes did not find a man was that he sought among his contemporaries the man of a time that no longer existed."

8. In the original manuscript, this sentence, which comes at the bottom of a page, is followed by a line beneath which Rousseau has written "*Fin du chapitre: il n'y a point de guerre contre les hommes; il n'y en a qu'entre les États.*" This seems to be a note that Rousseau wrote to remind himself of what to include at the end of the chapter. (See the section "Fundamental Distinctions" below.)

9. Rousseau's analysis of the self-preservation of states is parallel to his distinction between *amour de soi* and *amour propre*, which he explains in "note O" in the *Discourse on the Origin of Inequality*. See Rousseau, *Discourses*, 221–222; *OC*, III:219–220.

10. The bracketed paragraphs have been crossed out in the original.

11. In his "Extrait" of the Abbé de Saint Pierre's *Projet de paix perpétuelle*, Rousseau develops the idea that treaties signed between great powers are usually more like temporary truces than real signs of peace. See *OC*, III:568 or Appendix B.

12. Emphasis in this paragraph mine.

13. Rousseau's first argument in the *Social Contract* is that political right is based on conventions. See Rousseau, *Social Contract*, 47; *OC*, III:352.

APPENDIX B
ROUSSEAU'S "SUMMARY"

1. "After all the weapons have been put down, then let the human race consult with itself, and in turn let all the nations love one another." Translated by Frank Moretti. These lines from Lucan's *Pharsalia* appear as an epigraph to the published edition of Rousseau's text, but they do not appear in Rousseau's original manuscript.

2. The Amphictyons were various leagues of peoples in early Greek history who had agreed to unite for mutual protection and for the guardianship in common of a central sanctuary; the Iucomonies were territorial divisions of ancient Etruria united by a federal government; the *feriae* were holidays during which free Romans suspended their political and legal transactions, and slaves enjoyed a cessation of labor; the Cités were the chief towns of the subdivisions of Gaul, representatives of which met regularly and exerted considerable influence politically in the Roman Empire; and the Achean League or Confederation was the most highly developed form of federal government that has been handed down from antiquity. For the information contained here and in the following note, I am indebted to Shirley G. Patterson's edition of *L'État de Guerre and Projet de Paix Perpétuelle*, 84–86.

3. The union of Germanic states refers to the loosely organized confederation brought into existence by the Treaty of Westphalia; the Helvetian League was the name given to the union of Swiss cantons that formed in 1307 and

became recognized as an independent state in 1648; and the Estates-General were political assemblies of delegates from the three social orders in France that met sporadically from the fourteenth through the eighteenth centuries. As is evident from the variety of the groupings mentioned here, Rousseau is interested more in pursuing the general concept of confederation than in limiting his discussion to one specific form of political association.

4. "The respect for the Roman Empire has outlived its power to such an extent that many legal experts have questioned whether the Emperor of Germany wasn't perhaps the natural sovereign of the world; and Barthole has pushed this so far as to treat as heretical anyone who dares to doubt it. The books of the canonists are full of similar decisions about the temporal authority of the Roman church" (note by Rousseau).

5. Rousseau seems to be referring to "natural" revolutions here, such as the revolutions that mark the different stages in human development that he laid out in the *Discourse on the Origin of Inequality*.

6. In this passage, Rousseau is naively overlooking one of his own precepts concerning the importance of a state's constitution in its ability to remain at peace with its neighbors. It was precisely the weakness of her political "constitution" that was at the root of Germany's military aggressiveness during the first half of the twentieth century.

7. "Things have changed since I wrote this, but my principles will always be true. It is, for example, very easy to foresee that in twenty years from now England, with all her glory, will be ruined, and, moreover, will have lost the rest of her liberty. Everyone assures us that agriculture is flourishing in that isle, but I say that it is in decline. London is expanding every day; as a result, the surrounding countryside is becoming depopulated. The English wish to be conquerers; thus it will not be long before they are slaves" (note by Rousseau).

8. "Other objections may present themselves here, but since the author of the *Projet* did not address them, I have, after close examination, rejected them" (note by Rousseau).

9. Note that Rousseau's final argument for trying to limit war points to the harmful effects that international anarchy has on the internal politics of sovereign states.

APPENDIX C
ROUSSEAU'S "CRITIQUE"

1. French military dignitaries who acted as judges in disputes regarding points of personal honor. Cf. Patterson, ed., *État de Guerre and Projet de Paix Perpétuelle*, 89.

2. Here and elsewhere in the "Critique," I have added paragraph breaks in order to make Rousseau's exposition more clear.

3. Rousseau was obviously not aware, as scholars are today, that it was Sully, rather than Henri IV, who was largely responsible for conceiving of the "Grand Design" for a Christian Republic.

Bibliography

WORKS BY ROUSSEAU

Rousseau, Jean-Jacques. *Oeuvres complètes.* 4 vols. Édition sous la direction de Bernard Gagnebin et Marcel Raymond. Bibliothèque de la Pléiade. Paris: Gallimard, 1959–1969.

————. *The Political Writings of Jean-Jacques Rousseau.* 2 vols. Edited and with an Introduction and Notes by C. E. Vaughan. New York: Wiley, 1962.

————. *Political Writings.* Translated and edited by Frederick Watkins. Edinburgh: Thomas Nelson, 1953.

————. *Correspondance complète.* 43 vols. Geneva: Institut et Musé Voltaire, 1984.

————. *The First and Second Discourses.* Edited by Roger D. Masters; translated by Roger D. and Judith R. Masters. New York: St. Martin's Press, 1964.

————. *Discourses and Essay on the Origin of Languages.* Edited, translated, and annotated by Victor Gourevitch. New York: Harper & Row, 1986.

————. *L'État de Guerre and Projet de Paix Perpétuelle. Two Essays by Jean-Jacques Rousseau.* With Introduction and Notes by Shirley G. Patterson. New York: G. P. Putnam's, 1920.

————. *A Lasting Peace through the Federation of Europe and The State of War.* Translated by C. E. Vaughan. London: Constable, 1917.

————. *Politics and the Arts: Letter to M. d'Alembert on the Theater.* Translated and with an Introduction by Allan Bloom. Ithaca: Cornell University Press, 1960.

————. *On the Social Contract, with "Geneva Manuscript" and "Political Economy."* Edited by Roger D. Masters; translated by Judith R. Masters. New York: St. Martin's Press, 1978.

————. *The Social Contract.* Translated and with an Introduction by Maurice Cranston. Harmondsworth, England: Penguin, 1968.

————. *The Social Contract and Discourse on the Origin and Foundation of Inequality*

among Mankind. Edited and with an Introduction by Lester G. Crocker.
New York: Washington Square Press, 1967.
———. *Emile: or On Education*. Translated and with an Introduction and Notes
by Allan Bloom. New York: Basic Books, 1979.
———. *Emile*. Translated by Barbara Foxley. New York: Everyman's Library,
1974.
———. *The Minor Educational Writings of Jean Jacques Rousseau*. Selected and
translated by William Boyd. New York: Teachers College Press, 1962.
———. *Confessions*. Translated by J. M. Cohen. Harmondsworth, England:
Penguin, 1953.
———. *Rêveries du promeneur solitaire*. Extraits présentés et annotés par Pierre
Grosclaude. Paris: Librairie A. Hatier, 1958.

WORKS ABOUT ROUSSEAU

Barber, Benjamin. "How Swiss Is Rousseau?" *Political Theory* 13. no. 4. (November 1985): 475–495.
Beaulavon, Georges. "Les Idées de J.-J. Rousseau sur la guerre." *La Revue de Paris*, October 1917, 641–656.
Boyd, William. *The Educational Theory of Jean Jacques Rousseau*. New York: Russel & Russell, 1963.
Burgelin, Pierre. *La Philosophie de l'existence de J.-J. Rousseau*. Paris: Librairie Philosophique J. Vrin, 1973.
Carter, Christine Jane. *Rousseau and the Problem of War*. New York: Garland, 1987.
Cassirer, Ernst. *The Question of Jean-Jacques Rousseau*. Translated and edited by Peter Gay. Bloomington: Indiana University Press, 1967.
———. *Rousseau, Kant, and Goethe*. Two Essays. Translated by James Gutmann, Paul Oskar Kristeller, and John Herman Randall, Jr. Princeton: Princeton University Press, 1945.
Cell, Howard, and James I. MacAdam. *Rousseau's Response to Hobbes*. New York: Peter Lang, 1988.
Chapman, J. W. *Rousseau, Totalitarian or Liberal?* New York: Columbia University Press, 1956.
Cobban, Alfred. *Rousseau and the Modern State*. Hamden, Conn.: Anchor Books, 1964.
Cobban, Alfred, and R. S. Elmes. "A Disciple of Jean-Jacques Rousseau: The Comte d'Antraigues." *Revue d'histoire littéraire de la France*. Vol. 43 (1936).
Cohler, Anne M. *Rousseau and Nationalism*. New York: Basic Books, 1970.
Colletti, Lucio. *From Rousseau to Lenin: Studies in Ideology and Society*. New York: Monthly Review Press, 1972.
Cook, Terrence Edward. "Rousseau: Education and Politics." Ph.D. dissertation, Princeton University, 1971.
Cranston, Maurice. *Jean-Jacques: The Early Life and Work of Jean-Jacques Rousseau. 1712–1754*. New York: Norton, 1982.
Cranston, Maurice, and R. S. Peters. *Hobbes and Rousseau: A Collection of Critical Essays*. Garden City, N.Y.: Doubleday, 1972.

Crocker, Lester G. *Jean Jacques Rousseau*. Vol. 1, *The Quest, 1712–1758*. Vol. 2, *The Prophetic Voice, 1758–1778*. New York: Macmillan, 1973.

———. *Rousseau's "Social Contract": An Interpretive Essay*. Cleveland: Case Western Reserve University, 1968.

Daedalus, Summer 1978. Special Issue, "Rousseau for Our Time."

Davy, Georges. "Thomas Hobbes et J. J. Rousseau." *The Zaharoff Lectures for 1953*. Oxford: Clarendon Press, 1953.

de Man, Paul. *Allegories of Reading: Figural Language in Rousseau, Nietzsche, Rilke, and Proust*. New Haven: Yale University Press, 1979.

Derathé, Robert. "Jean-Jacques Rousseau et le progrès des idées humanitaires du XVIe au XVIIe siècle," *Revue internationale de la Croix Rouge*, October 1958, 523–543.

———. *Jean-Jacques Rousseau et la science politique de son temps*. Paris: Librairie Philosophique J. Vrin, 1970.

Ellenburg, Stephen. *Rousseau's Political Philosophy: An Interpretation from Within*. Ithaca: Cornell University Press, 1976.

Ellis, Madeleine B. *Rousseau's Socratic Aemilian Myths: A Literary Collation of Emile and the Social Contract*. Columbus: Ohio State University Press, 1977.

Fermon, Nicole. "The Politics of Sentiment: Rousseau's Teaching on the Family and the State." Ph.D. dissertation, Columbia University, 1988.

Fralin, Richard. *Rousseau and Representation: A Study of the Development of His Concept of Political Institutions*. New York: Columbia University Press, 1978.

Gildin, Hilail. *Rousseau's "Social Contract": The Design of the Argument*. Chicago: University of Chicago Press, 1983.

Guehenno, Jean. *Jean-Jacques Rousseau*. 2 vols. Translated by John and Doreen Weightman. New York: Columbia University Press, 1966.

Hendel, Charles W. *Jean-Jacques Rousseau: Moralist*. New York: Bobbs-Merrill, 1934.

Hofer, Cuno. *L'influence de J. J. Rousseau sur le droit de la guerre*. Geneva: Georg & Cie., 1916.

Hoffmann, Stanley. "Rousseau on War and Peace." *American Political Science Review* 17, no. 2 (June 1963): 317–353.

Hubert, René. *Rousseau et l'Encyclopédie: Essai sur la formation des idées politiques de Rousseau (1742–1756)*. Paris: J. Gamber, 1928.

Keohane, Nannerl O. "'The Masterpiece of Policy in Our Century': Rousseau on the Morality of the Enlightenment." *Political Theory* 6 (November 1978): 457–484.

LaFreniere, Gilbert F. "Rousseau's First Discourse and the Idea of Progress." *Willamette Journal*, Fall 1983.

Lassudrie-Duchène, Georges. *Jean-Jacques Rousseau et le droit des gens*. Paris: Imprimerie Henri Jouve, 1906.

Launay, Michel. *Jean-Jacques Rousseau, Écrivain politique (1712–1762)*. Grenoble: Association Pour une Coopérative d'Édition et de Recherche, 1971.

Masters, Roger. *The Political Philosophy of Rousseau*. Princeton: Princeton University Press, 1968.

McClintock, Robert O. "Rousseau and the Dilemma of Authority." *History of Education Quarterly*, Fall 1974.

McDonald, Joan. *Rousseau and the French Revolution, 1762–1791.* London: University of London, Althone Press, 1965.

Miller, James. *Rousseau, Dreamer of Democracy.* New Haven: Yale University Press, 1984.

Riley, Patrick. "The General Will Before Rousseau." *Political Theory* 6 (November 1978): 485–516.

Schwartz, Joel. *The Sexual Politics of Jean-Jacques Rousseau.* Chicago: University of Chicago Press, 1984.

Shklar, Judith. *Men and Citizens: A Study of Rousseau's Social Theory.* Cambridge: Cambridge University Press, 1969.

Starobinski, Jean. *Jean-Jacques Rousseau: La transparence et l'obstacle.* Suivi de sept essais sur Rousseau. Paris: Éditions Gallimard, 1971.

Windenberger, J. L. *Essai sur le système de politique étrangère de J.-J. Rousseau: La Republique Confédérative des petits États.* Paris: Alfonse Picard et Fils, 1900.

Witemeyer, Hugh. "George Eliot and Jean-Jacques Rousseau." *Comparative Literature Studies* 16, no. 1 (June 1979): 121–129.

Wright, E. H. *The Meaning of Rousseau.* New York: Russell and Russell, 1963.

RELATED SOURCES

Abbott, Philip. *The Family on Trial: Special Relationships in Modern Political Thought.* University Park, Pa.: Pennsylvania State University Press, 1981.

Arendt, Hannah. *On Revolution.* New York: Viking Press, 1963.

———. *The Origins of Totalitarianism.* New York: Meridian Books, 1960.

Aries, Philippe. *Centuries of Childhood: A Social History of the Family.* Translated by Robert Baldick. New York: Vintage Books, 1962.

Aristotle. *Nicomachean Ethics.* Translated and with an Introduction by Martin Ostwald. Indianapolis: Bobbs-Marrill, 1962.

———. *The Politics of Aristotle.* Translated with an Introduction, Notes, and Appendixes by Ernest Barker, New York: Oxford University Press, 1958.

Becker, Carl L. *The Heavenly City of the Eighteenth-Century Philosophers.* New Haven: Yale University Press, 1932.

Bellah, Robert N., et al. *Habits of the Heart: Individualism and Commitment in American Life.* Berkeley: University of California Press, 1985.

Boulding, Elise. *Building a Global Civic Culture: Education for an Interdependent World.* New York: Teachers College Press, 1988.

Boulding, Kenneth E. *Stable Peace.* Austin: University of Texas Press, 1981.

Bourne, Randolph S. *The Radical Will: Randolph Bourne—Selected Writings 1911–1918.* Edited with an Introduction by Olaf Hansen; Preface by Christopher Lasch. New York: Urizen Books, 1977.

———. *War and the Intellectuals: Collected Essays, 1915–1919.* Edited by Carl Resek. New York: Harper Torchbooks, 1964.

Bull, Hedley. *The Anarchical Society: A Study of Order in World Politics.* New York: Columbia University Press, 1977.

Camus, Albert. *Neither Victims nor Executioners.* Translated by Dwight Macdonald. Philadelphia: New Society Publishers, 1986.

Cassirer, Ernst. *The Philosophy of the Enlightenment*. Translated by Fritz C. A. Koelln and James P. Pettegrove. Princeton: Princeton University Press, 1951.

Condorcet, *Selected Writings*. Edited and with an Introduction by Keith Michael Baker. Indianapolis: Bobbs-Marrill, 1976.

Cook, Blanche Wiesen, Sandi E. Cooper, and Charles Chatfield, eds. *Peace Projects of the Eighteenth Century*. Garland Library of War and Peace. New York: Garland, 1982.

————. *Peace Projects of the Seventeenth Century*. Garland Library of War and Peace. New York: Garland, 1982.

Davies, Norman. *God's Playground: A History of Poland in Two Volumes. Vol 1, The Origins to 1795*. New York: Columbia University Press, 1982.

Der Derian, James. *On Diplomacy: A Genealogy of Western Estrangement*. Oxford: Basil Blackwell, 1987.

Dewey, John. *Democracy and Education*. New York: The Free Press, 1944.

————. *Dewey on Education: Selections*. Introduction and Notes by Martin S. Dworkin. New York: Teachers College Press, 1975.

Dobbs, Michael, K. S. Karol, and Dessa Travisan. *Poland, Solidarity, Walesa*. New York: McGraw-Hill, 1981.

Dyson, Freeman. *Weapons and Hope*. New York: Harper & Row, 1984.

Ellul, Jacques. *The Technological Society*. Translated by Robert K. Merton. New York: Vintage Books, 1964.

Elshtain, Jean Bethke. "Citizenship and Maternal Thinking II; Reflections on War and Political Discourse: Realism, Just War, and Feminism in a Nuclear Age." *Political Theory* 13, no. 1 (February 1985): 39–57.

————. *Meditations on Modern Political Thought: Masculine/Feminine Themes from Luther to Arendt*. New York: Praeger, 1986.

————. *Public Man, Private Woman: Women in Social and Political Thought*. Princeton: Princeton University Press, 1981.

————. *Women and War*. New York: Basic Books, 1987.

Encyclopédie ou Dictionnaire raisonné des sciences, des arts, et des métiers, par une société de gens de lettres. 36 vols. Lausanne and Berne, 1782.

Falk, Richard. *The Promise of World Order: Essays in Normative International Relations*. Philadelphia: Temple University Press, 1987.

Falk, Richard, Friedrich Kratochwil, and Saul H. Mendlovitz. *International Law: A Contemporary Perspective*. Boulder, Colo.: Westview Press, 1985.

Fellows, Otis E., and Norman L. Torrey, eds. *Diderot Studies*. Syracuse: Syracuse University Press, 1952.

Fischer, Dietrich. *Preventing War in the Nuclear Age*. Totowa, N.J.: Rowman & Allanheld, 1984.

Foner, Eric. *Tom Paine and Revolutionary America*. New York: Oxford University Press, 1976.

Forsyth, M. G., H. M. A. Keens-Soper, and P. Savigear. *The Theory of International Relations: Selected Texts from Gentili to Treitschke*. London: Allen and Unwin, 1970.

Franklin, Julian H. *John Locke and the Theory of Sovereignty: Mixed Monarchy and the Right of Resistance in the Political Thought of the English Revolution*. Cambridge: Cambridge University Press, 1981.

Gallie, W. B. *Philosophers of Peace and War: Kant, Clausewitz, Marx, Engels, and Tolstoy*. Cambridge: Cambridge University Press, 1978.

Gargaz, Pierre-André. *A Project of Universal and Perpetual Peace. Written by Pierre-André Gargaz, a former Galley-Slave, and Printed by Benjamin Franklin at Passy in the Year 1782*. Edited and with an Introduction by George Simpson Eddy. New York: By the Editor, 1922.

Gay, Peter. *The Enlightenment: An Interpretation*. 2 vols. New York: Knopf, 1966.

————, ed. *The Party of Humanity*. New York: Norton, 1971.

Gayer, Alan. *The Idea of Disarmament!: Rethinking the Unthinkable*. Elgin, Ill.: Brethren Press, 1982.

Grotius, Hugo. *De Jure Belli ac Pacis: Libri Tres*. 2 vols. Vol. 2 translated, by Francis W. Kelsy. The Classics of International Law series. Oxford: Clarendon Press, 1925.

Hinsley, F. H. *Power and the Pursuit of Peace: Theory and Practice in the History of Relations between States*. Cambridge: Cambridge University Press, 1963.

Hobbes, Thomas. *Leviathan*. Parts 1 and 2. Introduction by Herbert W. Schneider. New York: Liberal Arts Press, 1958.

————. *The Life of Mr. Thomas Hobbes of Malmesbury*. London: n.p., 1689.

————. *Man and Citizen*. Edited and with an Introduction by Bernard Gert. Garden City, N.Y.: Doubleday Anchor, 1972.

Hoffmann, Stanley. *Duties beyond Borders: On the Limits and Possibilities of Ethical International Politics*. Syracuse: Syracuse University Press, 1981.

Horkheimer, Max, and Theodor W. Adorno. *Dialectic of Enlightenment*. New York: Herder and Herder, 1972.

Howard, Michael. *War and the Liberal Conscience*. New Brunswick, N.J.: Rutgers University Press, 1986.

Jaeger, Werner. *Paideia: The Ideals of Greek Culture*. 2 vols. Translated by Gilbert Highet. New York: Oxford University Press, 1945.

Johnson, James Turner. *Ideology, Reason, and the Limitation of War: Religious and Secular Concepts, 1200–1740*. Princeton: Princeton University Press, 1975.

————. *Just War Tradition and the Restraint of War: A Moral and Historical Inquiry*. Princeton: Princeton University Press, 1981.

————. *The Quest for Peace: Three Moral Traditions in Western Cultural History*. Princeton: Princeton University Press, 1987.

Kant, Immanuel. *Critique of Pure Reason*. Translated by Norman Kemp Smith. New York: St. Martin's Press, 1965.

————. *Kant's Political Writings*. Edited with an Introduction by Hans Reiss; translated by H. B. Nisbet, Cambridge: Cambridge University Press, 1977.

————. *The Conflict of the Faculties*. Translated and with an Introduction by Mary J. Gregor. New York: Arabis Books, 1979.

Lane, Harlan. *The Wild Boy of Aveyron*. Cambridge: Harvard University Press, 1979.

Lasch, Christopher. *The Culture of Narcissism*. New York: Norton, 1979.

Leakey, Richard E., and Roger Lewin. *Origins*. New York: Dutton, 1977.

Locke, John. *The Educational Writings of John Locke*. A critical edition with Introduction and Notes by James L. Axtell. Cambridge: Cambridge University Press, 1968.

――――. *An Essay Concerning Human Understanding*. Edited and with an Introduction by Peter H. Nidditch. Oxford: Oxford University Press, 1975.

――――. *John Locke on Education*. Edited and with an Introduction by Peter Gay. New York: Teachers College Press, 1964.

――――. *Locke's Two Treatises of Government*. A critical edition with Introduction and Notes by Peter Laslett. Cambridge: Cambridge University Press, 1967.

――――. *Some Thoughts Concerning Education*. Abridged and edited with an Introduction by F. W. Garforth. Woodbury, N.Y.: Barron's Educational Series, 1964.

Machiavelli, Niccolò. *The Prince and the Discourses*. New York: Modern Library, 1950.

MacIntyre, Alasdair. *After Virtue: A Study in Moral Theory*. Notre Dame: University of Notre Dame Press, 1984.

Macpherson, C. B. *The Political Theory of Possessive Individualism: Hobbes to Locke*. Oxford: Oxford University Press, 1962.

Manuel, Frank E., ed. *The Enlightenment*. Englewood Cliffs, N.J.: Prentice-Hall, 1965.

Masters, Roger. "World Politics as a Primitive Political System." *World Politics* 16, no. 4 (July 1964).

McPhee, John. *La Place de la Concorde Suisse*. New York: Farrar, Straus and Giroux, 1983.

Melman, Seymour. *The Permanent War Economy: American Capitalism in Decline*. New York: Simon and Schuster, 1974.

Montesquieu. *The Spirit of the Laws*. Translated by Thomas Nugent, with an Introduction by Franz Neumann. New York: Hafner, 1949.

Morgenthau, Hans J. *Politics among Nations: The Struggle for Power and Peace*. New York: Knopf, 1960.

Okin, Susan Muller. *Women in Western Political Thought*. Princeton: Princeton University Press, 1979.

Passmore, John. *The Perfectibility of Man*. New York: Scribner's, 1970.

Perkins, Merle. *The Moral and Political Philosophy of the Abbé de Saint-Pierre*. Geneva: Librairie E. Droz, 1959.

――――. "Voltaire's concept of international order." *Studies on Voltaire and the Eighteenth Century*. Vol. 36. Geneva: Institut et Musée Voltaire, 1965.

Plato. *Protagoras and Meno*. Translated by W. K. C. Guthrie. Harmondsworth, England: Penguin, 1956.

――――. *The Republic of Plato*. Translated with Notes and an Interpretive Essay by Allan Bloom. New York: Basic Books, 1958.

Pocock, J. G. A. *The Machiavellian Moment: Florentine Political Thought and the Atlantic Republican Tradition*. Princeton: Princeton University Press, 1975.

Pounds, Norman J. G. *Poland between East and West*. Princeton: Van Nostrand, 1964.

Reardon, Betty A. *Comprehensive Peace Education: Educating for Global Responsibility*. New York: Teachers College Press, 1988.

Recueil d'Essais: Hommages á Marcel Raymond. *De Ronsard á Breton*. Paris: Librairie José Corti, 1967.

Roosevelt, Grace G. "A Reconstruction of Rousseau's Fragments on the State of War." *History of Political Thought* 8 (Summer 1987); 225–244.

Roosevelt, Jinx (Grace G.). "Randolph Bourne: The Education of a Critic—An Interpretation." *History of Education Quarterly*, Fall 1977, 257–274.

Sabine, George H. *A History of Political Theory*. New York: Holt, Rinehart and Winston, 1961.

Saint-Pierre, Charles Irénée Castel de, *Projet pour rendre la paix perpétuelle en Europe*. Presenté par Simone Goyard-Fabre. Paris: Éditions Garnier Frères, 1981.

Schell, Jonathan. *The Fate of the Earth*. New York: Knopf, 1982.

Soboul, Albert. *A Short History of the French Revolution, 1789–1795*. Berkeley: University of California Press, 1977.

Souleyman, Elizabeth V. *The Vision of World Peace in Seventeenth and Eighteenth-Century France*. New York: G. P. Putnam's, 1941.

Talmon, J. L. *The Origins of Totalitarian Democracy*. New York: Praeger, 1951.

Tolstoy, Leo. *War and Peace*. Translated by Constance Garnett. New York: Milestone Editions, n.d.

Viotti, Paul R., and Mark V. Kauppi. *International Relations Theory: Realism, Pluralism, Globalism*. New York: Macmillan, 1988.

Voltaire. *The Portable Voltaire*. Edited and with an Introduction by Ben Ray Redman. Harmondsworth, England: Penguin, 1949.

Wade, Nicholas. *The Ultimate Experiment: Man-Made Evolution*. New York: Walker, 1977.

Waltz, Kenneth N. *Man, the State, and War: A Theoretical Analysis*. New York: Columbia University Press, 1954.

Walzer, Michael. *Just and Unjust Wars: A Moral Argument with Historical Illustrations*. New York: Basic Books, 1977.

Wien, Barbara J., ed. *Peace and World Order Studies: A Curriculum Guide*. New York: World Policy Institute, 1984.

Wilber, Charles K., ed. *The Political Economy of Development and Underdevelopment*. New York: Random House, 1973.

Wilson, Arthur M. *Diderot*. New York: Oxford University Press, 1982.

Wolin, Sheldon S. *Politics and Vision: Continuity and Innovation in Western Political Thought*. Boston: Little, Brown, 1960.

Wollstonecraft, Mary. *Vindication of the Rights of Woman*. Harmondsworth, England: Penguin, 1985.

Zampaglione, Gerardo. *The Idea of Peace in Antiquity*. Translated by Richard Dunn. Notre Dame: University of Notre Dame Press, 1973.

Index

Abbé de Saint-Pierre. *See* Saint-Pierre, Charles Castel, Abbé de
Adeimantus, 80–81
adolescence, and education, 158, 159, 163
Aesop's fables, 156
aggression, 53, 82, 131, 133, 142, 173; origins of, 37–38, 111, 153, 178
aggressiveness, 29, 38, 177; and *amour propre*, 110, 163. *See also* aggression
agriculture, 138, 140, 161
Alembert, d', 71
alliance: military, 6; for peace, 94, 102
amour de soi, 37, 51, 118, 178, 257 n.9; definition of, 29–30; and individual integrity, 30, 146, 150, 157, 163–164, 165; and national autonomy, 131–132, 136, 141, 145
amour propre: in *Considerations on Poland*, 131–132, 136–137, 145; in *Discourse on Inequality*, 29–30, 32; in *Emile*, 145, 147, 150, 153, 162, 163–164, 167–168; and international relations, 37, 110–113, 118, 178–179
anarchy, 34, 79, 115, 130, 132; international, 8, 23, 107, 118, 119, 180
ancien régime, 115, 125, 145, 147
Antraigues, Louis-Emmanuel Henri Alexandre Launay, Count d', 10–13, 116–117, 235–236 n.20, n.21
Arendt, Hannah, 241 n.26, 243 n.1
Argenson, René-Louis de Voyer, Marquis d', 47, 54, 251 n.51

Aristotle, 49, 127, 160, 239 n.44
art: of education, 96, 163, 164; of politics, 36, 81, 82, 99, 179
association: of individuals, 42, 81–82, 83–87, 112; political, 7, 41, 118, 180; of states, 94, 100, 101, 106
authority, 146, 149, 154, 155
autonomy, 136, 164; military, 180

balance of power, system of, 94, 99, 105, 116, 129, 135
Barbeyrac, Jean, 50
Barker, Ernest, 239 n.44
Bastide, Jean-François, 107–108
Bellah, Robert N., 245 n.27
Bentham, Jeremy, 108, 248 n.30
Bloom, Allan, 3
Bordes, Charles M., 53
Boulding, Elise, 255 n.35
Bourne, Randolph, 38
Boyd, William, 252 n.2
Bull, Hedley, 247 n.17
Burlamaqui, Fabrice, 50

Carter, Christine Jane, 234 n.13, 241 n.32
Cassirer, Ernst, 235 n.14, 256 n.57
Catherine the Great, of Russia, 124, 144
Cell, Howard R., 237 n.2
child, education of: in infancy, 152–153; in early childhood, 154–156; in youth,

Switzerland, 143, 252 n.64
system, of international relations, 6, 8,
9, 34, 55, 131, 132, 133, 137, 140, 153,
180. *See also* state system; war system

Tacitus, 44–45, 54
teacher, in *Emile*, 155, 157, 163, 164,
169, 170
Thielemann, Leland, 243 n.4
third world countries, 140
Treaty of Westphalia, 94, 99
Truffaut, François, 254 n.20
tutor, 172; Rousseau as, 149, 253 n.10.
See also teacher, in *Emile*
twentieth century, 56, 63, 94, 109, 133,
159, 181

unhappiness, source of, 152, 156, 168
United Nations, 8, 74, 86, 94, 100
United States, 56, 140, 141, 180
utility, principle of, in education, 154,
159, 160
Utrecht, 94; Council of, 101

Vattel, Emérich de, 49, 56
Vaughan, C. E., 7, 12, 14, 66, 124,
235 n.14, 243–244 n.6, 244 n.9,
248 n.31, 249 n.1, 256 n.3
Venice, 11, 71, 91, 117, 118
Victoria, Franciscus de, 49, 74, 242 n.38
virtue, 53, 136, 137, 156, 170; civic, 127,
129, 132, 142, 146, 180; geopolitical,
146, 158
Voltaire, 54, 108, 240 n.10

Wade, Nicholas, 255 n.37
Waltz, Kenneth N., 8, 9, 238 n.32

war, 56, 57, 64, 94–96, 99, 113, 117,
234 n.13; declaration of, 47, 48, 58, 60,
62, 103, 178; definition of, 14, 52, 54–
59, 61, 62, 66, 69; economic costs of,
105, 106; in *Emile*, 5, 147, 171; of every
man against every man, 21, 23, 33,
39, 54, 65, 81, 82; and human nature,
14, 15, 16, 21, 31, 42, 54; ideological
dimensions of, 56, 59; legitimate, 15,
16, 61, 65, 70, 178; limitations on, 6,
58, 69, 74, 98; methods of, 15; modern, 54; origins of, 31, 33–39, 42, 55,
69, 70, 179, 180; as political institution, 55–57, 60, 63, 69; prevention of,
by confederation, 98, 103, 119, 169,
179; Rousseau's writings on, 66, 69;
and the state, 15, 38, 42, 43, 61, 129,
131–132, 177–179; and the state of war,
distinction between, 15, 16, 56; structural persistence of, 9; thermonuclear,
62, 180; and tyranny, 5, 111–112, 171
war and peace: Grotius's theories of, 52;
Rousseau's writings on, 4, 5–7, 8, 9,
10, 12, 21, 109, 116, 118, 153, 170,
171, 177, 179
War of the Austrian Succession, 11
War of the Spanish Succession, 94
war system, 6, 8, 131, 138, 164
Warens, Mme. de, née Françoise-Louise
de la Tour, 22, 26
wars, 65, 113, 167
Watkins, Frederick M., 245 n.24,
249 n.1, 250 n.10, 252 n.66
weakness, 29, 135, 152–153, 157, 165
Wielhorski, Count Michel, 124, 125
Windenberger, J. L., 7, 12, 14, 235 n.20
Wokler, Robert, 238 n.25
Wollstonecraft, Mary, 253 n.12
world order, 180
World War I, 8, 38
World War II, 109